# CLASSIC CARS
100 of the greatest cars from 1886 to the present day

Published by Collins
An imprint of HarperCollins Publishers
Robroyston Gate,
Glasgow
G33 1JN
www.harpercollins.co.uk

HarperCollins Publishers
Macken House,
39/40 Mayor Street Upper,
Dublin 1, D01 C9W8, Ireland

1st edition 2025

© HarperCollins Publishers 2025

Collins® is a registered trademark of HarperCollins Publishers Ltd

All rights reserved. No part of this publication may be reproduced, stored in a retrieval system, or transmitted, in any form or by any means, electronic, mechanical, photocopying, recording or otherwise without the prior permission in writing of the publisher and copyright owners.

The contents of this publication are believed correct at the time of printing. Nevertheless the publisher can accept no responsibility for errors or omissions, changes in the detail given or for any expense or loss thereby caused.

HarperCollins does not warrant that any website mentioned in this title will be provided uninterrupted, that any website will be error free, that defects will be corrected, or that the website or the server that makes it available are free of viruses or bugs. For full terms and conditions please refer to the site terms provided on the website.

A catalogue record for this book is available from the British Library.

ISBN 978 0 00 870524 4

10 9 8 7 6 5 4 3 2 1

Printed in India

If you would like to comment on any aspect of this book, please contact us at the above address or online.
e-mail: collins.reference@harpercollins.co.uk

This book contains FSC™ certified paper and other controlled sources to ensure responsible forest management.

For more information visit: www.harpercollins.co.uk/green

# CONTENTS

| | |
|---|---|
| INTRODUCTION | 4 |
| THE PIONEERS | 6 |
| POST-WAR PROGRESS | 36 |
| THE SWINGING SIXTIES | 86 |
| OIL CRISIS AND UNREST | 140 |
| THE BOOM IS BACK | 186 |
| TO A NEW CENTURY | 222 |
| INDEX | 254 |
| ACKNOWLEDGEMENTS | 256 |

# Introduction

What turns a car into a classic? Every enthusiast, dealer and journalist will have their own answer. Some might base their judgement on something practical and tangible, like a great innovation in technology, or a step forward in styling, or both – think of the Citroën DS or the Mini. To that we can add success and longevity, like the Ford Model T or the Volkswagen Beetle. Think of those with astonishing speed, either in motorsport or on the street. That accounts for a great many, from the AC Cobra to the Ferrari F40. Sometimes a car doesn't have to be anything other than beautiful, though being fast and affordable certainly helped the Jaguar E-type and the Alfa Romeo Spider.

But there are also those cars that are part of our childhood memories, or are now best known for an appearance in a movie or a TV show, or which are just so striking to look at that once you've seen one, you'll never forget it. In the end, the only thing that defines a car as a classic is its following: if it has owners and fans who worship and work on their cars, attend shows, and form clubs and social media groups, it qualifies.

If you already have a love of old cars, you'll understand how difficult it was to get our selection for this book down to the round number of 100. If you're new to the subject, you might be amazed we can think of so many. Either way, some explanation is in order as to what makes a car worthy of an entry in this book.

We've taken a slice through the twentieth century, starting with a car that was out of date even by 1900 and ending with a couple that showed the way things would go after the year 2000. In between, you'll find six chapters selecting the finest classic machinery from each era, explaining what made them special and why they are sought-after today. Each car gets its own double-page spread, and the real stars merit a more in-depth four-page entry. All of this is, of course, accompanied by photographs to drool over, and that's not all; for each car, you'll find a detailed specification table with enough raw data to satisfy anyone with a thirst for technical knowledge.

As well as the car entries, you'll find various histories of the most famous car-makers from around the world. Ever wondered which luxury car brand is named after the salesman's daughter, or which diminutive British saloon links the origins of BMW and Jaguar?

Classic-car ownership is an aspirational hobby. We can't buy them all – even a single dream car can be hard to attain – but dreaming is important, and for the next 250 pages that's exactly what we hope you'll do. Here are the keys . . . now it's time to decide which cars will find a place in your fantasy garage.

Classic and vintage cars should be enjoyed! Here is the author's 1923 Alvis 12/40 by the Anglo-Scottish border at Norham.

# THE PIONEERS
## 1886 TO 1939

# Benz Patent Motorwagen

The word 'patent' in this machine's name is significant – none of those involved in its creation could have imagined the change that the automobile would bring to our lives, but they knew the importance of claiming an invention. Carl Benz, like many innovators, stood on the shoulders of fellow forward-thinkers as he combined many ideas into one world-changing invention.

Although the four-stroke internal combustion engine (patented in 1876 by Nicolaus Otto, Gottlieb Daimler and Wilhelm Maybach) later became the default choice for almost all road vehicles, Carl Benz took a different route. Possibly by working on earlier ideas from British inventors Joseph Day and Dugald Clerk, he patented a two-stroke engine in 1880. A simpler, lighter but noisier design, two-stroke motors are the type that later found homes in motorcycles, lawnmowers, chainsaws, and in some smaller cars. Benz used a two-stroke engine to create his light, three-wheeled 'Motorwagen', for which he filed a patent on 29 January 1886.

This patent became a famous document, describing the general characteristics of a 'light cart' with a 'small gas engine, of any system', and it is the first well-considered written description of what a car should be. Benz's Motorwagen was driven by a single-cylinder two-stroke engine of just 954 cc capacity, lying on its side and revving to just 400 rpm – less than the idle speed of modern cars. This little motor turned a large flywheel to maintain the car's momentum and the engine's smoothness, and drove the two large rear wheels via chains and an idler pulley that used a leather belt. This, when shifted to the driveshaft pulley via a lever, acted as a clutch.

Even with Carl Benz's clever design and construction, the Motorwagen may have been forgotten without the actions of his wife, Bertha Benz. Carl had given the car a modest demonstration on a street in his home town of Mannheim the year the patent was granted, but orders failed to materialise. Bertha Benz, whose own money had been invested in Benz's work, saw the need for publicity, so in August 1888 she set off in his third Motorwagen construction to visit her mother in Pforzheim, 106 km (66 miles) away.

She had not told her husband, much less warned the authorities. Along the way she managed to find suitable solvents to use as fuel at chemists' shops, had the chain repaired by a blacksmith, cleared the fuel line with her hat pin and, most significantly of all, invented brake linings when she arranged for a cobbler to make leather pads to improve the wooden brakes. The journey took all day and generated much attention and publicity, showing that cars really were a viable mode of cross-country travel. Bertha's resourcefulness is commemorated by the signposted Bertha Benz Memorial Route, showing her historic round trip.

| 1886 Benz Patent Motorwagen ||
|---|---|
| Length | 2,700 mm |
| Width | 1,400 mm |
| Weight | 265 kg |
| Wheelbase | 1,450 mm |
| Suspension | None (front); full-elliptic leaf springs, no dampers (rear) |
| Brakes | Hand lever, leather pads acting on belt pulley |
| Engine | 954 cc horizontal single-cylinder two-stroke, water cooled |
| Power | 0.66 bhp @ 400 rpm |
| Torque | n/a, but c.1 lb-ft |
| Transmission | Idler pulley, leather drive belt, chain final drive |
| 0–60 mph | n/a |
| Top speed | 10 mph |
| Cost new | c.£200 |
| Value today | £50,000 for recent replica; one of the 25 originals would be priceless |

TOP: Carl Benz seated on his invention.

BOTTOM: A tool-room copy of the original Patent Motorwagen on display at the Technik Museum Sinsheim, Germany.

# ROLLS-ROYCE 40/50 HP 'SILVER GHOST'

| Rolls-Royce 40/50 hp 'Silver Ghost' (figures for 1909 model) | |
| --- | --- |
| Length | 4,572 mm |
| Width | 1,722 mm |
| Weight | 1,569 kg |
| Wheelbase | 3,442 mm |
| Suspension | Semi-elliptic leaf springs (front); three-quarter-elliptic leaf springs (rear) |
| Brakes | Rear drums and transmission brake (later deleted), front-wheel brakes from 1924 |
| Engine | 7,046 cc straight-six, sidevalve |
| Power | 50 bhp @ 1,250 rpm |
| Torque | n/a |
| Transmission | Four-speed manual, overdrive top gear |
| 0–60 mph | 40 sec. (est.) |
| Top speed | 65 mph |
| Cost new | £985 (chassis only) |
| Value today | £100,000–£3 million (AX 201 could be £50 million!) |

This famous model is correctly known as the 40/50 hp, as the name Silver Ghost was originally applied to just one car, which was registered AX 201 and finished in aluminium paint. It was used by Rolls-Royce for a year of arduous testing and record breaking, covering more than 15,000 miles in the summer of 1907 alone, including an extraordinary 14,371 miles non-stop, observed by the Royal Automobile Club as an extended reliability trial. At this time, cars were widely regarded as dirty, noisy, smelly and, above all, unreliable: you spent more time mending them than driving them. Rolls-Royce showed the world it didn't have to be like that and, eventually, all 40/50 hp models became known as Silver Ghosts.

The Silver Ghost's design was a leap forward in so many ways – power, smoothness, durability, silence, comfort – that it represented a step change, especially for a company with a top-of-the-range model that was giving trouble: the six-cylinder Rolls-Royce 30 hp. Henry Royce tackled the problem head-on by designing a new model to replace it, lengthening the chassis to give passengers more room and lightening the steering by moving the engine behind the front axle line. He increased the size of the engine to just over seven litres and based it on a huge cast-aluminium crankcase that was stiff enough to support a sturdy new crankshaft with a highly advanced feature – pressure lubrication.

Drilling oilways down the centre of a crankshaft allowed an oil pump to supply the crank's bearings with lubrication, which allowed them to run cooler, more reliably and at higher speed. The 40/50 hp was probably the first production car with this feature, which is taken for granted now, though some makers continued with simple 'splash' lubrication inside the sump until the late 1940s. Royce's new engine was rated in the 40 hp class: a road tax bracket based on piston area and not really a measure of horsepower. Engines were rapidly becoming more efficient, as indicated by the '50' in the second half of the name – a brake horsepower figure that rose to 80 bhp or more as the engine was developed.

The first Silver Ghosts used a four-speed gearbox, but such was the engine's torque, or low-down pulling power, that a three-speed version was soon deemed adequate – only for a four-speed version to be reintroduced in 1913, after a Ghost had struggled to climb a mountain pass on the 1912 Alpine Trial. A year later, the Silver Ghost chassis and engine were used to create the Rolls-Royce armoured car, of which 120 were built for the First World War. Too heavy for muddy trench warfare, they did well in the deserts of the Middle East, where Royce's superlative engineering kept them running in demanding conditions.

Soon after the 40/50 hp was introduced, production of the other Rolls-Royce models ceased. The Silver Ghost's instant success was enough to keep the company busy for many years. Indeed, such was the demand for the car that Rolls-Royce took the radical step of building a factory in America. In January 1921, the first of more than 1,700 Silver Ghosts was completed by the new plant in Springfield, Massachusetts, adding to more than 6,000 British-built cars. The Springfield plant remained open until 1931, when the Great Depression took hold, by which time the Silver Ghost had been replaced by the Rolls-Royce Phantom.

Here, though, was another remarkable thing about the Silver Ghost: its lifespan of almost 20 years. Most cars from 1906 would have seemed clattering, antiquated

embarrassments to motorists in 1925, but not the Ghost. Subtly and continuously upgraded, it was always fast enough, quiet enough and strong enough to fulfil any role. Like most marques at this time Rolls-Royce did not build its own bodywork, leaving coachbuilding firms to clothe their chassis, and it soon showed itself equally suitable as a limousine, touring car or even sports car. Indeed, the only significant change between the Silver Ghost and its replacement, the Phantom was the adoption of overhead valves, rather than the sidevalves of the Ghost.

Today, Silver Ghosts are still highly sought-after. There are very few other cars of their era that can be driven comfortably in modern traffic, cruising at 55 mph (more for the sporty Alpine Eagle or London to Edinburgh models), making no fuss in traffic and even stopping promptly – though such a weighty car needs forethought as most have only rear-wheel brakes. The strong, relatively simple engine, with its ignition system of two spark plugs in each cylinder, driven by two different systems, means it's unusual for it to break down – or 'fail to proceed' as Rolls-Royce would have put it. The soft springs and tall tyres are often combined with sumptuous seats to make the ride as comfortable as any modern luxury car, and a lot more characterful.

Above all, they still turn heads. One glimpse of that majestic radiator and people know they are in the presence of the best car in the world.

PREVIOUS PAGE: A 1918 Alpine Eagle tourer.

TOP: The original 'Silver Ghost'.

# Ford Model T

The Model T is the most significant car of the twentieth century, and it might even be the most important machine ever created. Its list of achievements is mind boggling. For instance, it proved the concept of the moving assembly line, influencing every other manufacturing industry, and it transformed the car from an eccentric toy for the rich into something the emerging middle class could afford. From 1908 it mobilised first America and then much of the rest of the world, bringing mechanical power to rural locations that previously had none. You could buy devices to turn Model Ts into tractors, railcars or snowploughs, and they were used to power sawmills, threshers, water pumps, generators and all kinds of farm machinery. By 1918, half the cars in America were Model T Fords: a couple of years later it was half the cars in the world.

Remarkably, the price kept falling. The Model T has perhaps two things in common with the Rolls-Royce Silver Ghost: it was continually updated and improved while in production, and it lived an unusually long life at a time when cars were evolving rapidly. Henry Ford and his staff were continually finding ways to cut production costs by simplifying the design, selecting the most cost-effective components (the famous black-only colour scheme Ford used from 1914 to 1925 happened because black was the cheapest paint pigment) and, above all, by improving the production line. Once Ford's new Highland Park plant in Michigan opened in 1910, almost nothing but raw materials was bought in: iron ore, wood and leather went in at one end, Model Ts emerged from the other. Before Highland Park, each Ford took 12½ hours to build. By 1914, that figure was down to 93 minutes, and a new Model T came off the line every three minutes.

Why was it so popular? Ford had judged the vehicle's size very well: not too large and heavy, not too small and feeble. It came with a choice of open and closed bodywork and there was a pickup truck option. It was also remarkably easy to drive by 1908 standards. Instead of a gear lever and some tricky, unsynchronised gears to manage, drivers selected low, high or reverse gears with foot pedals and controlled the engine speed with a hand throttle. One footbrake and a handbrake lever were used to stop. It feels alien to anyone used to driving a more modern car, but oddly enough that helped keep it in production. Millions of buyers had only ever driven a Model T and couldn't face relearning how to drive, so they kept buying them as long as Ford kept making them, right up to May 1927.

More than 15 million Model Ts were built, a number no car overtook until the VW Beetle in 1972. Ford had expanded Model T production around the world, making them in England, Canada, Argentina, Australia, Belgium, Brazil, Denmark, France, Japan, Mexico, Norway and Spain, creating the first global car. For better or worse, cars became part of everyday life because of the Ford Model T.

| 1924 Ford Model T roadster | |
|---|---|
| Length | 3,404 mm |
| Width | 1,676 mm |
| Weight | 725 kg |
| Wheelbase | 2,540 mm |
| Suspension | Single transverse semi-elliptic leaf springs (front and rear) |
| Brakes | Transmission brake via foot pedal, rear drums via handbrake lever |
| Engine | 2,896 cc in-line four, sidevalve |
| Power | 20 bhp @ 1,800 rpm |
| Torque | 83 lb-ft @ 900 rpm |
| Transmission | Two-speed epicyclic and reverse |
| 0–60 mph | n/a |
| Top speed | 45 mph |
| Cost new | £110 |
| Value today | £10,000–£50,000 |

TOP: A 1926 Model T in Tudor saloon form.

BOTTOM: A Model T during production testing at Ford's Detroit factory in 1908.

# Austin Seven

The Austin Seven, or 'Baby Austin', is often compared to the Model T Ford for its success at mobilising the masses, but the two were never in direct competition. By the time the Austin Seven was announced in 1922 the Model T was almost 15 years old and had been assembled in Britain since 1911. The Model T was also larger, thirstier and in a very different road tax bracket – 20 hp as opposed to 7 hp. So while the Ford was cheap to buy, it was not especially cheap to own.

Sir Herbert Austin saw the need for something different, and so did a great many others. In the UK this meant a boom in cyclecars that began in the years before the First World War. Tiny, lightweight constructions sometimes using motorcycle engines (hence the name), these were supposed to create affordable four-wheeled transport. However, in practice they were often flimsy, slow and no more weatherproof than a motorbike. Austin, with two successful models in the 20 hp and 12/4, knew he could do better.

Some of his first sketches for this 'car of the people' were reputedly laid out at life-size on his billiard table, which gives an idea of the Seven's compact dimensions. The design worked because it was a large car in miniature, not a motorised go-kart dressed as a car. There was a single transverse front leaf spring, like a Model T Ford, and a tiny four-cylinder sidevalve engine, like a Peugeot Quadrilette: a French model launched in 1921 with a similar aim. The Seven had brakes on all four wheels at a time when many larger cars had rear-wheel brakes only. The performance was remarkable, considering the little 696 cc engine (soon raised to 747 cc) – 50 mph and 50 mpg were possible, though not at the same time. You could order an electric starter and feel superior to the owners of many more expensive machines who were obliged to heave on a cranking handle.

The final nail in the coffin for the Seven's cyclecar rivals was the quality of bodywork. The original 'Chummy' tourer had a decent folding roof and side screens, and then in 1926 Austin introduced a proper, steel-panelled saloon. Selling at just £150, complete with Triplex glass, it made a nonsense of roofless alternatives. Back then, the average wage was around £250 a year, equivalent to £19,100 in 2025. A new Austin Seven's price translates to £11,400 today and, of course, they soon began appearing on the second-hand market, at which point car ownership really was open to almost everyone.

A vast range of Seven variants developed, including sporting models such as the EA or Ulster, which gave many people their first taste of motorsport. Indeed, such was the supply of ageing Sevens in the years after the Second World War (290,000 were made up to 1939), that whole classes and clubs sprang from amateur builders constructing their own 'specials' with the little Austin as a base. Today, the Austin Seven forms a hugely popular entry route to vintage motoring and competition in the UK, and it's one of the few cars of this era to be rising in value.

| 1926 Austin Seven Tourer | |
|---|---|
| Length | 2,794 mm |
| Width | 1,168 mm |
| Weight | 457 kg |
| Wheelbase | 1,905 mm |
| Suspension | Single semi-elliptic leaf spring, transverse (front); live axle with quarter-elliptic leaf springs and trailing arms (rear) |
| Brakes | Mechanical drum brakes, front and rear |
| Engine | 747 cc in-line four, sidevalve, water cooled |
| Power | 10 bhp @ 2,400 rpm |
| Torque | n/a |
| Transmission | Three-speed manual, synchromesh |
| 0–60 mph | n/a |
| Top speed | 51 mph |
| Cost new | £145 |
| Value today | £3,000–£25,000 |

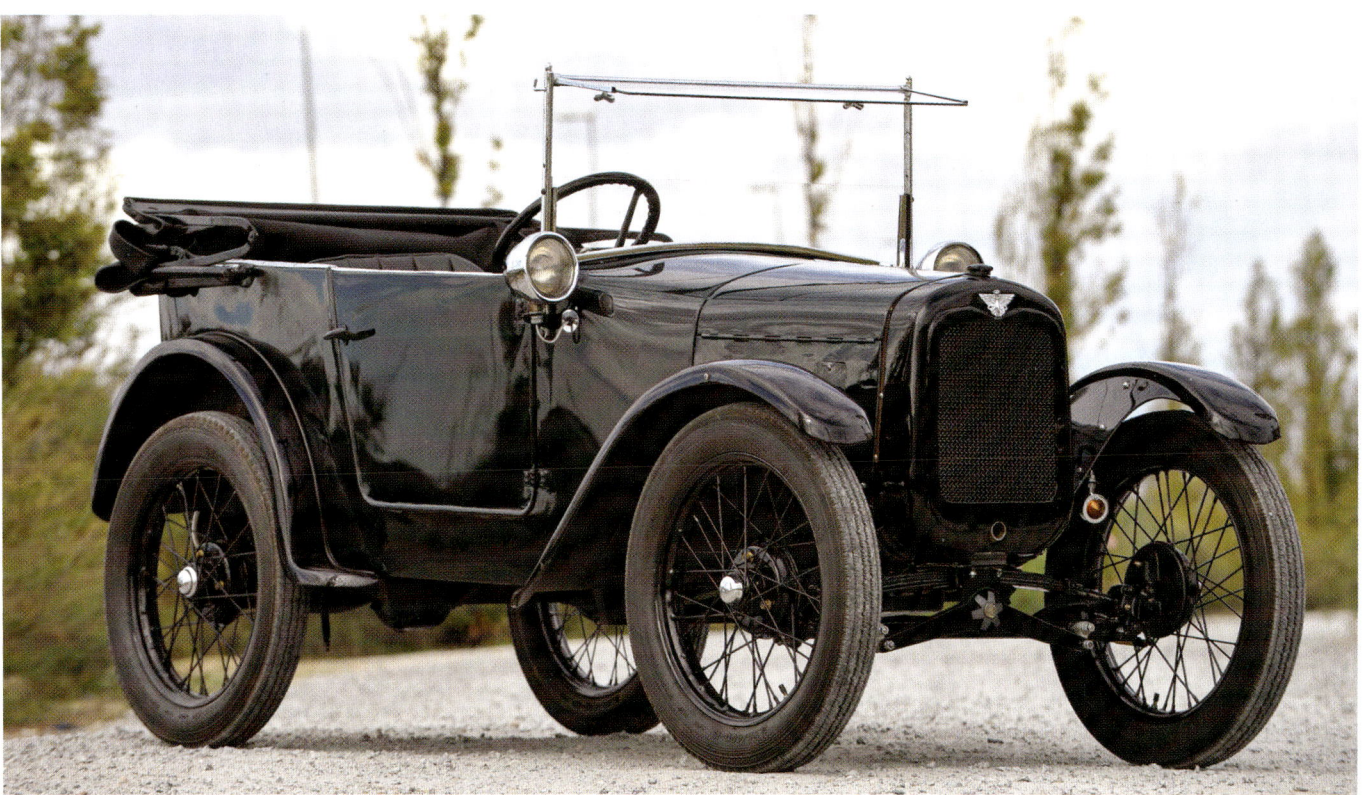

TOP: A 1934 Austin Seven saloon.

BOTTOM: The Chummy tourer, here in 'AD' form as introduced in 1926.

# Mercedes-Benz

Here is a name with a direct connection to the dawn of motoring. Carl Benz, aided by his wife Bertha, showed that the internal combustion engine could successfully power a small road vehicle. By the end of the nineteenth century, Benz & Cie. was the largest car-maker in a small industry, producing 572 vehicles in 1899 alone. Another pioneer, Gottlieb Daimler, had built his own company with his colleague Wilhelm Maybach. Soon after Daimler died in 1900, Maybach entered an agreement with a customer-turned-salesman called Emil Jellinek, based in the French Riviera. Jellinek specified features of a new, more sporting Daimler for Maybach to build, naming it after his daughter Mercedes. It was startlingly fast for the time – almost 40 mph – and boosted Daimler's sales enormously. Later, in 1923, both Benz and Daimler were suffering in the economic hardship of Germany after the First World War and agreed to merge. Daimler-Benz would make and sell cars called Mercedes-Benz, in honour of that pivotal early success.

From quite early on, Daimler-Benz made a range of Mercedes models across different sizes and classes, but it was the mighty 7.1-litre supercharged Sports models like the SSK that built the company's prestige. Indeed, the 770-series 'Grosser' Mercedes became the most popular choice amongst high-ranking Nazi officials in the 1930s, when Mercedes startled the world with its 'Silver Arrow' racing cars. Alongside these straight-eight, 180 mph machines, Mercedes launched something far more significant in the long run: the 260D, an early diesel-engined production car.

Daimler-Benz was much better placed than many German car firms in the post-war years, immediately retaking its place as the leading builder of Germany's luxury cars. Some key figures, including designer Friedrich Geiger, returned to work at Stuttgart and created the amazing 300SL 'Gullwing', among others. Just as in pre-war years, Mercedes maintained a range of solid if rather unexciting mid-market saloons as well as their eye-catching luxury products, providing a profitable base to develop ever-better range-topping machines. The S-class saloons, beginning with the W116 in 1971, were launch pads for technology that would eventually reach other Mercedes models and the rest of the industry.

Like BMW, Mercedes had something of a golden age from the 1960s to the 1980s, where the enduring company image was formed: these cars were beautifully built, comfortable, durable, quiet and always significantly more expensive than apparent rivals, which almost became a point of prestige in its own right. Styling changed slowly, rather like Rolls-Royce: a car that makes little effort to follow fads and fashions will still look good when fashions change.

Where BMW had its M-Division, Mercedes had AMG, an external tuning company later brought in-house. High-powered versions of standard coupés, saloons and latterly even SUVs became valuable additions to the range. Eventually, AMG-specific models like the SLS, a gullwing-doored tribute to the 300SL, gave Mercedes something to rival Porsche, Ferrari and Bentley. Mercedes is still innovating, and in 2022 showed the EQXX, an elegant EV saloon with a range of 1,000 km. Carl Benz and Gottlieb Daimler would be impressed.

# THROUGH THE YEARS

**CLOCKWISE FROM TOP LEFT:** A Daimler 'Mercedes'; SSK roadster; 300SL cabriolet; SLS Black; W116 S-class saloon; 260D saloon.

# Bugatti Type 35

In the 1920s, the difference between a fine road-going sports car and a Grand Prix car was quite slight, especially if winning races was a higher priority than road use. Such was the origin of the Bugatti Type 35, which, even 100 years on, would be some people's choice for the greatest sporting car of all time.

Many different variants evolved from one original model. This car featured a simple two-seater body powered by a 2-litre straight-eight engine with some impressive features for 1924: three valves per cylinder, an overhead camshaft and roller bearings on the crankshaft that allowed it to spin up to 6,000 rpm. Most other cars of the time were getting breathless at half that speed. Ettore Bugatti's genius extended beyond the engine; this car had a low-slung tubular chassis, a hollow front axle and alloy wheels to reduce unsprung weight, and numerous jewel-like details that contributed to the highest build quality – and high prices.

The Type 35 began winning races almost as soon as it was introduced in 1924, and from 1925 the first of many variants emerged. This was the 35A, simplified for those who only wanted a road car – yet soon 35As were winning races too. The 35T gained a larger 2.3-litre engine for road races like the gruelling Targa Florio in Sicily, and then came supercharged versions: 35C (2-litre) and 35B (2.3-litre). Bugatti found there was a market for less powerful versions with the same joyous handling and splendid design, so the Type 37 (a four-cylinder, 1.5-litre version) and Type 39 (eight cylinders, still 1.5-litre) came too.

Only 340 Type 35s left the factory in Molsheim, eastern France between 1924 and 1931, and a total of 300 Type 37s and 39s. Yet Type 35s and their derivatives won more than 2,000 races between 1924 and 1930, according to a historical piece published by Bugatti themselves in 2019. This almost certainly makes it the most successful racing model of all time, yet the majority were also used as road cars – especially when they ceased to be so dominant.

Three remarkable characteristics make any Type 35 a thrilling car to drive. First, the eight-cylinder engine delivers smooth, seamless power that no other vintage car of its size and era can surpass, and it does so with a famously exciting exhaust note. It was often compared to the sound of tearing calico, a coarse cotton cloth, but much louder! Second is the gearbox, which has a reversed and mirrored H-pattern, with first gear upper right and fourth gear lower left. It requires concentration to use but the change quality is amazing – light, precise and free of crunches, though it has no synchromesh. Third, and most impressive of all, is the car's handling. It steers so beautifully that it calls to mind a Lotus Elan of the 1960s – 40 years younger and an icon in its own right amongst drivers' cars. Now vastly valued and much imitated, the Type 35 is the car that made Bugatti a great name and, for a while, set standards no rival could meet.

| 1926 Bugatti Type 35B | |
|---|---|
| Length | 3,820 mm |
| Width | 1,506 mm |
| Weight | 762 kg |
| Wheelbase | 2,400 mm |
| Suspension | Semi-elliptic leaf springs and friction dampers (front); live axle with quarter-elliptic leaf springs and trailing links (rear axle) |
| Brakes | Integral aluminium drum brakes, mechanical operation, front and rear |
| Engine | 2,262 cc in-line eight, overhead camshaft, four valves per cylinder |
| Power | 140 bhp @ 5,300 rpm |
| Torque | n/a |
| Transmission | Four-speed manual, rear-wheel drive |
| 0–60 mph | n/a |
| Top speed | 130 mph |
| Cost new | n/a |
| Value today (any Type 35) | £500,000–£5 million |

**TOP:** The distinctive horseshoe grill has remained a trademark of Bugatti cars – though it has shrunk somewhat over the years.

**BOTTOM:** As graceful on the street as at the racetrack.

# Morgan Aero / Super Sports 'Three-Wheeler'

The little Morgans shouldn't have survived. They were products of the cyclecar boom of the years just before the First World War, and by the mid-1920s there were plenty of good small cars, like the Austin Seven, that rendered the clattering, flimsy cyclecars obsolete. Yet the Morgan had not one but two aces up its sleeve: sporting performance and that missing wheel.

Henry Frederick Stanley Morgan, usually known as HFS or Harry, put his first three-wheeler into production in 1910. This original tricycle set the basic pattern for all that followed: a large (by motorcycle standards) V-twin engine mounted across the nose, driving the single rear wheel by dog clutches and chains, based on a tubular backbone chassis. The front wheels were given independent front suspension by stub axles sliding on pillars. This combination resulted in good roadholding and surprisingly high speeds, so the little Morgans immediately found favour in competition. Nonetheless, calling a new model of 1914 the Grand Prix was perhaps a little hopeful.

When peace came in 1918, production continued and the model range expanded – taking in both two-seater and (rather snug!) four-seater versions with a choice of engines from J. A. P. and Blackburne – as record-setting and competition success continued to keep the Morgan name in favour among sporting types on a budget. That missing wheel meant that not only could owners drive one with a motorcycle licence, but that the vehicle dipped under an 8 cwt (*c*.400 kg) weight limit, attracting a discounted road tax: a Morgan paid £4 a year, while an Austin Seven might be twice as much. If these sound like tiny savings, remember that a great many people could barely afford a motorcycle; a Morgan that cost no more to run and could get away from most sports cars was a tempting prospect. By 1927, the Super Sports model could hit 80 mph in standard form.

Morgan continued to develop his little oddities, first moving from a two-speed to a three-speed gearbox, with better brakes, electric starting and lighter steering. Eventually he tried a more civilised approach with the F-type, using a four-cylinder car engine up front, borrowed from a Ford 8. In 1935, feeling the pressure from the increasing number of small, affordable sports cars from the likes of MG and Singer, he bowed to the inevitable and introduced his own four-wheeled model, the 4/4. But the three-wheeler refused to die, finding fans right to the end of the V-twin's UK production in 1939, while the F-type trike lasted until 1952.

By then, the Morgan Three-Wheeler Club had been formed, and the cars have retained an enthusiastic following ever since. They remain remarkably competitive with far larger, more powerful machines, and seeing them dice with gigantic vintage Bentleys on a racetrack is a treat. On the road, any V-twin Morgan offers a unique experience, rather like taxiing in a vintage biplane that's lost its wings. As each 'thump' from a firing cylinder pushes you down the road, you can't help but feel grateful that such an eccentric anomaly survived for so long.

**TOP:** A 1927 Morgan Aero with a sidevalve water-cooled J. A. P. engine.

**BOTTOM:** All Morgans used a single rear wheel until 1935, and the 'trike' survived into the 1950s.

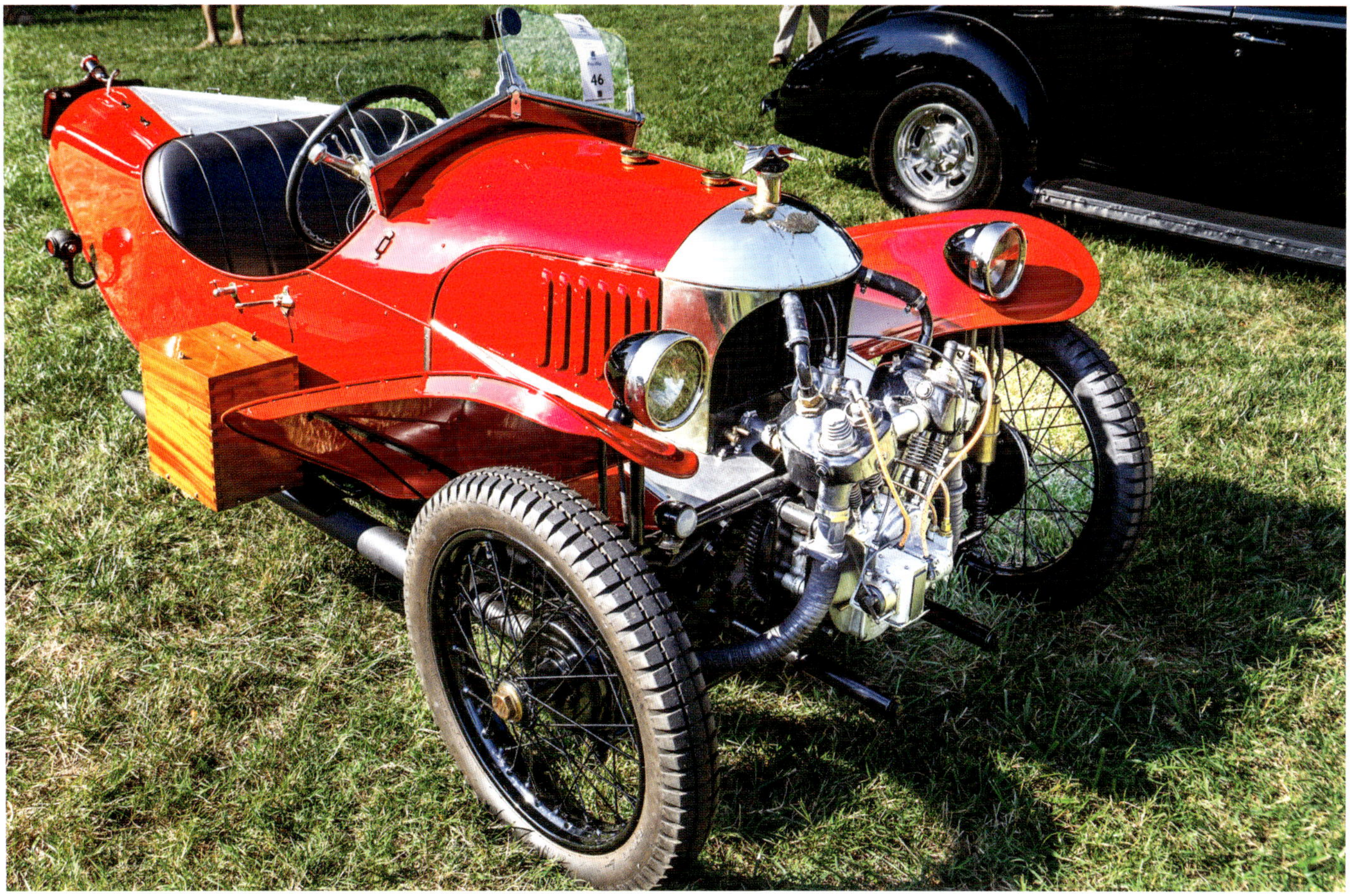

| 1935 Morgan Super Sports | |
|---|---|
| Length | 3,150 mm |
| Width | 1,499 mm |
| Weight | 406 kg |
| Wheelbase | 2,159 mm |
| Suspension | Independent via coil springs and sliding stub axles (front); trailing yoke and quarter-elliptic leaf springs (rear) |
| Brakes | Mechanical drum brakes, front and rear |
| Engine | 990 cc V-twin, overhead valve, air cooled |
| Power | 39 bhp @ 4,200 rpm |
| Torque | 50 lb-ft @ 2,400 rpm |
| Transmission | Three-speed manual, synchromesh |
| 0–60 mph | 14 sec. |
| Top speed | 85 mph |
| Cost new | £127 |
| Value today | £20,000–£45,000 |

# Duesenberg Model J

Ever heard the saying 'It's a doozie', meaning something extra special? Here's the origin: 'doozie' is short for Duesenberg, one of the greatest names in American motoring history, despite it being gone almost 90 years. Why? Because in the company's brief lifespan it was famous for making the most desirable machines money could buy, and its reputation lives on today. The list of achievements is startling too: Duesenberg built the first American car to win a Grand Prix, only a year after making their first car, and won the Indianapolis 500 in 1922, 1924, 1925 and 1927.

Fred and August Duesenberg, like Henry Royce, W. O. Bentley and Ettore Bugatti, were engineers rather than businessmen or management experts. They had been in and around the world of car-engine design since the early 1900s, eventually specialising in racing engines, and then marine and aero engines during the First World War. In 1920 they established themselves in Indianapolis itself and created a racing car with a Bugatti-inspired 3-litre straight-eight engine with three valves per cylinder and an overhead camshaft. It beat the French on their own turf, winning the 1921 French Grand Prix. Alongside racing cars, they also entered the world of high-luxury road cars.

Duesenberg's 4.2-litre Model A was the first American production car with a straight-eight engine (a feature that would later become almost standard across the industry), but innovation didn't stop there: it was a couple of decades ahead of everyone else with its four-wheel hydraulic brakes. In 1928 a successor came along, grander, faster and more excessive in every way: the Model J. It was like a Grand Prix car, with a 6.9-litre straight-eight engine with twin overhead camshafts and four valves per cylinder, and it had Grand Prix power: 265 bhp, which dwarfed any contemporary rival, and the supercharged version made even more. It offered only a three-speed manual gearbox, but with 89 mph available in second gear and 116 mph in top, it needed no more. Coachbuilders clamoured for the task of bodying such a marvellous chassis and stars from Hollywood's Golden Age queued up to buy them. The catalogue price of up to $17,950, twice the price of the V16 Cadillac introduced in 1930, wasn't enough to put off Mae West, Clark Gable, Gary Cooper, Elizabeth Arden, William Randolph Hearst and the royal families of Italy and Spain.

By 1930, though, the Wall Street Crash had marked the end of the Roaring Twenties and the beginning of the Great Depression. Most of the 481 Model Js that would be sold had already been built; it would take Duesenberg seven more years to shift them all, though it was a minor miracle the company survived the Depression at all – many luxury marques did not. In the end, it was the demise of parent company Cord (which had taken control in 1926) that brought down Duesenberg, whose great name and even greater products continue to be regarded as the finest cars in America. In 2017 a short-chassis supercharged SSJ model from 1935, ordered new by Gary Cooper, was estimated to sell at auction for $10 million. The hammer finally fell at $22 million: the Duesenberg legend is as strong as ever.

TOP: The twin-cam, straight-eight, 6.9-litre engine gave tremendous performance.

BOTTOM: A 1929 Duesenberg Model J Convertible Berline, bodied by Murphy.

| 1929 Duesenberg Model J | |
|---|---|
| Length | 6,248 mm |
| Width | 1,880 mm |
| Weight | 2,905 kg |
| Wheelbase | 3,899 mm |
| Suspension | Semi-elliptic leaf springs and friction dampers (front and rear) |
| Brakes | Hydraulic drum brakes, front and rear |
| Engine | 6,878 cc straight-eight, double overhead camshaft, four valves per cylinder |
| Power | 265 bhp @ 4,740 rpm |
| Torque | n/a |
| Transmission | Three-speed manual, rear-wheel drive |
| 0–60 mph | 9.8 sec. |
| Top speed | 106 mph |
| Cost new (SSJ) | $17,950 (c.£4,000) |
| Value today | £2 million–£20 million |

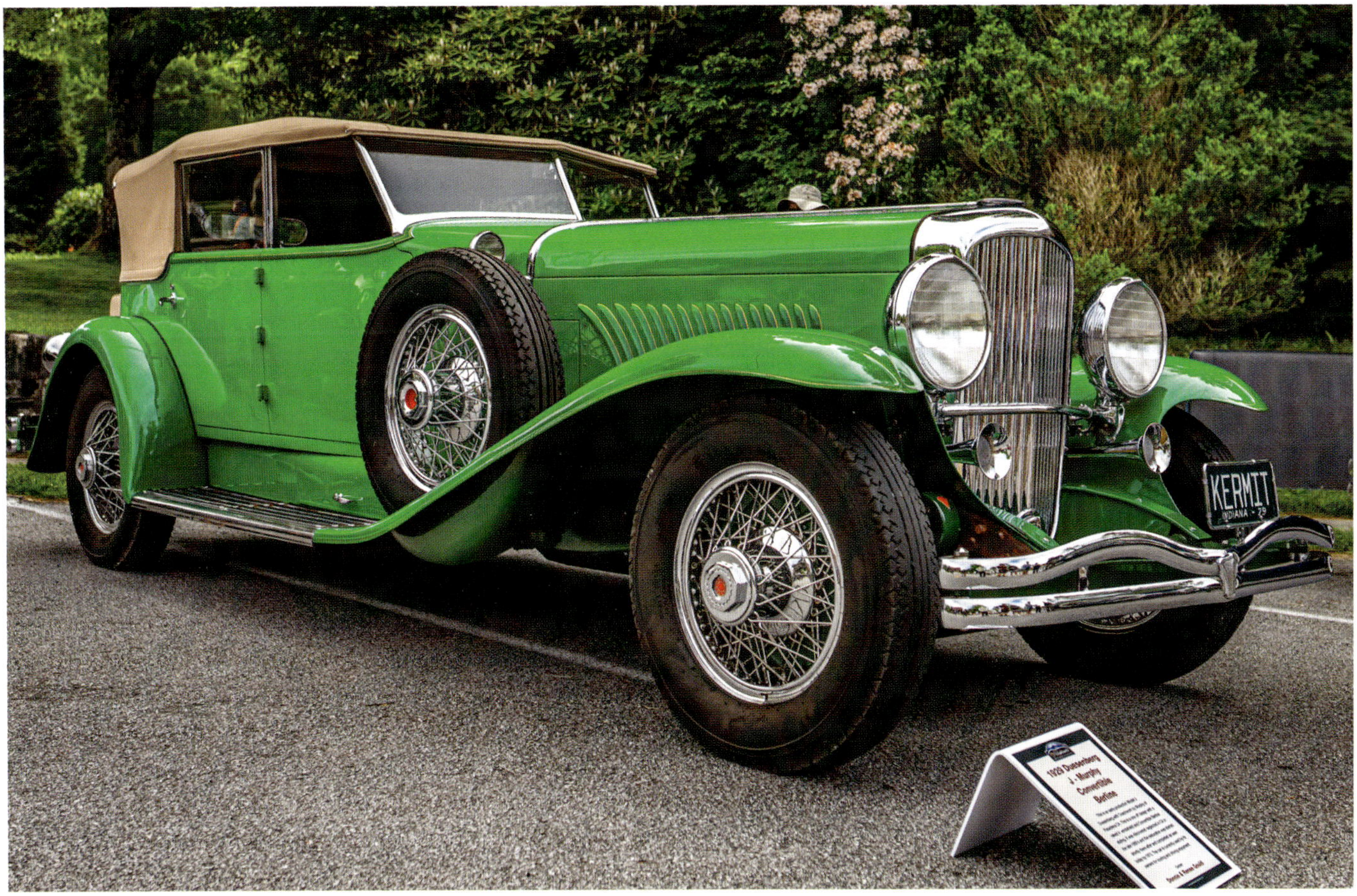

# Bentley 4½-litre 'Blower'

Walter Owen Bentley had raced cars and motorcycles before the First World War and designed successful aero engines during the conflict, including the Bentley rotary that powered many Sopwith Camels. He sought to apply what he'd learned from competition and aero engineering to the creation of a high-quality road car, and the first Bentley 3-litre emerged in 1921.

It was very advanced, with a four-cylinder overhead camshaft engine that used four valves per cylinder, like the 16-valve 'hot hatches' of the 1980s and 1990s. But cars of 100 years ago were very different in form, with the Bentley chassis usually bodied as a sporting open tourer or sensible, upright saloon. Bentleys were sturdily built and were accused of being too heavy, but they made durable long-distance racing cars, winning the Le Mans 24-hour race for the first time in 1924. This race was key to Bentley's prestige and success. The increasing speed of the competition and the increasing weight of saloon coachwork were reasons for expanding the 3-litre engine to create the 4½-litre model in 1927.

It was an instant classic. Although it won only one of Bentley's five Le Mans victories between 1924 and 1930, it was immensely popular with private owners and club racers, and many 3-litres have since been modified to the 4½-litre specification. One of the famous 'Bentley Boy' racing drivers, Sir Henry 'Tim' Birkin, felt it could be still faster and more successful with the use of supercharging. This is the principle of forcing more air/fuel mixture into the cylinders with a compressor driven by the engine, already in use by other makers, notably Mercedes. W. O. Bentley hated the idea of supercharging his cars so Birkin pursued the project himself, employing Amherst Villiers, a young expert on supercharger technology.

With a large supercharger or 'blower' emerging from the base of the radiator at the front of the car, the installation wasn't subtle. It wasn't a reliable one either, at least to begin with, but it did make prodigious power when it was on song, and Birkin eventually persuaded Bentley to make the 50 production examples necessary for an entry at Le Mans. They achieved this for 1930, but the two Blowers wore themselves out chasing down Rudolf Caracciola's supercharged Mercedes, which also retired, leaving the larger, heavier but unsupercharged Bentley Speed Six of Woolf Barnato and Glen Kidston to win. Soon after, Bentley Motors faced a financial crisis and was acquired by Rolls-Royce, and the Blower and its sister models disappeared into history.

Since then, original Blower Bentleys have become hugely valued and imitated, so much so that Bentley themselves decided to build a run of 12 exact copies of the supercharged 4½-litre, completed in 2023, at a price of around £1.5 million each. Noisy, heavy to drive, thirsty and vastly expensive, a true Blower is also one of the most exciting experiences any driver can hope for. The car's status might outweigh its achievements, but such details can't spoil the legend.

**TOP:** The front-mounted supercharger boosted power but made the potent Bentley less reliable.

**MIDDLE:** The cockpit of a Blower Bentley.

**BOTTOM:** The 'blower' sends compressed mixture back to inlet ports on the offside of the engine.

| 1930 Bentley 4½-litre 'Blower' ||
|---|---|
| Length | 4,445 mm |
| Width | 1,739 mm |
| Weight | 1,930 kg |
| Wheelbase | 2,985 mm |
| Suspension | Semi-elliptic leaf springs and Hartford friction dampers (front and rear) |
| Brakes | Bentley-Perrot mechanical drum brakes, front and rear |
| Engine | 4,398 cc in-line four, overhead camshaft, four valves per cylinder |
| Power | 175 bhp @ 3,500 rpm (standard) to 240 bhp @ 4,200 rpm (race) |
| Torque | (est.) 300 lb-ft @ 1,800 rpm |
| Transmission | Four-speed manual, unsynchronised |
| 0–60 mph | 12 sec. (race) to 15 sec. (standard) |
| Top speed | 98 mph (standard) to 130 mph (race) |
| Cost new | £1,720 (standard) |
| Value today | £2.75 million–£10 million |

# Rolls-Royce

Henry Royce was an unusually gifted electrical and mechanical engineer who built his first car in 1904, a few months before he was introduced to the Hon. Charles Rolls, an aristocratic young motoring enthusiast and owner of a car dealership. Their original agreement was for Royce to design and manufacture four models (of two, three, four and six cylinders) and for Rolls to sell them through his dealership in London. By 1906 the two men had agreed to form a company together to build cars and Rolls-Royce Limited began construction of a factory in Derby.

Never has one car built a firm's reputation like the Rolls-Royce Silver Ghost, as shown on p. 10. It made an extraordinarily bold claim in early advertising: it promised, after being described as such in a magazine, to be the best car in the world. Before long, those who tried it agreed it really was, and its reputation spread. That phrase – the Best Car in the World – has stuck to Rolls-Royce ever since, proving to be truer for some models than others. Rolls-Royce never did anything in a hurry and it was more than 15 years before they launched a smaller model, the 20 hp, to slot in beneath the imperious Ghost. It was a success and gave rise to several more generations of 'small' Rolls-Royces, while the Ghost evolved into the New Phantom, Phantom II and the impressive V12 Phantom III.

When Rolls-Royce bought the struggling Bentley Motors in 1931, the fates of the two marques were intertwined for the rest of the century. Initially Bentley thrived, first with the superb Derby models of the 1930s and then with the Mk VI and R-type, especially in Continental form. Rolls-Royce's base at Crewe, a wartime 'shadow factory' tasked with making aero engines, was profitable enough through the 1950s for the company to invest a great deal in exploring new models, including various prototypes for smaller saloons and coupés to capture more sales, probably under the Bentley name. In the end, none were produced and the differences between Rolls-Royce and Bentley were eroded: by the 1960s Bentley sales were falling away. Ironically, it was a crisis within Rolls-Royce's aero-engine business that put the company in peril and forced a separation, with Rolls-Royce Motors (including Bentley) spun off from the nationalised Rolls-Royce Ltd in 1973.

Bentley's image wasn't rescued until the Turbo models arrived in the 1980s, and by the 1990s it was Rolls-Royce that seemed threatened. The Silver Spirit and Turbo R looked very dated and their replacements, the Rolls-Royce Silver Seraph and the Bentley Arnage, were barely launched before the company was put up for sale and bought by Volkswagen. Or so VW thought. It turned out that while they had bought the Crewe works and the rights to build Bentleys, the rights to the Rolls-Royce brand and logo were still owned by the aero-engine maker … which sold them to BMW. So in 1998 the two marques split at last, with BMW constructing a new factory at Goodwood and taking Rolls-Royce into the twenty-first century as a 'House of Luxury' as well as a car marque, and with record sales success.

# THROUGH THE YEARS

**CLOCKWISE FROM TOP LEFT:** A Phantom II; Silver Shadow; Silver Cloud II; Phantom VII; Silver Spur.

# Citroën Traction Avant

Sometimes pioneering cars are not famous for being the very first, but for being the first to make an idea successful. So it was for the Citroën Traction Avant and front-wheel drive. The idea of a car pulling itself along the road with its front wheels rather than driving from the back had been around almost as long as cars themselves, and several manufacturers had front-drive models in production before Citroën. These, however, were either too expensive to develop and build to turn a profit (such as the offerings from Alvis and Tracta) or tiny entry-level machines (like those made by DKW in Germany), but André Citroën showed it could work for a mass-market family car. It changed the motoring landscape forever, but it also caused his downfall.

The brilliant designer André Lefèbvre joined Citroën in early 1933 and found the front-wheel drive project underway. Thus, not every innovative feature of the Traction Avant was his, but when added together they make a remarkable list: front-wheel drive, the daring chassis-less approach of monocoque construction, hydraulic brakes and all-round independent suspension by torsion bars. It nearly went a step further, as André Citroën only abandoned his ambition for automatic transmission at the last minute. Unhappily, he kept faith in a new type of constant-velocity joint in the driveshafts. They seized, and sorting out the problem after investing so heavily in the new car's production bankrupted Citroën. Only eight months after launching the Traction Avant, André Citroën was ousted and his company taken over by its main creditor, Michelin. He died six months later.

His creation, by contrast, went from strength to strength. Michelin's hard-nosed approach made the cars reliable and profitable, so by the time war came in 1939 it was an established success in mainland Europe and in the UK, where right-hand drive examples were built in Slough. During the war it became a favourite not only of the Gestapo but of the French Resistance, as it offered a mix of comfort, performance and safety unknown in other mass-produced models. First came the small-engined 7A, 7B and 7C, but it was the *Onze* (11) with 1,911 cc that became the classic of the range – it was offered in *Legère* (lightweight) or *Normale* form, the latter being longer, wider and roomier. The boot grew bigger and interesting multi-role bodies like the *Commerciale* (a combination van and estate car) and *Familiale* (an eight-seat people carrier), plus glamourous coupés and convertibles made sure there was a Traction for everyone.

It became a fixture on French streets for decades, while technical innovation continued too. A six-cylinder version tested the luxury market: in 1954 this model served as a try-out for the new oleo-pneumatic suspension that would soon be launched on the Citroën DS. The Traction Avant still feels great fun to drive, with an impressively lively feel from an engine output and three-speed gearbox that don't look exciting on paper. Few cars of its time could be used as daily transport now, but the Traction Avant is nothing if not a survivor – and it'll survive modern traffic just fine.

| 1948 Citroën Light Fifteen (English-built *Onze Legère*) | |
| --- | --- |
| Length | 4,318 mm |
| Width | 1,651 mm |
| Weight | 1,115 kg |
| Wheelbase | 2,908 mm |
| Suspension | Independent by lower links and torsion bars (front); by transverse torsion bar and trailing links (rear) |
| Brakes | Hydraulic drums, front and rear |
| Engine | 1,911 cc in-line four, overhead valve, water cooled |
| Power | 55 bhp @ 4,250 rpm |
| Torque | 90 lb-ft @ 2,200 rpm |
| Transmission | Three-speed manual |
| 0–60 mph | 20.6 sec. |
| Top speed | 76 mph |
| Cost new | £573 |
| Value today | £10,000–£40,000 |

TOP: A cabriolet model.

BOTTOM: The *Onze Normale*, slightly wider and longer than the *Legère* model.

# Tatra 77 and 87

If the Citroën Traction Avant seemed advanced in 1934, the Tatra 77 was positively futuristic. This was the height of the streamlining craze, but for almost all other manufacturers the fad was only skin-deep: British and French coachbuilders created sleek, teardrop-like shapes with fastback rooflines and faired-in headlamps, yet underneath were the same channel-section chassis and heavy, slow-revving engines. The Chrysler Airflow, launched the same year, was based on a more advanced monocoque structure with no separate chassis, but its mechanical features were conventional.

The Tatra, then, was very different, but Tatras had always been different. At first glance the cars created by chief design engineer Hans Ledwinka looked like other 1920s vehicles, but underneath they were not. From 1923 he established a pattern, using a central tubular backbone chassis, an air-cooled engine and independent swing-axle rear suspension. A wide range of cars, from economy models to luxury limousines, grew from this, but it was the influence of Hungarian airship designer Paul Jaray that would shift Tatra's fate.

From 1914 Jaray worked for Zeppelin at Friedrichshafen in southern Germany, developing the streamlining of vast airships, but in the 1920s he founded Stromlinien Karosserie Gesellschaft (Streamlined Coachwork Company). His ideas caught Tatra's attention, especially that of Hans Ledwinka, and Jaray was commissioned to design some streamlined prototypes. Meanwhile, Ledwinka was developing his own bold ideas, switching from front- to rear-engined layouts and creating a light, powerful, air-cooled V8 engine with a 3-litre capacity.

Though it only produced 60 bhp in the first Tatra 77, Jaray's low-drag bodywork meant the new car could pass 90 mph. Ledwinka embarked on a rapid redesign to improve the car's handling and boost power; these features came together with the mildly restyled Tatra 87 of 2.9-litres and 85 bhp, giving near-100 mph performance. More than 3,000 Tatra 87s were produced between 1936 and 1950, but it's Tatra's wartime story that is most often remembered now, for two reasons.

First, despite Ledwinka's redesign to improve weight distribution, the handling of the deceptively fast and smooth T87 could catch out the unaware. Arrive at a corner too quickly and the swing-axle rear suspension could lose grip when the car leaned hard to one side and, combined with the weight of engine and gearbox at the rear, the back end could slither round in an uncatchable skid. There was a persistent but probably inaccurate story that the German Army banned officers from driving captured or stolen T87s after a series of accidents, leading to the car being nicknamed the 'Czech secret weapon'.

Second, there was Ledwinka's working relationship with Ferdinand Porsche and his encounters with Adolf Hitler. This almost certainly meant the creation of the original Volkswagen was influenced by Jaray's streamlining and Ledwinka's design for a four-cylinder sibling to the T87. Tatra launched a lawsuit in 1938, which was settled by Volkswagen only in 1965. So while Tatra's far-sighted principles conquered the world through one of the most successful cars ever built, the relative obscurity of the T87 is unjust; it should be as famous as the Citroën Traction Avant.

| 1947 Tatra 87 | |
|---|---|
| Length | 4,740 mm |
| Width | 1,670 mm |
| Weight | 1,370 kg |
| Wheelbase | 2,850 mm |
| Suspension | Independent via transverse leaf spring, double wishbones (front); independent by swing axles and transverse leaf spring (rear) |
| Brakes | Hydraulic drum brakes, front and rear |
| Engine | 2,969 cc V8, overhead camshaft, air cooled |
| Power | 74 bhp @ 3,900 rpm |
| Torque | n/a |
| Transmission | Four-speed manual, rear-wheel drive |
| 0–60 mph | 16 sec. |
| Top speed | 103 mph |
| Cost new | n/a |
| Value today | £30,000–£90,000 |

TOP: The Tatra 77's streamlined form was revolutionary in the mid 1930s.

BOTTOM: The rear fin of the 87.

# Alvis 4.3-litre Vanden Plas Tourer

The second half of the 1930s represented a golden age for a new type of car. The first really good, fast roads were spreading out across Europe, and in the UK the speed limit (a widely ignored 20 mph) was removed altogether by the 1930 Road Traffic Act. Now cars capable of continuous, comfortable high-speed cruising were not only desirable but useful. Many manufacturers aimed to provide exactly this, with the likes of Mercedes, Bugatti, Delahaye and Alfa Romeo among the best known on the Continent, while in Britain the leading examples came from Bentley, Lagonda and Alvis.

Alvis was established in Coventry in 1919 and soon gained a reputation for building high-quality cars for the sporting driver at a sensible price, a reputation cemented by the splendid four-cylinder 12/50. But they also risked much on innovation, introducing a front-wheel drive car with all-independent suspension in 1928, six years before the Citroën Traction Avant. They were pioneers of the synchromesh gearbox, which makes it possible to change gear quickly and silently without needing to judge engine speed or double-declutch. By 1934 their six-cylinder Speed 20 model was the first to boast synchromesh on all four gears.

The Speed 20 developed into the larger, faster 3.5-litre, then the Speed 25 and, finally, in 1937, the 4.3-litre model. These were genuine 100 mph cars when fitted with lighter open bodywork. They were available in two different wheelbases, and a dozen of the shorter chassis were clothed by coachbuilder Vanden Plas in a gorgeous two-door, four-seat touring body. The car's stunning looks and high performance were backed up with the comfort and good road manners produced by independent front suspension, still unusual at that time.

Any 'Speed Model' Alvis is an exciting car to drive, with a smooth six-cylinder engine and a sporting connection to the road. The 4.3-litre model adds a distinctly post-war level of performance; it is both faster and more powerful than, say, a large six-cylinder Vauxhall or Ford saloon of the 1960s. The steering wheel is huge – there is no power assistance so you need the leverage – and you sit low, looking down a bonnet that seems even longer than it really is. The huge Lucas P100 headlamps give an extra point of reference for aiming the car down the road, and all you need then is the right kind of journey. In France such cars were once called *Grande Routières*, translating roughly as Grand Tourers, and they did indeed seem built for the grand routes.

Today, they are being built once again. The Alvis Car Company ceased production in 1967 but its workshop stores were preserved and the site became the headquarters of a leading Alvis specialist. Now re-awakened, the Alvis Car Company has started a Continuation Series of 25 Vanden Plas Tourers, only very slightly modernised to comply with regulations. Here is how *The Autocar* judged it in 1938:

'There are cars, good cars and super cars. When a car can be put into the last of these categories and yet is not by any means in the highest-priced class, considerable praise is due to the makers. The model in question is the latest 4.3-litre Alvis sports tourer.'

| 1938 Alvis 4.3-litre Vanden Plas Tourer | |
|---|---|
| Length | 4,851 mm |
| Width | 1,778 mm |
| Weight | 1,730 kg |
| Wheelbase | 3,149 mm |
| Suspension | Semi-elliptic leaf springs and Luvax adjustable dampers (front and rear) |
| Brakes | Mechanical drum brakes, front and rear |
| Engine | 4,387 cc in-line six, overhead valve, water cooled |
| Power | 137 bhp @ 3,600 rpm |
| Torque | n/a |
| Transmission | Four-speed manual, synchromesh |
| 0–60 mph | 10.5 sec. |
| Top speed | 105 mph |
| Cost new | £995 |
| Value today | £200,000–£350,000 |

TOP: George Hartwell leads the LCC 3-hour Sports Car Race at Brooklands on 16 July 1938 in an Alvis 4.3.

BOTTOM: A 1937 4.3-litre Tourer resplendent in two-tone paintwork at the Bicester Heritage Centre.

# POST-WAR PROGRESS
## 1945 TO 1959

# Volkswagen Type 1 'Beetle'

The VW Beetle might be the most recognisable car in the world. An early batch was built for testing as far back as 1937 and it remained in full-time production from 1945 to 2003, with more than 21.5 million cars built. Ninety years after it was conceived, the original Volkswagen is still known and widely seen on the roads of every continent in the world, short of Antarctica.

The car's origins are rooted in the Third Reich, when Adolf Hitler became convinced of the German people's need for a simple, affordable car – Volkswagen means 'people's car' – to help mobilise the country via the network of new *autobahnen*, or motorways. The contract went to Ferdinand Porsche and he in turn employed a team of designers and engineers, though the ideas for the car's layout and general appearance may well have been 'borrowed' from several others who were not credited (see the entry for the Tatra 77 and 87, p. 32). The new car would be called the KdF-Wagen, short for *Kraft durch Freude*, meaning strength through joy. The factory was built at a new town, itself named Stadt des KdF-Wagens bei Fallersleben, or KdF-Stadt for short.

The outbreak of war put a stop to car production as the factory turned over to building military vehicles based on KdF-Wagen components, chiefly the Kübelwagen. This high-chassis, Jeep-like machine was built in such numbers (more than 50,000) that, despite heavy bombing, the factory remained a valuable facility when peace came. However, no British car manufacturers could be persuaded to take it on or to move production to the UK, so an enterprising British Army officer, Major Ivan Hirst, persuaded the Army to order 20,000 cars for its own use. Production began, the KdF-Wagen became the Volkswagen and KdF-Stadt became Wolfsburg. By the end of 1946, 10,020 cars had been completed. It would be another three years before the factory was handed back to German control, by which time the military orders had been succeeded by commercial production. Volkswagens were being sold to private customers at home and, crucially, abroad too.

For the first nine years of production the Beetle (Käfer in German, Bug to Americans) whirred along with the same 1,131 cc air-cooled flat-four engine developed for the Kübelwagen. With only 25 bhp, performance was low on thrills, but the car's unusually streamlined shape allowed a 60 mph cruising speed. This rose slightly from 1954 as the engine size grew to 1,192 cc and power to around 33 bhp, when a new model made its debut, with an oval rear window replacing the split-screen original. In 1965 the rear window again grew larger, and this time a host of different models and engine sizes became available, reflecting the car's vast success. The Wolfsburg plant was larger than ever, and the company's crucial American market sales hit a real high in the 1960s, after ten patient years waiting for acceptance.

The Volkswagen was about as different from America's homegrown automobiles as it could be: light, small, rear-engined and economical, with a steady refusal to change its appearance in a market that demanded a new look every single year. It became an alternative form of motoring, giving mobility to those who couldn't afford to buy and run a gas-guzzler, or who simply preferred something a little more manageable on city streets. It became a part of American culture and counter-culture, identified with the hippy movement while also spawning a new phenomenon – the beach buggy.

The Beetle's chassis, a flat punt with gearbox and engine at the rear and simple, compact torsion-bar suspension, made an ideal basis on which to build different bodywork – especially when glass-fibre construction became cheaply and widely available. VWs were drag raced, modified, turned into off-road machines for desert racing and customised for street use. The Cal-look approach, developed in southern California in the late 1960s, saw VWs lowered and de-bumpered, often with Porsche-style wheels fitted, and it's since become popular across the world. In the UK and Europe, the huge supply of affordable, ageing Beetles gave rise to a new kit-car industry, with VW underpinnings supporting numerous replicas and bold new designs.

If it needed any help finding its way into the hearts of buyers in America and the rest of the world, a starring role in a film called *The Love Bug* (1969) clinched it. The story of a little white VW with a mind of its own was a huge success, and Herbie starred in four sequels. Model variations increased in number, and in 1970 the wheelbase was lengthened by an inch as the front suspension in the 1302 and 1303 models changed from torsion bars to more conventional coil spring and damper struts.

Knowing the Beetle couldn't last forever, in the 1970s Volkswagen expanded away from purely Beetle-based, air-cooled models for the first time. Production at Wolfsburg ceased in 1974 when the new Golf was introduced, but demand elsewhere was undeniable and production continued in Australia, Mexico and Nigeria. Of these, the Mexican plant lasted longest, producing its final Beetle on 30 July 2003, six years after the introduction of the Golf-based New Beetle, a retro-inspired model that itself lasted until 2019.

The influence of the VW Beetle is difficult to overstate. For instance, no Volkswagen would have meant no Porsche, and no VW Type 2, the original camper van or hippy bus, plus all its descendants (see p. 56). The company built around the Beetle is now the largest car-maker in the world, by worldwide sales, encompassing VW itself, Audi, Seat, Porsche, Lamborghini, Bentley, Bugatti, Skoda and the truck makers MAN and Scania. In 2022 it made a net income of €15.8 billion from a revenue of €280 billion. It created a city of 125,000 people – Wolfsburg – and as an example of how deeply VW is part of German life, you can buy Volkswagen sausages (actually currywurst) in supermarkets and football stadiums. The sausage even has its own VW part number! All because a stubborn British Army officer wouldn't let a good product die.

**TOP:** A 1972 Beetle.

**BOTTOM:** A 1951 Beetle with the distinctive split rear screen just visible.

**FOLLOWING PAGE:** Beetles conquered the world – this convertible model is in Indonesia.

| Volkswagen Type 1 'Beetle' (figures for 1949 model) ||
|---|---|
| Length | 4,039 mm |
| Width | 1,549 mm |
| Weight | 708 kg |
| Wheelbase | 2,400 mm |
| Suspension | Upper and lower trailing links and torsion bars, telescopic dampers (front); swing axles, trailing arms, torsion bars (rear) |
| Brakes | Hydraulic drums, front and rear |
| Engine | 1,131 cc horizontally opposed four-cylinder, overhead valve, air cooled |
| Power | 25 bhp @ 3,300 rpm |
| Torque | 49 lb-ft @ 2,000 rpm |
| Transmission | Four-speed manual, rear-wheel drive |
| 0–60 mph | 37.2 sec. |
| Top speed | 66 mph |
| Cost new | *c.*£200 |
| Value today | £10,000–£30,000 |

# Land Rover

It's another of the immortals – along with the VW Beetle and the Mini, the Land Rover is a vehicle whose influence is all around us. Indeed, examples of even the first generation are still in daily use around the world, as well as being restored and cherished as classics. Like the Citroën it wasn't quite the first of its type, but it was the one that made such vehicles a success and opened up new markets.

The Land Rover was created after a conversation between two brothers, Maurice and Spencer Wilks, chief designer and managing director of long-established British car-maker Rover. Maurice had a farm on Anglesey, North Wales, where he was using a war-surplus Willys Jeep, and when Spencer asked him in 1947 what he would do when the battered Jeep gave out, Maurice said, 'Buy another one, I suppose. There isn't anything else.'

This, so the legend goes, got them thinking. They saw a gap in the market and needed a new product to keep their large post-war factory busy, so they sent designer Gordon Bashford to buy two more ex-Army Jeeps and begin work on a prototype. It made for a capable off-road tool, but for production the Jeep chassis and axles were ditched, and they used the four-speed gearbox and 1.6-litre engine from the Rover 75 'P3' saloon. It was launched in 1948 as a basic agricultural or light industrial vehicle, with decent on-road performance too. 'Basic' was the right word for the specification – door tops and a canvas roof were extras – but it cost only £450, as it dodged the purchase tax applied to road cars.

Land Rovers became the obvious tool for petrol- (or diesel-) powered exploration where there were no roads, and their military potential was clear from the start. As private vehicles they evolved through a second series, introduced in 1958 with some minor styling changes, a Series IIA in 1961 that brought in a larger 2.25-litre diesel, then a Series III in 1971 that had its headlamps in the wings rather than the grille, a feature introduced in the last two years of SIIA production.

The remarkably unaltered basic design received an upgrade in 1983 when the 90 and 110 were launched with coil springs instead of leaf springs, and a much more modern interior. These were renamed the Defender in 1990, when an improved turbo-diesel engine, the 200TDi, began to account for the vast majority of Land Rovers sold. The Defender lasted until January 2016, not quite making 70 years since the first Land Rover was built, but still a remarkable achievement. Always comparatively slow, noisy and heavy to drive, Land Rovers nonetheless have a charm and rugged appeal that later (and in many ways, better) Japanese rivals struggle to match. The fact that the Land Rover gave rise to so many long-lived imitators, especially the Toyota Land Cruiser, shows just how cleverly the Wilks brothers filled that immense gap in the market.

**TOP:** A 1948 Series I, with the headlamps behind the grille, unique to 1948-1950 models.

**BOTTOM:** A Series III pickup making easy work of the rugged terrain of the Dominican Republic.

| 1955 Land Rover Station Wagon ||
|---|---|
| Length | 3,574 mm |
| Width | 1,588 mm |
| Weight | 1,347 kg |
| Wheelbase | 2,184 mm (86 in) |
| Suspension | Live axles with semi-elliptic leaf springs and telescopic dampers (front and rear) |
| Brakes | Hydraulic drums, front and rear |
| Engine | 1,997 cc in-line four-cylinder, IOE, water cooled |
| Power | 52 bhp @ 4,000 rpm |
| Torque | 101 lb-ft @ 1,500 rpm |
| Transmission | Four-speed manual, four-wheel drive |
| 0–50 mph | 24.9 sec. |
| Top speed | 59.5 mph |
| Cost new | c.£590 |
| Value today | £15,000–£35,000 |

# Jaguar XK120

It's rare for a car to emerge that trumps its rivals in every department – looks, performance, even price – but the Jaguar XK120 did just that. It set standards of speed and acceleration for post-war sports cars that even the Italians could only match in full race trim, and its long, graceful curves made British rivals look dumpy. Yet it cost just £1,263, a figure that wasn't much more than half the price of a Bristol 400 or an Aston Martin DB1, and still several hundred pounds cheaper than an Alvis TB21, and it was quicker than all three. The Healey Silverstone and Cadillac-engined Allard J2 would have given the XK120 a run for its money, selling at similar prices, but these were not far from bare-bones competition machines, and they won no beauty contests.

The XK120 was styled by Jaguar boss William Lyons, the body built on a shortened chassis from a Jaguar Mk V saloon but with torsion-bar suspension via wishbones at the front. It was powered by the XK engine, which would change Jaguar's fortunes. The unit was conceived while Lyons and his engineers Bill Heynes, Walter Hassan and Claude Bailey were supposed to be on fire-watching duty at the SS-Jaguar factory in Coventry in the last years of the war. Lyons wanted a twin-cam engine – an expensive, complex design only then found in racing cars or the most expensive exotics from Bugatti and Alfa Romeo – and left the engineers to get on with it.

This they did, in both four-cylinder and six-cylinder forms, and as late as 1949 you could find advertisements for the new 'Jaguar Super Sports in 2-litre and 3½-litre form'. In the end, only the six-cylinder 3.4-litre version was built. Getting hold of one was difficult, though. Lyons thought few would sell and, rather than tooling up for pressed-steel body panels, he had the first 200 cars coachbuilt in aluminium, after which the rave reception made tooling up for larger-scale production very urgent. Even then, almost all production went to the USA in the post-war 'export-or-die' craving for foreign currency.

This was tantalising in the extreme for British sports-car lovers, who saw the XK's remarkable road-test results (the '120' referred to a genuine 120+ mph top speed) and instant competition success – including circuit racing and three Alpine Rally wins on the trot – plus an eye-catching speed record that saw Jaguar raise the mark for production cars to 132.6 mph in May 1949. Meanwhile, the first production example went to Hollywood in the hands of Clark Gable. Jaguar had the glamour to match the 'go'.

The XK120 led directly to the C-type, Le Mans success, the D-type and the E-type, creating a lineage of sporting greatness on track and off that still feeds Jaguar's brand image today. Perhaps more importantly to classic car lovers, they still feel thrilling to drive, requiring a mixture of delicacy (that huge steering wheel, the crunchy Moss gearbox!) and bravery, if you're to exploit the car's impressive power. As a benchmark for the sports-car experience, it's hard to match.

| 1950 Jaguar XK120 | |
|---|---|
| Length | 4,394 mm |
| Width | 1,562 mm |
| Weight | 1,325 kg |
| Wheelbase | 2,591 mm |
| Suspension | Independent by wishbones and torsion bars, telescopic dampers (front); live axle, leaf springs, telescopic dampers (rear) |
| Brakes | Hydraulic drums, front and rear |
| Engine | 3,442 cc in-line six-cylinder, DOHC, water cooled |
| Power | 160 bhp @ 5,100 rpm |
| Torque | 195 lb-ft @ 2,500 rpm |
| Transmission | Four-speed manual, rear-wheel drive |
| 0–60 mph | 12 sec. |
| Top speed | 126 mph |
| Cost new | £1,263 |
| Value today | £60,000–£130,000 |

TOP: The OTS variant showcases the XK120's lines well.

MIDDLE: The engine of a 1953 XK120.

BOTTOM: Drophead Coupé, Coupé and Open Top Sports versions, side by side.

# Citroën 2CV

The years following the Second World War saw the production of many small, affordable people's cars, most notably the original – the Volkswagen. What was remarkable about many of them, when you consider that they had to be reliable and also cheap to buy and run, is how innovative they were. None was more so than the Citroën 2CV.

Citroën were used to innovation, having changed the motoring landscape with the Traction Avant in 1934. Only two years later, Pierre Boulanger (soon to be Citroën's president) started the development of the *Toute Petite Voiture*, which would become the 2CV. As well as a front-mounted, air-cooled, flat-twin engine driving the front wheels, the 2CV used a platform chassis with compact, simple but very clever suspension. The bodywork was made from the most basic panels, initially corrugated and only available in grey. All were quickly and easily removable for repair or replacement, and even the seats could be taken out to make room for larger loads, or to use as picnic furniture. Here was a car designed without compromise for an unusual target – it had to transport four people and 50 kg of farm goods to market at 30 mph, and be able to carry a basket of eggs across a ploughed field … without breaking any of the eggs!

This gave rise to that marvellous suspension. Each front wheel was mounted on an arm leading forward from a chassis cross-member, and each rear wheel on an arm trailing back from a cross-member. These arms were connected to coil springs contained in cylinders lying along the side of the floor, one spring pulled forward by a front wheel, one pulled back by the rear wheel. Crucially, being housed in the same cylinder meant they were interlinked: go over a bump with the front wheel, and the wheel rises while the suspension pushes the rear wheel on that side down, resisting any pitching effect and making the car's ride amazingly level over uneven ground. The rather long, soft springs mean the overall ride is soft and the car has lots of wheel travel.

That little engine (initially just 375 cc and making 9 bhp, or 2 *Cheval Vapeur*, meaning roughly 'steam horsepower') was designed to run at full throttle all day long without suffering, and a four-speed gearbox had synchromesh on every ratio, making the car easy to drive. From 1955 buyers could choose a larger 425 cc engine and the car was available with a centrifugal clutch, like a moped, making it easier still for novice drivers to operate. In 1965 a still larger 602 cc engine became available, lasting to the end of production in France in 1988, and in Portugal in 1990.

The 2CV was always the butt of jokes and nicknames, but it was enduringly popular wherever economical motoring was required, becoming associated with a kind of counter-culture of its own, like the VW Beetle. Yes, it's slow, thrifty, basic and noisy, and in corners it leans over like a dinghy in a gale, but it's impossible to drive a 2CV without smiling. Which is what makes it so well loved to this day.

| 1953 Citroën 2CV | |
|---|---|
| Length | 3,777 mm |
| Width | 1,476 mm |
| Weight | 499 kg |
| Wheelbase | 2,370 mm |
| Suspension | Longitudinal paired coil springs operated by tie-rods; friction dampers on cross-members (front and rear) |
| Brakes | Hydraulic drums, front (inboard) and rear |
| Engine | 375 cc flat-twin, overhead valve, air cooled |
| Power | 9 bhp @ 3,500 rpm |
| Torque | 16 lb-ft @ 1,800 rpm |
| Transmission | Four-speed manual, front-wheel drive |
| 0–60 mph | n/a |
| Top speed | 41 mph |
| Cost new | £565 |
| Value today | £5,000–£25,000 |

TOP: A 1955 example with 'ripple' bonnet.

BOTTOM: Two Citroëns side by side, with the 2CV's predecessor, the TPV, in front.

# Bristol 401

Bristol Cars was born from not one but two world wars. Sir Stanley White, director of the Bristol Aeroplane Company, had lived through an uncomfortable time after the First World War, when demand for aeroplanes and aero engines plummeted, and he struggled to keep his factories busy. Before the end of the Second World War, he and his son George White were in discussions with the Aldington brothers of Frazer-Nash, who had been distributors of BMW cars before the war, badged 'Frazer Nash-BMW', and plans developed for Bristol to manufacture the cars at its Filton plant. As the new model was developed – essentially a BMW 327-like body on a 326 chassis with a 328 engine – boardroom changes meant Bristol Cars would sell this new machine as an independent entity and the Frazer-Nash name would no longer appear.

The new model was well received for the performance of its lively BMW straight-six engine and clever independent suspension, but it was yet to find its own identity. That came in 1948 with the 401. For the first time, Bristol had a distinctive look of its own, even if the BMW-style paired radiator grilles remained. The styling was neither German nor British but Italian, with Carrozzeria Touring of Milan providing the streamlined fastback shape. It looked a more sporting car than the 400, yet had great seating room, a huge boot and a much-improved interior, with a proper heater and well-thought-out pockets and storage compartments.

It was on the road that the new Bristol really showed itself off. Rather like the Bentley Continental that would emerge in 1952, a sleek body built in aluminium allowed a high top speed, in this case 97 mph from an engine of just 1,971 cc: a 2.1-litre, six-cylinder Rover saloon of 1948 would top out at 75 mph. But more than that, the Bristol's torsion-bar rear suspension and well-controlled transverse leaf front-springing worked so sure-footedly with the car's accurate steering that road testers ran out of superlatives. Here's Laurence Pomeroy of *The Motor*:

'The particular merit of the 401 is a combination of virtues which may not be equalled in any other motor car in the world. It will comfortably carry four people, in addition to them it will swallow an almost fabulous volume of luggage. It will sustain 80–90 mph from dawn until the cows come home; and then on into the night. I feel that if, unhappily, one were confined to drive one car for all occasions … the Bristol would be the best buy in the world today, taking into account fuel economy, high average speeds, safety and reliability.'

The 401 gave rise to a long line of successors, evolving into several variations of a two-door saloon or coupé shape and switching from the BMW-derived engine to Chrysler V8s in 1961. Thus they remained, changing infrequently, into the twenty-first century. Always individual, expensive and something of an acquired taste, you either 'get' Bristols or you don't, and those that do can be almost evangelical about these uniquely British grand tourers.

| 1952 Bristol 401 | |
|---|---|
| Length | 4,864 mm |
| Width | 1,702 mm |
| Weight | 1,264 kg |
| Wheelbase | 2,896 mm |
| Suspension | Independent via transverse leaf and upper links (front); live axle with longitudinal torsion bars (rear) |
| Brakes | Hydraulic drums, front and rear |
| Engine | 1,971 cc in-line six, overhead valve, water cooled |
| Power | 85 bhp @ 4,500 rpm |
| Torque | 107 lb-ft @ 3,500 rpm |
| Transmission | Four-speed manual, rear-wheel drive |
| 0–60 mph | 17.4 sec. |
| Top speed | 97 mph |
| Cost new | £3,214 |
| Value today | £20,000–£60,000 |

TOP: The distinctive rear of the 401.

BOTTOM: The Bristol 401 evolved into the identical-looking 403, with improvements to power output, handling and braking.

# Morris Minor

Yet another in the post-war surge of people's cars, for cost reasons the Minor ended up rather more conventional than its designer intended. That designer, of course, was Alec Issigonis. Though he is better remembered for creating the Mini, his approach to packing people inside a car and making that car easy and pleasant to drive were plain to see in the original Minor.

Issigonis's design for the Morris Ten's proposed independent front suspension in 1937 was ditched for reasons of expense. However, his ideas got him noticed and he was allowed to head up the design work for a new small-car project, started as far back as 1941. The concept, nicknamed Mosquito, had the familiar Minor shape and advanced technical features: all-independent suspension by torsion bars in a chassis-less monocoque structure, rack-and-pinion steering and an 800 cc flat-four engine, perhaps influenced by what was known of the KdF-Wagen (VW Beetle) at that time.

Lord Nuffield, Morris's chief, disliked both Issigonis and the Mosquito/Minor project, referring to the car as 'the poached egg'. It was almost a compliment in disguise – the Minor's short, wide, rounded shape was unlike the narrow, upright, old-fashioned Ford Popular and other small cars of the 1940s, and it provided as much space for occupants as much larger cars. But Nuffield's impatience with growing costs, and a rush to launch the Minor at the first post-war London Motor Show in 1948, meant the engine development was cancelled and the rear suspension became a simple live-axle design on leaf springs.

It wasn't enough to spoil the Minor MM, that first model with the headlamps next to the radiator grille and a sidevalve engine. It still had better roadholding and nicer steering that any rival, with a spacious, comfy interior and a good ride, thanks to the specially commissioned 14-inch wheels, three inches smaller and much lighter than the old Morris 8s. In 1952 the Minor's enduring look arrived with the Series II, the headlamps now high up on the front of the wings and the old sidevalve engine replaced by the 803 cc Austin A-series overhead valve unit. However, with 30 bhp it was still a pedestrian performer and it wasn't until the Minor 1000 was launched in 1956 that the definitive Minor arrived.

Minors soon became part of the landscape, as almost the default second car for households affluent enough to own two and a much-loved first car for millions of working families. A convertible tourer version offered open-topped motoring with four seats, while the Traveller – a half-timbered two-door estate launched in 1953 – offered still more space and versatility. Van and pickup versions made ideal small commercial vehicles, as nice to drive and cheap to run as the four-seat versions.

Today, Minors are probably the most popular classic cars in Britain, with well over 20,000 examples surviving, many cared for by members of the Morris Minor Owners' Club. When production ended in 1971, more than 1.6 million Minors had been built, and their pet-like appeal, pleasing road manners and outstanding specialist support still make them a gateway to the classic car scene for thousands of people.

TOP: An original 1950 'low-light' model.

MIDDLE: The Traveller body was popular, seen here on a 1968 example.

BOTTOM: The spartan interior of a 1970 Morris Minor.

| 1957 Morris Minor 1000 | |
|---|---|
| Length | 3,759 mm |
| Width | 1,549 mm |
| Weight | 800 kg |
| Wheelbase | 2,184 mm |
| Suspension | Independent via longitudinal torsion bars, lever-arm dampers (front); live axle, leaf springs, lever-arm dampers (rear) |
| Brakes | Hydraulic drums, front and rear |
| Engine | 948 cc in-line four-cylinder, overhead valve, water cooled |
| Power | 37 bhp @ 4,750 rpm |
| Torque | 48 lb-ft @ 3,000 rpm |
| Transmission | Four-speed manual, rear-wheel drive |
| 0–60 mph | 31.3 sec. |
| Top speed | 75 mph |
| Cost new | £603 |
| Value today | £2,000–£25,000 |

# Porsche 356

For a company that became so famous and successful, Porsche's car production started very quietly. Ferdinand Porsche himself was highly accomplished and very well known, having designed not only competition cars like the Mercedes-Benz SSK and the Auto-Unions, but also tanks. Most of all he was known for the KdF-Wagen that became the Volkswagen Beetle. He was imprisoned for three years after the Second World War, during which time his son Ferry Porsche kept the family's consultancy business going and started work on a new design, the 356, setting up small-scale production in an old sawmill in Gmünd, Austria. Only 50 were built here, bodied by hand in aluminium.

From 1950 production began in earnest, when the Porsche family moved back to Stuttgart, and the 356 became a standardised product with a steel body built by coachbuilder Reutter. It used VW suspension and engine components on a VW-like (but new) chassis, plus a streamlined body shaped by long-time Porsche colleague Erwin Komenda. From the beginning Porsche knew the route to success was through motorsport and this efficient little car won its class at Le Mans on the first attempt, in 1951. Further success soon followed at the Mille Miglia, Nürburgring, Targa Florio and even the gruelling Carrera Panamericana in Mexico.

Those VW components soon evolved into Porsche's own as the engines grew to 1.3- and then 1.5-litre, while the bodies developed too. A cabriolet was offered from 1951 and the initial two-piece split windscreen became a single piece of bent glass in 1952, then a single piece of curved glass in the 356A of 1955: a sleeker, more mature update of the body shape. Porsche offered the 356 in various states of tune, always aware of the model's continued use in motorsport, so a 356A could be bought as Standard (60 bhp), Super (75 bhp) or even Carrera (100 bhp, thanks to twin overhead camshafts on each bank of cylinders).

Porsche also saw the importance of the growing US market both to Volkswagen and to their British and European sports-car rivals, so they created the Speedster with America in mind. This was a lightened roadster version of the 356A, with a cut-down screen and good performance, and is now one of the most sought-after 356s of all. The 356 lasted well into the 1960s with the 356B (1959) and 356C (1963) adding larger, more powerful engines – and eventually disc brakes and better steering – though driving a 356 quickly always remained something of an art. The swing-axle rear suspension means cornering just a bit too hard can lead to a sudden loss of grip at the rear wheels, causing a spin. But the steering – light, sensitive and full of feel – and the supple, rather elastic suspension let you press on fast enough to surprise much more powerful cars.

That was always the 356's appeal: a sporting underdog that eventually gave rise to a whole family of sports cars, supercars and racing machines. Nowadays they're valued much higher than their four-cylinder engines and modest performance figures would suggest, but as the first of a mighty breed, they will always be revered by Porsche fans.

TOP: The B model in cabriolet form.

MIDDLE: The view from the driver's seat.

BOTTOM: A 'pre-A' model from 1953.

| 1954 Porsche 356 Super | |
|---|---|
| Length | 3,848 mm |
| Width | 1,661 mm |
| Weight | 844 kg |
| Wheelbase | 2,108 mm |
| Suspension | Independent via trailing arms and torsion bars with telescopic dampers (front); swing axles with torsion blades and telescopic dampers (rear) |
| Brakes | Hydraulic drums, front and rear |
| Engine | 1,488 cc flat-four, overhead valve, air cooled |
| Power | 70 bhp @ 5,000 rpm |
| Torque | 79 lb-ft @ 3,600 rpm |
| Transmission | Four-speed manual, rear-wheel drive |
| 0–60 mph | 12.4 sec. |
| Top speed | 107 mph |
| Cost new (356A) | £1,891 |
| Value today | £40,000–£120,000 (Speedster and Carrera models much more) |

# Jaguar

What sets Jaguar apart from other car-makers is William Lyons himself. The company's founder and long-time chairman was responsible for the styling of every new car that Swallow Sidecars and then Jaguar introduced, though some of the key models in the 1950s and 1960s were shaped by aerodynamicist Malcolm Sayer. Not even Enzo Ferrari took much of a hand in design, leaving the body styling to coachbuilders. He did, though, share one quality with William Lyons – an ability to spot talent.

Lyons formed Swallow Sidecars with business partner William Walmsley in 1922, establishing a factory in Blackpool. Within a few years they were making bodies for cars too, and their streamlined Austin Seven Swallow was a particular hit. Lyons took the bold step of creating a car under the Swallow Sidecars name, and in 1931 introduced the SS1. Powered by a six-cylinder Standard engine and wearing a range of swooping bodies designed by Lyons, the SS1 developed a reputation for looking much more expensive than it was. Success came fast; Swallow Sidecars became SS Cars Ltd, and the products became faster and still more dashing, notably the low-slung SS100. The Jaguar formula was there before the name: good looks, good performance, low price.

After the Second World War the name SS was dropped because of the obvious association with the Schutzstaffel, the Nazi paramilitary force. Lyons had gathered a fine team of engineers around him, some of whom collaborated to create the superb XK engine. This powered all Jaguar models for the next 25 years and was still in use into the 1990s, proving perhaps the most versatile and successful British engine of the post-war years.

At this time, motorsport added a great deal to Jaguar's legend, and particularly the 24 Hours of Le Mans race. The streamlined C-type won in 1951 and 1953, then the more powerful D-type with a fin behind the driver conquered all in 1955, 1956 and 1957. Such an achievement meant the boot badge on the XK150 stated 'WINNER, LE MANS' and listed all five years beneath. Jaguar also did well in saloon-car racing, especially with the Mk 1 and Mk 2 saloons. Lyons always knew the importance of a diverse range; while the XKs and E-types got the headlines, it was the saloons that kept the company in business.

Yet even Jaguar had its struggles by the mid-1960s. Jaguar bodies were made by Pressed Steel and when this company was bought by the British Motor Corporation, Lyons was concerned for the future of the marque and agreed to merge with BMC. Soon after this, though, the resulting company was merged with Leyland, and British Leyland was formed. This began a darker time in Jaguar's history, and Lyons retired in 1972. Jaguar regained some independence in 1984, when it was floated as a separate company, but was then bought by Ford in 1989. This at least allowed investment in cars like the XK8 and its new V8 engine, which powered the firm towards the next century. Ownership changed again with a sale to Indian conglomerate Tata in 2008, but the core values – grace, space, pace – remained.

# THROUGH THE YEARS

**CLOCKWISE FROM TOP LEFT:** An SS 100; Mk 2 Saloon; C-Type; XJS 3.6-litre; Mk IX.

# Volkswagen Type 2

For such a familiar vehicle the VW Type 2 goes by a multitude of names: Camper, Caravelle, Kombi, Microbus, Dormobile, Westfalia, Splittie, Bay Window and so on. Some of these are general descriptions, others are nicknames, model names or the names of the firms that carried out conversion work. But it's what was underneath that mattered: the mechanical parts from a small family car were used to create an incredibly versatile van-like vehicle that could fulfil all kinds of roles.

While Citroën's innovative H-van, launched in 1947, revolutionised van design it would never make a people carrier. The Type 2 was ready to fulfil both roles when the first two models were launched early in 1950: the Commercial was a van, while the Kombi had side windows and removable rear seats. The Microbus, with more windows and seating for eight, arrived a few months later.

The design of the VW Type 2 was a team effort, but the original concept probably came from a Dutch VW importer called Ben Pon. On a visit to the factory in 1946 he saw an improvised flatbed parts-mover on a Type 1 (Beetle) chassis and sketched an enclosed van on the same basis. The Type 1 platform wasn't stiff enough, so Volkswagen created a van-type unitary body with built-in chassis rails, while VW's engineers avoided the need for a new engine by using the reduction gear from the wartime all-terrain Kübelwagen. However, a 1,131 cc flat-four with just 24 bhp made for sluggish progress.

Engine size and power increased steadily, as did the variety of bodies: single- and double-cab pickups soon arrived, plus the famous and now sought-after Samba, a more luxurious Microbus with a row of small windows down each side of the roof. By the early 1960s the Type 2 was becoming so popular and successful around the world that many car-makers introduced their own forward-control minibus/van, and it became a staple part of the range for several marques, especially in America.

The Microbus had started to play a significant part in American culture. It was an affordable, practical way to move more people and luggage than you could fit into a car. Often hand-painted, it became associated not only with hippies and hitch-hikers, but also with the Civil Rights movement, transporting people to marches or spreading education about the right to vote. In Europe it made its biggest impact as a campervan, opening up freewheeling, long-distance holidays to many families for the first time. The German coachbuilder Westfalia (eventually absorbed by Volkswagen) is the best known, but many other companies also offered folding beds, hammocks, cookers, fridges and tables, often with a pop-up roof for extra space.

The original split-screen van was replaced in 1967 by the Bay Window version known as the Transporter 2 or T2, which felt more capable and was more stable at speed. This in turn lasted until 1979 (far beyond in Brazilian factories). The concept was too good to die, so since then we've had the rear-engined T3, the front-engined T4, T5 and T6, and now the latest electric e-Transporter. Though it never rivalled the Beetle for overall sales, the original Type 2 became just as much the foundation of Volkswagen's immense worldwide success.

**TOP:** VW soon replaced the split windscreen with a single piece of glass, as seen on this Camper.

**BOTTOM:** An early Microbus.

## 1956 Volkswagen Type 2 Microbus

| | |
|---|---|
| Length | 4,191 mm |
| Width | 1,761 mm |
| Weight | 1,103 kg |
| Wheelbase | 2,400 mm |
| Suspension | Independent via trailing arms and torsion bars with telescopic dampers (front); swing axles with torsion blades and telescopic dampers (rear) |
| Brakes | Hydraulic drums, front and rear |
| Engine | 1,192 cc flat-four, overhead valve, air cooled |
| Power | 36 bhp @ 3,700 rpm |
| Torque | 56 lb-ft @ 2,000 rpm |
| Transmission | Four-speed manual, rear-wheel drive |
| 0–60 mph | 30.6 sec. |
| Top speed | 59 mph |
| Cost new | £880 |
| Value today | £15,000–£80,000 |

# Lancia Aurelia B20 GT

Lancia and Citroën were arguably the most innovative car-makers in the world between 1925 and 1955. While the French firm made a success of front-wheel drive, re-invented the small car with the 2CV and redefined ride quality with the oleo-pneumatic DS (see p. 66), Lancia had been pioneering chassis-less construction in the 1920s with the Lambda, developing narrow-angle V4 and V8 engines, and offering five-speed gearboxes in the Ardea, a small family car, as early as 1948. The Aurelia, first introduced in saloon form in 1950 and then as the coupé B20 GT in 1951, was eventually regarded as Lancia's greatest classic of all.

The Aurelia offered some startling features. The new engine was a V6, a format rarely tried before and yet full of promise. It had the power of an in-line six but was as light as an in-line four, especially if, like in the Aurelia, it was made of aluminium. The clutch and gearbox were between the rear wheels, with the rear brakes also gathered inboard near this transaxle. Weight distribution could therefore be evenly split between front and rear wheels for improved handling. This, teamed with independent suspension all round – by trailing arms at the rear and Lancia's own sliding pillar arrangement at the front – made for delightful road manners. The car's simple, full-width styling finished the job, placing it a decade ahead of most opposition.

A sporting version, therefore, was an obvious next step. The B20's fastback shape, even purer than that of the saloon, was created by Felice Mario Boano for Ghia, but the bodies were built by Viotti and then Pininfarina. Francesco de Virgilio's engine design (one of nine versions he created during the Aurelia's development!) was expanded from 1.8 litres to 2.0 litres and given two Weber carburettors. Seventy-five bhp may not sound much today, but it sent the B20 to 100 mph and was teamed with such good aerodynamics, fine handling and effective brakes that in 1951 it was enough to win races – not least a clean sweep of the 2-litre class at the Mille Miglia on its first attempt.

The Aurelia B20 GT evolved through six different series; rather typical of Lancia's obsession with constant tinkering and improvement, a habit that eventually drove them into financial trouble and takeover by Fiat. But for the B20, it meant styling tweaks: small tail fins disappeared from the third series when engine size increased to 2.5-litres, plus other technical changes like a switch to a de Dion rear axle design for the fourth series. Drivers who disliked the column change for the gearbox could fit a Nardi floor-change conversion.

Whichever version you drive, an Aurelia B20 is a memorable, satisfying machine. It feels willing and maintains high speeds easily, even if the outright power and acceleration isn't blinding. Coming into its own on twisty roads, those Michelin X tyres (it was the first car fitted with radials as standard) and the superb suspension give a supple grace that encourages you to push the musical V6 engine that bit harder. A truly great classic sporting car.

A 1962 B20 GT series 6.

'It is of interest ... to all who can appreciate fine machinery and enterprising design.'

*Autocar* magazine, 8 November 1957

| 1955 Lancia Aurelia B20 GT Series 3 | |
|---|---|
| Length | 4,267 mm |
| Width | 1,549 mm |
| Weight | 1,195 kg |
| Wheelbase | 2,652 mm |
| Suspension | Independent via sliding pillars and integrated dampers (front); swing axles with trailing Y-arms, coil springs and lever-arm dampers (rear) |
| Brakes | Hydraulic drums, front and rear |
| Engine | 2,451 cc V6, overhead valve, water cooled |
| Power | 118 bhp @ 5,000 rpm |
| Torque | 134 lb-ft @ 3,500 rpm |
| Transmission | Four-speed manual, rear-wheel drive |
| 0–60 mph | 12.3 sec. |
| Top speed | 112 mph |
| Cost new | £3,472 |
| Value today | £60,000–£140,000 |

# Bentley R-type Continental

Sometimes science and art come together to form the most beautiful shapes. The R-type Continental's form was devised by Rolls-Royce's Ivan Evernden and John Polwhele Blatchley, and carried forward by Evernden with Stanley Watts and George Moseley of H. J. Mulliner, the coachbuilder responsible for building the body. Evernden used Rolls-Royce's wind tunnel at their aero-engine plant in Hucknall, Nottinghamshire to tweak this slippery, low-drag shape suited to high-speed touring, and he wanted it to have a rounded nose rather than the traditional bluff Bentley radiator. Rolls-Royce said no, but did allow him to reduce its height by an inch and a half.

The R-type saloon chassis was used with no change to the wheelbase and made for a hefty starting point, but the sleek aluminium panels supported by a slender steel frame saved around 160 kg over the saloon car. This was vital to ensure the tyres could cope with the new car's 120 mph top speed, achieved only by a slight increase in engine tune (higher compression ratio, more sporting carburetion) and taller gearing. It was enough to make the R-type Continental the fastest four-seater car in the world.

The R-type was also one of the most glamorous and most expensive cars. The asking price of £7,608 at launch put it on a par with the cost of a large house in one of London's better neighbourhoods, or equivalent to about six Jaguar XK120s. The name 'Continental' harked back to another model on which Evernden had worked: the Rolls-Royce Phantom II Continental of the early 1930s. This was a shortened, high-geared model also aimed at fast foreign touring, and as Bentley was the more sporting of the two marques under Rolls-Royce's control, it was natural that Bentley should offer this latest development of the idea.

Soon, though, the idea of the Continental – low weight, special tuning and a purity of design – was eroded. The cars were offered with small, lightweight seats rather than the usual Bentley armchairs, but owners were asking for the more comfortable option, as well as chunky valve radios and automatic transmission too, once it became available with the larger 4.9-litre engine. When the next generation of Bentley came along (the S1), the fastback Continental remained largely unchanged in looks but was never as light and lithe as the first cars. By the time the S2 and S3 generations arrived with V8 engines, there was little, if any, difference in the state of tune and the gearing. You could even buy the S3 version with Rolls-Royce grilles and badges. The Continental nameplate had become much more about style than substance, which is why the first cars are now so valued and respected – they offered both.

An R-type Continental doesn't reveal its true character until shown an open road. Around town it's another large, gracious Bentley, but stretching its legs to overtake slower traffic, ideally on an arrow-straight French *route nationale* lined with poplar trees and dappled with sunshine, gives a glimpse of 1950s high life at its very finest.

| 1952 Bentley R-type Continental | |
|---|---|
| Length | 5,245 mm |
| Width | 1,816 mm |
| Weight | 1,700 kg |
| Wheelbase | 3,048 mm |
| Suspension | Independent via wishbones, coil springs and hydraulic dampers (front); live axle with leaf springs and hydraulic dampers (rear) |
| Brakes | Hydraulic drums, front and rear |
| Engine | 4,566 cc in-line six, IOE, water cooled |
| Power | 153 bhp @ 4,000 rpm |
| Torque | 20 lb-ft @ 2,500 rpm (est.) |
| Transmission | Four-speed manual, rear-wheel drive |
| 0–60 mph | 13.6 sec. |
| Top speed | 120 mph |
| Cost new | £7,608 |
| Value today | £375,000–£700,000 |

TOP: The interior of a 1954 R-type Continental.

BOTTOM: An American-market R-type Continental looking glamorous on whitewall tyres.

# Austin-Healey 100

The Austin-Healey, that most British of hairy-chested sports cars, came into being almost entirely because of the American market. Leonard Lord, boss of Austin, was convinced by the 'export or die' philosophy of post-war years and expended much energy on making suitable models to sell in America for hard currency. His Austin A40, styled like a shrunken Chrysler, did quite well over there, as did its sports version, a little two-door convertible built by Jensen. But the larger A90 Atlantic of 1948, gaudy and overdone, was a flop. It left Lord needing a larger sports car to take on the MG, the Triumph 1800 roadster and even the Jaguar XK120.

Donald Healey, an ex-Triumph engineer, had been building his own sports cars since 1946, trying Riley engines and then an Alvis straight-six and a larger Nash equivalent for the American market. When he presented a new idea – a car powered by the Austin A90's beefy 2.6-litre in-line four and clothed in a pretty roadster body styled by Gerry Coker – it was the hit of the 1952 London Motor Show. Leonard Lord rapidly made a deal with Healey, arranging assembly of the cars at the Austin plant in Longbridge after Jensen created the chassis and body assemblies. Production began in May 1953.

It was an instant hit. With a three-speed manual gearbox (really a four-speed box from the Austin A70, but with the low-ratio first gear selector left out) and overdrive on second and third, it gave sporting drivers five speeds to play with. The combination of a large, torquey engine in a relatively light car made it feel even quicker than the road tests suggested, while the sharp handling put it a generation ahead of cars with pre-war origins, such as the Triumph Roadster. It was pretty cheap too – at £1,064, it undercut other convertible options like the Alvis TB14 and TB21, Lea-Francis 2½-litre Sports and indeed the XK120. But buying one in the UK was a struggle – only 5 per cent of production stayed at home while 80 per cent went to America, and the remaining 15 per cent found an enthusiastic reception in other export markets around the world. It slotted in very neatly below the XK120 in performance terms – but not far below – and it could outrun almost everything else. Soon Austin was building 400 of them a month.

Motorsport success followed, naturally enough, bringing the arrival of the tuned 100M in 1955 and the lighter, faster and very rare 100S, the first production sports car to have four-wheel disc brakes. By 1956, Austin's engineers were itching to update the gruff old four-cylinder engine and introduced the 100/6, using the smoother six-cylinder 2.6-litre engine from the new Austin Westminster. It wasn't as popular as the 100/4 until Austin expanded the engine in 1959 to create the Austin-Healey 3000. Despite the ageing shape staying largely unchanged, the 3000 became the most successful of all Big Healeys, lasting to 1968. But for simple pleasures and wind-in-the-hair fun, the original Healey 100 still takes a lot of beating.

TOP: The original 100/4.

BOTTOM: The quicker 100M, with windscreen folded to reduce drag.

| 1953 Austin-Healey 100 | |
|---|---|
| Length | 3,848 mm |
| Width | 1,537 mm |
| Weight | 953 kg |
| Wheelbase | 2,286 mm |
| Suspension | Independent via wishbones, coil springs and hydraulic dampers (front); live axle with leaf springs and hydraulic dampers (rear) |
| Brakes | Hydraulic drums, front and rear |
| Engine | 2,660 cc in-line four, overhead valve, water cooled |
| Power | 90 bhp @ 4,000 rpm |
| Torque | 144 lb-ft @ 2,500 rpm |
| Transmission | Three-speed manual plus overdrive, rear-wheel drive |
| 0–60 mph | 10.3 sec. |
| Top speed | 119 mph |
| Cost new | £1,064 |
| Value today | £20,000–£80,000 |

# Mercedes-Benz 300SL 'Gullwing'

For anyone who wasn't around in 1954, it's difficult to understand the astonishment generated by the launch of the Mercedes-Benz 300SL. In post-war Europe most countries were still in the grip of austerity, with motoring options to match. The few new cars that had started to appear still looked like they were born in the 1930s – from lordly machines like the Rolls-Royce Silver Wraith via the mid-market Triumph Renown to the basic Ford Popular 103E. The Gullwing, by contrast, looked like it had landed from Mars.

Its performance numbers would have seemed other-worldly too. A realistic top speed of 145–150 mph was astounding … and this in a car that came with a luxurious cockpit and fitted luggage. And then there were those doors. Mercedes chose to use the roof-hinged gullwing doors to allow larger, stiffer sill sections, but there's no denying it had a striking effect as a styling feature.

The 300SL was not a fresh design on a clean sheet of paper, rather it was the evolution of a competition car, the W194. Rudolf Uhlenhaut had created the W194 in 1952 for sports-car racing, with an emphasis on streamlining and low weight. The engine was borrowed from the 300 'Adenauer' saloon, a 3-litre straight-six. The breakthrough for the engine installation in the W194 racer was to tilt it 50 degrees over to the left and convert it to a dry-sump system, reducing the overall height to allow a very low, sleek nose and a small frontal area.

Exactly the same approach was adopted for the Gullwing, but turning the W194 into a road car involved much more than adding comfy seats and chrome bumpers. The engine was reworked with fuel injection and produced 40 bhp more than the racer, while the body was, in fact, completely new. Friedrich Geiger's work on the shape of the 300SL was a breakthrough for the brand, modernising the older upright radiator of previous saloons yet leaving the car instantly recognisable as a Mercedes. More than 25,000 were sold, four in five of them in the USA, and when the Gullwing was replaced in 1957 it was with a roadster equivalent.

Though the Gullwing was electrifyingly quick, its road manners were not perfect. The rear suspension design meant the tyre tread was only squarely planted on the road when the wheel was at its resting ride height. When the car leaned over in hard cornering, the rear wheels could lose grip rather suddenly. However, that was a nitpicking complaint to most drivers of the time, because even at speeds well beyond the legal limit and the limits of other contemporary sports cars, the Gullwing was barely getting into its stride.

You don't need a spacesuit to drive one, but you might need a spaceship to match the sense of occasion: the delicate pop-out handle, the wing rising on its hydraulic struts, the steering wheel folding out of the way so you can fall into the bucket seat over that wide, high sill and pull the door down like you're closing the canopy on a fighter jet. All that before you've even started the engine. It's no surprise that the Gullwing remains high on the list of all-time greats for any serious collector.

| 1955 Mercedes-Benz 300SL 'Gullwing' ||
|---|---|
| Length | 4,463 mm |
| Width | 1,793 mm |
| Weight | 1,343 kg |
| Wheelbase | 2,400 mm |
| Suspension | Independent via wishbones, coil springs and hydraulic dampers (front); swing axle with coil springs and hydraulic dampers (rear) |
| Brakes | Power-assisted hydraulic drums, front and rear |
| Engine | 2,996 cc in-line six, OHC, water cooled |
| Power | 243 bhp @ 6,100 rpm |
| Torque | 217 lb-ft @ 4,800 rpm |
| Transmission | Four-speed manual, rear-wheel drive |
| 0–60 mph | 8.2 sec. |
| Top speed | 146 mph |
| Cost new | £4,393 |
| Value today | £900,000–£1.4 million |

TOP: The 300SL was descended from the Mercedes race team's W194, seen here in a retro rally event.

BOTTOM: The iconic gullwing doors made the 300SL unmistakeable.

# Citroën DS

If the 1954 Mercedes 300SL Gullwing looked like it landed from Mars, Citroën's DS of 1955 must have originated in a different galaxy – or a different time. The styling of the DS paid no heed at all to any previous Citroën, or indeed any previous car. It included pure streamlining principles such as a wide, sleek nose tapering to a narrower tail, like a teardrop, but added touches of sci-fi, like the rear turn signals in pods either side of the lightweight glass-fibre roof, and the bright steel C-pillar.

Though most would never guess, the styling of the DS originated from Flaminio Bertoni, the same man who had already designed two previous Citroën icons: the Traction Avant and the 2CV. Bertoni was remarkable, maintaining a career as a sculptor and inventor alongside his work for Citroën. The year before the DS was launched, he won first prize for sculpture at a show in Paris, and the year after he patented a new system for the rapid construction of family houses.

Technical design for the DS was overseen by André Lefèbvre: if anything, an even greater genius. Having arrived at Citroën in time to see the Traction Avant into production, he engineered the 2CV and the HY van, before developing the DS with suspension engineer Paul Magès. Magès had created hydro-pneumatic (or oleo-pneumatic) suspension, which appeared in 1954 on the six-cylinder version of the Traction Avant, offered with self-levelling rear suspension to see if the idea could survive daily use. It did, so Lefèbvre forged ahead with a much more radical use of high-pressure hydraulics on the new DS.

There was self-levelling, height-adjustable suspension at front and rear, hydraulic power steering, high-pressure hydraulic brakes and even semi-automatic transmission, which used a lever sprouting from the top of the steering column to operate a powered hydraulic shift mechanism. The key to all this innovation was that none of it was simply a gimmick; everything worked together to create a remarkable driving experience. The suspension gave a better ride than any luxury limousine but did not allow the car to wallow in corners. The steering was fingertip light, very fast and accurate, while the brakes – discs at the front – were exceptionally powerful with hardly any pressure required on the button-like floor pedal.

The only major aspect of the car that wasn't innovative was under the bonnet, where buyers found the old 1.9-litre four-cylinder engine from the Traction Avant. Money to develop a new air-cooled flat-six had not been forthcoming. Nonetheless, the DS was a landmark and set new standards overnight. For Citroën the way forward was clear – the smallest models would remain based on the 2CV, but a new mid-sized model (the GS) and a Maserati-powered grand tourer called the SM would all continue with oleo-pneumatic suspension and brakes, as would the ensuing CX, BX and XM.

The ideas in the DS were never widely mimicked by other makers, but they defined three generations of Citroën now seen as a high-water mark for individuality, ride quality and style.

| 1956 Citroën DS 19 | |
|---|---|
| Length | 4,801 mm |
| Width | 1,783 mm |
| Weight | 1,238 kg |
| Wheelbase | 3,124 mm |
| Suspension | Height-adjustable, independent via twin leading arms and oleo-pneumatic rams (front); single trailing arms and oleo-pneumatic rams (rear) |
| Brakes | High-pressure hydraulic inboard discs (front); drums (rear) |
| Engine | 1,911 cc in-line four, overhead valve, water cooled |
| Power | 75 bhp @ 4,500 rpm |
| Torque | 101 lb-ft @ 3,000 rpm |
| Transmission | Four-speed semi-auto, front-wheel drive |
| 0–60 mph | 22.1 sec. |
| Top speed | 88 mph |
| Cost new | £1,486 |
| Value today | £15,000–£40,000 |

TOP: A period advert for the ID.

BOTTOM: The futuristic shape of the DS is instantly recognisable.

# Rolls-Royce Silver Cloud

In an age when other cars were changing fast, even embracing the space race in styling terms (in America in particular), Rolls-Royce had a problem. Their aristocratic customers were not likely to enjoy such fads, nor be impressed by change unless it transformed the car for the better. In the mid-1950s Rolls-Royce buyers were often the same people who were placing the orders 20, 30 and even 40 years before, and they expected a car with the same feel, even the same aesthetic. How to satisfy the need for a new, better Rolls-Royce without alienating those who fundamentally disliked change?

The answer was subtle. Rolls-Royce's designers, led by John Polwhele Blatchley, looked at some of the saloon shapes developed by independent coachbuilders on the Bentley Mk VI and R-type chassis and created something deliberately restrained, even a little behind the times. By launching a car that was already somewhat outdated when new, Rolls-Royce avoided the danger of a trendy design going rapidly out of fashion.

The Silver Cloud wasn't nearly as bold a shape as the dramatic fastback Bentley R-type Continental, launched in 1952, yet it looked more up to date than previous Rolls-Royces, which was perfectly good enough for a new model. The car it replaced, the Silver Dawn, was a Rolls-Royce-badged version of the Bentley R-type saloon, very little changed from the Mk VI saloon of 1946. The only other Rolls-Royce on offer in 1955 was the Silver Wraith, a traditional model aimed at the chauffeur-driven market and sold as a chassis to be clothed by a coachbuilder, almost always with a body that would look at home in the late 1930s.

Underneath, the Silver Cloud was an evolution of the R-type, which was a minor development of the Mk VI. The strong, silent, straight-six engine was still there, now expanded to 4.9-litres, and the brakes were improved from a hydro-mechanical set-up to full hydraulics. The new car was rather longer than the R-type and the extra space was well used, making entry and exit easier, especially to the back seats. The lengthy wheelbase (even greater if you opted for an extended version, either with or without a limousine division) helped emphasise the car's wonderfully soft and supple ride, while automatic transmission and optional power steering made it effortless to drive.

Yet Rolls-Royce knew they had to maintain the company tradition of continuous improvement. Having launched this artful confection of old values, they worked up a new V8 engine thought to be vital to the marque's survival in the USA, where only budget family sedans had six-cylinder engines. The V8 arrived with the Silver Cloud II in 1959, which was virtually indistinguishable from the first Cloud. The Silver Cloud III (1962) wore quad headlamps, but otherwise this graceful old form, already less than new in 1955, lasted to 1965 – and it gave rise to the mighty Phantom V and Phantom VI limousines that ran all the way to the 1990s. Durable, delightful, and still everyone's idea of a classic Rolls-Royce, the Silver Cloud and its Bentley S-series equivalent were masterpieces of understatement from a company where quality was far, far more important than fashion.

| 1958 Rolls-Royce Silver Cloud ||
|---|---|
| Length | 5,377 mm |
| Width | 1,897 mm |
| Weight | 1,881 kg |
| Wheelbase | 3,124 mm |
| Suspension | Independent via wishbones, coil springs and hydraulic dampers (front); live axle with leaf springs and hydraulic dampers (rear) |
| Brakes | Hydraulic drums, front and rear |
| Engine | 4,887 cc in-line six, IOE, water cooled |
| Power | 180 bhp @ 4,000 rpm |
| Torque | 280 lb-ft @ 2,000 rpm |
| Transmission | Four-speed automatic, rear-wheel drive |
| 0–60 mph | 13 sec. |
| Top speed | 106 mph |
| Cost new | £5,693 |
| Value today | £20,000–£80,000 |

TOP: A big grille, long bonnet and spacious interior – it can only be a Rolls Royce.

BOTTOM: The plush interior, with walnut dashboard and trim.

# Volvo 121 'Amazon'

Volvo is a long-established name in Sweden, with a history of car production going back to 1927, which is earlier than the rest of the world might realise. It was only in the 1950s that Volvos were exported in any number, and they already had a distinctive look and character. The PV 444 was a sturdy, rather bluff and beetle-backed machine that soon established a reputation for durability and toughness. But it had a more surprising edge: it made quite a successful rally car. This was exactly the foundation the new model, initially called 'Amason' with an 's', would build on.

Volvo made the jump from the old 1940s look of separate wings and a 'coffin' bonnet to full-width styling in 1956. Mechanically there was little change from the PV 544, with a 1.6-litre version of Volvo's overhead-valve four-cylinder engine powering the new car, but to find the secret of the Amazon's success you have to look further than the specification. After all, nothing really stands out – unitary construction, an all-synchro manual gearbox and hydraulic brakes were up to date but not remarkable. The choice of four-door and two-door saloons, plus a Combi or estate car option, doesn't seem likely to turn heads. But it was so much more than the sum of its parts.

First, the styling was well-judged. Even though it was directly influenced by American cars of the time, it seemed slow to date when translated to the smaller form of a European saloon. Second, Volvo's early emphasis on both passive and active safety began to build a reputation that lasts to this day. The Amazon was the first car offered with front seatbelts as standard, and later was the first with three-point seatbelts. The unusually light and accurate steering and strong brakes gave you a better chance of avoiding an accident in the first place than in almost any rival. Finally, Volvo added a performance edge quite early, introducing the twin-carburettor 122S version in 1958, the same year they launched the car in the USA. Amazons weren't just reliable and practical, they were fun.

The Amazon also lasted incredibly well. In damp, salty climates like the UK it was normal for a mid-price family saloon to fall victim to body corrosion after a few years, with most in the scrapyard before their tenth birthday. But Volvo used higher-quality steel, treated to ensure better paint adhesion and then extensively undercoated. They rusted eventually, but it took two, three or four times as long as a rival Vauxhall or Ford from the same era.

Volvo kept the old PV going as a lower-cost sibling of the Amazon right up to 1965, but in 1961 they had launched the dashing, low-slung P1800 sports coupé. It used Amazon/122 mechanical components and gave Volvo a significant image boost, though a far stronger legacy came from the saloon. The next Volvo, the 140 series, was the first of the brick-like shapes that made the Swedish firm a byword for rather dull Scandinavian safety, but it's the Amazon that came to be seen as the classic. To this day they remain among the most popular choices for long-distance historic rally events, and still make practical daily drivers.

| 1958 Volvo 'Amazon' 121 ||
|---|---|
| Length | 4,394 mm |
| Width | 1,588 mm |
| Weight | 1,067 kg |
| Wheelbase | 2,604 mm |
| Suspension | Independent via wishbones, coil springs and hydraulic dampers (front); live axle with coil springs and hydraulic dampers (rear) |
| Brakes | Hydraulic drums, front and rear |
| Engine | 1,583 cc in-line four, overhead valve, water cooled |
| Power | 85 bhp @ 5,500 rpm |
| Torque | 87 lb-ft @ 3,500 rpm |
| Transmission | Four-speed manual, rear-wheel drive |
| 0–60 mph | 14 sec. |
| Top speed | 94 mph |
| Cost new | £1,201 |
| Value today | £4,000–£25,000 |

TOP: Volvo is best known for its estates – and it started early.

MIDDLE: Green leatherette for miles: an Amazon interior.

BOTTOM: The 121 in two-door saloon form, a popular basis for a rally car.

# Lotus Seven

The craze for building Ford 'specials' blossomed in the UK from the early 1950s, when the chassis and sidevalve engines of small pre-war and post-war Ford models became cheaply available in scrapyards. Most of these specials were crude, amounting to no more than a rough glass-reinforced plastic (GRP) sports body on the old Ford chassis. As far back as 1952, though, there was a car you could buy in kit form that put such concoctions to shame. The Lotus Mk 6 used its own semi-spaceframe chassis, a Ford front axle split to give rudimentary independent suspension and Ford Ten mechanical parts. Its designer, Colin Chapman, put it into production after winning almost every race he entered.

About 100 were built in five years, before Chapman's wife Hazel suggested the need for a successor. Chapman and his employee Gilbert 'Mac' Mackintosh did the stress calculations one Sunday evening and a week later had built the first car. It had a new spaceframe with a stressed floor and transmission tunnel, borrowing the rear suspension and steering from the Lotus Eleven racing car and the double-wishbone independent front suspension from the Lotus Twelve Formula Two car. Again, it was offered in kit form and soon with an increasing choice of power: Ford Ten sidevalve, BMC A-series, or in Super Seven form, the Coventry Climax OHC engine.

It took club racing by storm, offering true racing-car handling (and performance, with the more powerful engines) for £399 plus the cost of an engine and back axle, as cars in kit form avoided a heavy purchase tax. It was just as happy dicing through city traffic or beating all-comers on country roads, so many young owners were able to compete – and win – in their daily driver.

In 1960 a Series 2 version appeared with a simplified chassis, flared glass-fibre front wings and overhead-valve Ford 105E power, while the Super Seven was updated the year after with a Cosworth-tuned Ford 109E engine making 95 bhp. The S3 of 1968 used Ford Cortina 1600 power, or the fabulous Lotus twin-cam engine as a rare option. In 1970, the Seven S4 used a simpler, cheaper chassis and suspension layout, and an all-new glass-fibre body, but still the same Cortina and twin-cam engine options. Then, shortly before production ended, the Seven's fate changed forever.

When Lotus announced its intention to discontinue the Seven, the owner of successful Lotus dealer Caterham Cars, Graham Nearn, bought the rights to continue production. The Series 3 shape soon proved to be more popular than the wider, softer Series 4, and Caterham began production that continues to evolve to this day, its numerous models far outstripping total Lotus production. In addition, well over 100 other constructors and imitators around the world have built Seven-esque kits and production cars. Why? For all-out thrills, for the purest sports-car driving experience you can enjoy, there is still nothing better. Call it a four-wheeled motorbike or a racing car for the road, the Seven is both those things and more – it's the best small sports car in history.

**TOP:** The Lotus Seven in Series 3 form, which proved the most enduring shape.

**MIDDLE:** The first Lotus Seven prototype makes its competition debut at the Brighton Speed Trials, September 1957.

**BOTTOM:** A modern Caterham Seven, which differs very little from the original Lotus.

| 1957 Lotus Seven ||
|---|---|
| Length | 3,353 mm |
| Width | 1,481 mm |
| Weight | 440 kg |
| Wheelbase | 2,519 mm |
| Suspension | Independent via wishbones, coil springs and hydraulic dampers (front); live axle with upper and lower trailing arms, coil springs and hydraulic dampers (rear) |
| Brakes | Hydraulic drums, front and rear |
| Engine | 1,172 cc in-line four, sidevalve, water cooled |
| Power | 40 bhp @ 4,600 rpm |
| Torque | 52 lb-ft @ 2,500 rpm |
| Transmission | Four-speed manual, rear-wheel drive |
| 0–60 mph | 14.2 sec. |
| Top speed | 98 mph |
| Cost new | £399 (kit, minus engine) |
| Value today | £20,000–£60,000 |

# Ferrari

The first car-makers often evolved from bicycle manufacturers or industrial concerns, or moved from making components to constructing whole cars. Very few grew directly from racing teams, but that's how Enzo Ferrari started what would become the most famous marque of all.

His team, Scuderia Ferrari, was established over a dinner in Bologna one night in 1929. Enzo Ferrari, then 33, was a racing driver for Alfa Romeo. In the early 1930s they withdrew their factory racing effort because of economic difficulties, and Ferrari took over the running of their highly competitive, eight-cylinder racing cars. Later, it was a falling-out with Alfa Romeo that convinced Ferrari to start work on his own car, but eventually Alfa Romeo would buy Scuderia Ferrari and take racing back under factory control.

The first product from Ferrari's works at Maranello was a somewhat dumpy little roadster, the Tipo 125, but under its bonnet was the key to Ferrari's future. The 125's small-capacity V12, designed by Gioacchino Colombo, would provide excellent performance and the basis for generations of larger, louder and more powerful V12s, and a vast number of race wins.

For the first ten years Ferrari only built road cars to help fund their racing efforts, which shows in the tiny numbers produced – just a few hundred in that first decade. They were clothed by coachbuilders such as Pininfarina, Vignale, Ghia and Carrozzeria Touring, and came at a high price. By the late 1950s, though, *Il Commendatore*, as Enzo Ferrari was known, knew the market for costly, beautiful and luxurious sports cars was growing ever larger. From the early 1960s onwards, Ferrari's image as a builder of road cars would outstrip even its fame as a Formula One team. No small feat, as at the time of writing Scuderia Ferrari has 15 drivers' world championships to its name, and 16 constructors' championships.

Throughout the 1960s, luxurious grand tourers and convertibles sold in far higher numbers than the early coachbuilt cars, and by the 1970s Ferrari had models filling several different niches, from the small V6 Dino – originally not even badged as a Ferrari, and with an engine built by Fiat – to the large 2+2 GTs available with automatic gearboxes, up to the fastest range-topping two-seaters like the 'Daytona' and the mid-engined 365 Boxer.

Mid-engined designs dominated production in the 1980s and 1990s, as a succession of V8-engined cars led on from the 308 GT4 and 308 GTB, while the Boxer's flat-12 engine powered two generations of the Testarossa until Ferrari brought back the front-engined V12 with the 456 and 550 Maranello. Alongside, Ferrari maintained a series of headline-grabbing 'halo' models, such as the F40, F50, Enzo and LaFerrari, which were never the core of the business but helped build this famous marque ever higher. Enzo Ferrari died in 1988 at the age of 90, having seen the F40 into production. What he would have made of today's mould-breaking hybrids and SUVs – the SF90 and the Purosangue – can only be guessed at. But his name and his brand seem immortal.

# THROUGH THE YEARS

**CLOCKWISE FROM TOP LEFT:** A 125 S; 166 MM; Dino 246 GTS; Enzo; 308 GTB; 250 Lusso.

# Chevrolet Bel Air

The sheer daring and ambition of American car styling in the 1950s – tail fins, lashings of chrome, grilles like a mouthful of teeth and tail-lamps like rocket pods – still makes our eyes pop now. Sometimes glorious, sometimes far over the top, not every designer's dream machine would achieve success. The Chevrolet models of 1955 to 1957, though, stood out for all the right reasons.

These three years of production are collectively referred to as the Tri-Five Chevys, and fans of the era have their own favourite, but it's the last of them that's gained the greatest fame: of the 1957s, with their taller fins and toothier grin, it's the top-of-the-range Bel Air that people want. The range started with the 150 trim level, which did without two-tone paint or the large side trim 'beauty panel' that extended the length of the rear wing. The 210 series gained the panel and a slightly richer interior, but the choice of six-cylinder and V8 engines was the same.

The Bel Air had all the extra glitz: silver anodized aluminium beauty panel, three gold chevrons on each front wing, a gold grille insert, gold Bel Air script, more brightwork edging on various panels, sumptuous two-tone interiors and two-tone paint. A dizzying range of extra-cost options asked buyers to pick from three different motors in a total of nine optional power outputs and six gearbox selections, while power brakes, power steering, radios, air conditioning, spotlights, tinted glass, an electric clock, tissue dispensers and dozens of other boxes could also be ticked.

This was the American dream in four-wheeled form. America had come out of the Second World War with a buoyant economy and a national sense of optimism that even the conflict in Korea could not dent. Every year, customers expected and received more for their money – more convenience, more power, more luxury, more excitement – and nowhere was this more evident than the car industry. This dream sold in incredible numbers: Chevrolet made almost 1.4 million cars in 1957. Of those, 702,220 were Bel Air models. The four-door Bel Air sedan on its own accounted for more than a quarter of a million sales, starting at a temptingly affordable $2,290, with every dealer eager to offer credit to anyone who could handle a modest monthly payment. And with unemployment so low, almost everyone could.

But the era in which these cars were born is crucial to their popularity now: they were the prettiest mass-market cars of their day but, more importantly, they soon came to represent a golden age for America. Rock 'n' roll music was new and fresh, and despite Elvis Presley's effect on crowds of fainting teenage girls, it was all rather harmless. It really was a more innocent time, before economic setbacks, the Vietnam War and the rebellion of the counter-culture or the war on drugs. To drive a 1957 Chevy is to take a holiday in a simpler, happier, better life – and who doesn't want that?

| 1957 Chevrolet Bel Air convertible ||
|---|---|
| Length | 5,080 mm |
| Width | 1,881 mm |
| Weight | 1,546 kg |
| Wheelbase | 2,980 mm |
| Suspension | Independent via wishbones, coil springs and hydraulic dampers (front); live axle with leaf springs and hydraulic dampers (rear) |
| Brakes | Hydraulic drums, front and rear |
| Engine | 4,638 cc V8, overhead valve, water cooled |
| Power | 270 bhp @ 4,800 rpm |
| Torque | 320 lb-ft @ 3,000 rpm |
| Transmission | Two-speed 'Powerglide' automatic, rear-wheel drive |
| 0–60 mph | 9.9 sec. |
| Top speed | 98 mph |
| Cost new | $2,611 (c.£936, before options) |
| Value today | £25,000–£65,000 |

TOP: The huge chrome-ringed 'mouth' of a 1957 Bel Air, typical of American cars in the 1950s.

BOTTOM: A convertible Bel Air, almost as dramatic as the Oregon scenery.

# 1959 Cadillac Coupe de Ville

If a 1957 Chevy was an accessible dream machine for Middle America, the 1959 Cadillac was something only a lucky few would sample. Nonetheless, 'few' by American standards was still nearly 22,000 Coupe de Villes in this year alone, along with a great many more sedans, hard-tops and convertibles. But at two-and-a- half times the price of a Chevy, only your boss's boss drove a Cadillac. Everyone else just stared when one of these amazing machines ghosted past.

Cadillacs had been growing fins on the ends of their rear wings since the 1940s, and the original inspiration was said to be stylist Frank Hershey's view of a Lockheed P-38 Lightning fighter, which had a twin-boom fuselage with a tail fin on each. General Motor's styling chief Harley Earl didn't like them but was persuaded to let Hershey have his way, and by the mid-1950s every rival was following suit. By 1958 and 1959, some of these rivals were trying to out-do Cadillac for the size, shape or angle of the fins, yet the results were never as a harmonious as those you see here.

The fins had long since ceased to look like aircraft tail fins; these owed more to the intergalactic craft you might see in a comic book. They were also pure theatre because they had no function at all, except perhaps adding a little directional stability for anyone in the habit of cruising at 100 mph. From an aesthetic point of view, they added apparent length to an already huge car – Cadillacs, like other American automobiles, had been getting longer and lower for the previous ten years as fashions evolved. The fins also added a sense of movement, making the car look as though it were in motion when it was standing still. Or you could see them as a bird's wings, raised and ready for take off.

The 1959 Cadillacs are revered as the high point of the fins 'n' chrome era because they represented a literal peak: the tallest fins Cadillac ever offered, and the last year when such things were on the increase. From 1960 fins began to shrink and become slimmer, with some manufacturers dropping them rapidly for fear of being behind the times. Cadillac, though, kept with them throughout the new decade.

Under the outrageous exterior the 1959 Cadillac was a relatively sophisticated car, with a lot of options European luxury machines wouldn't include for many years: auto-dipping headlamps, rain-sensitive wipers, cruise control, central locking. It was also rather faster than Mercedes-Benz or Rolls-Royce equivalents, thanks to a brawny but well-silenced 6.4-litre V8 engine, while the ride was a softly sprung boat trip, though with better control in corners than its reputation suggests. It was also very well built, and because Cadillacs were often cherished as Sunday cars they still turn up in remarkable condition. Perhaps surprisingly for a car that seemed only to be about style, the 1959 Cadillac scored high in all departments and represented excellent value. Today, it stands as a monument to how exciting cars can be … if you let the styling department do as it pleases!

| 1959 Cadillac Coupe de Ville | |
|---|---|
| Length | 5,715 mm |
| Width | 2,057 mm |
| Weight | 2,145 kg |
| Wheelbase | 3,276 mm |
| Suspension | Independent via wishbones, coil springs and hydraulic dampers (front); live axle with trailing arms, coil springs and hydraulic dampers (rear) |
| Brakes | Hydraulic drums, front and rear |
| Engine | 6,390 cc V8, overhead valve, water cooled |
| Power | 325 bhp @ 4,800 rpm |
| Torque | 430 lb-ft @ 3,100 rpm |
| Transmission | Dual-range 'Hydramatic' automatic, rear-wheel drive |
| 0–60 mph | 10.2 sec. |
| Top speed | 115 mph |
| Cost new | $5,252 (c.£1,870, before options) |
| Value today | £30,000–£100,000 |

TOP: The rear fins of the Cadillac are, if anything, even more dramatic than the Chevrolet competition.

BOTTOM: The wide, sleek nose of the 1959 Coupe de Ville.

# AUSTIN / MORRIS MINI

| Morris Mini-Minor (figures for 1959 model) ||
|---|---|
| Length | 3,048 mm |
| Width | 1,410 mm |
| Weight | 607 kg |
| Wheelbase | 2,032 mm |
| Suspension | Independent via transverse links, rubber cones and hydraulic dampers (front); trailing arms with pushrod to rubber cones, hydraulic dampers (rear) |
| Brakes | Hydraulic drums, front and rear |
| Engine | 848 cc in-line four, overhead valve, water cooled |
| Power | 37 bhp @ 5,500 rpm |
| Torque | 44 lb-ft @ 2,900 rpm |
| Transmission | Four-speed manual, front-wheel drive |
| 0–60 mph | 26.5 sec. |
| Top speed | 74.5 mph |
| Cost new | £497 |
| Value today | £10,000–£35,000 (Mk 1 Mini) |

If you want to know how influential the Mini really was, just look around you. The next family car you see, even the next van, will probably have its engine mounted transversely – across the car, not along it – and driving the front wheels. It's become the standard format for almost everything, and while the Mini wasn't the very first car to use this approach, it's the one that showed what huge advantages such a layout gives.

There was, of course, one man driving this radical new idea: Alec Issigonis. Already known for creating the Morris Minor, he had left Morris Motors when it merged with Austin to form BMC in 1952, moving to Alvis. Here he offered several bold designs, but it became apparent Alvis would never have the funds to develop them, and Sir Leonard Lord, chairman of BMC, persuaded him to return in 1955 to work on three new experimental models. Then, in September 1956, Egypt's Colonel Nasser decided to nationalise the Suez Canal; in the ensuing crisis, oil prices shot up and petrol rationing returned to the UK.

By 1957 buyers were seeking the most economical vehicles possible, allowing little motorcycle-engined bubble cars and British equivalents from the likes of Reliant, Berkeley and Bond to find favour. At BMC, Issigonis's new job became focused on creating a small car to beat them all. He and his fellow engineers Jack Daniels and Chris Kingham had prototypes built and even running by mid-1957, which was incredibly quick progress bearing in mind the innovations they introduced. One of the most important was the solution to packaging the drivetrain, as described above. Issigonis knew he could fit the engine and gearbox into a space only two feet long by turning them sideways, but in a car only four feet wide, how would such an arrangement fit across the car? Issigonis hit on the solution early in the design process: the gearbox would not be mounted on one end of the engine, it would live underneath, in the oil sump.

Two other technical innovations would define the Mini, and along with the transverse engine, those technical developments allowed the passenger compartment to gain the largest possible volume from a small 'footprint'. First, Issigonis insisted on wheels of only ten inches in diameter, demanding specially made tyres by Dunlop. This kept wheel arch sizes right down, meaning less space was wasted. Second was the Mini's remarkable rubber suspension.

Dr Alex Moulton was a truly original thinker, like Issigonis, but with a special interest in suspension. He came up with the idea of using rubber cones in place of coil or leaf springs, and this allowed a very compact suspension design contained in front and rear subframes. At the front, a short transverse link acted on a cone mounted above, while at the rear, a trailing arm each side acted on a horizontal pushrod compressing a cone also fitted horizontally, the whole thing fitting underneath the floor below the back seat. What of the passengers themselves? The designers placed car seats on the floor of the factory to find out how much room four adults needed to sit comfortably and still have room to open a map. Chalk marks indicated the result – surprisingly little.

Mini production began in May 1959, ahead of launch that August. Initially sold as the Austin Seven and the Morris Mini-Minor, BMC soon found their main problem wasn't getting this radical little machine accepted by the public, but building enough of them to keep up with demand. The Mini was an instant hit because it did everything it was designed to do, and more, yet sold at the bargain price of £497. This almost certainly meant BMC was building them at a loss, but it undercut Ford's new Anglia 105E and gave the Mini the start it needed. There were unexpected perks with Issigonis's design. First, the Mini had character, thanks to the puppyish appeal of the looks and the way its tiny dimensions allowed drivers to dash through gaps in the traffic and park in smaller spaces than any 'proper' cars. Second, the Mini was great fun to drive, with neat handling, sure-footed roadholding, low body roll and decent performance.

Enter John Cooper. He was an experienced racing-car builder and team owner, and an innovator in his own right – the reason grand prix cars moved their engines from in front of the driver to behind was to keep up with Cooper's rear-engined Formula One car. He knew about tuning the A-series engine as well as the performance potential of the Mini, and he approached Issigonis as early as 1960, eventually getting the go-ahead from Issigonis's boss to build a fast Mini. The Mini Cooper was launched in September 1961 and added a vital new string to BMC's bow. Suddenly, the Mini was more than a city runabout or a shopping car for a stay-at-home mum: it was a giant-killer at some of the most prestigious sporting events. Minis won the Monte Carlo rally three times, eventually taking to the track in saloon-car racing and dicing with American Ford Galaxies many times their size.

Adoption by pop stars and celebrities as a chic accessory in 1960s Swinging London was the final piece of the puzzle for the Mini. It had become universal and almost classless, not unlike the Land Rover, and outlasted its rivals and its own sister models one after another. Sales landmarks of one million (1965), two million (1969), three million (1972), four million (1976) and five million (1986) came and went, and even when Leyland launched the Metro in 1980, the car intended to succeed the Mini, the cheeky little original kept on selling … outlasting its own replacement. The last Mini was built at Longbridge, Birmingham in 2000. By then it was badged as a Rover, though the Mini name was owned by BMW. The German marque started making its own Mini, related to the original by name only, the following year.

Today, the classic Mini has a huge international following and values of the earliest cars are still rising. Not every idea it introduced proved popular – those rubber suspension cones were not adopted elsewhere – but with 65 years of hindsight it's tempting to see this perfectly packaged, transverse-engined, front-wheel drive marvel as the first truly modern car.

**PREVIOUS PAGE:** A classic Mk 1 Mini.

**TOP:** Competing in the 1970 RAC Rally.

**BOTTOM:** A 1977 Clubman estate.

# Daimler SP250 'Dart'

The SP250's looks have always divided enthusiasts. It was perhaps too bold and fashion-conscious for the time, with a chrome-laden nose and significant fins at the rear, both of which would start to look outmoded early in the car's life. But while the looks now add some character and period appeal, it's the little Daimler's engine, construction and performance that mark it out as an important car.

The SP250 is commonly known as the Daimler Dart, even though that name was removed soon after the car was launched in 1959, when American firm Chrysler threatened legal action. It was Daimler's rather late entry to the stiff competition for US sales in the two-seat roadster market, which already featured numerous British offerings, from the least costly MG to the most glamorous Jaguar XK150. Daimler was able to borrow the chassis from another such car, the Triumph TR3, as Triumph and Daimler were both owned by BSA. Another great benefit of the association with Triumph came in the form of gifted engine designer Edward Turner.

In 1956, a feasibility study on V8 car engines produced 2.5-litre and 4.5-litre versions, notable for their hemispherical combustion chambers – these 'hemi' cylinder heads offered improved gas flow over other pushrod designs. Turner specified an unusually high grade of cast iron for the block and very high-quality crankshafts, which made the engines expensive to produce but extraordinarily strong. Decades later, drag racers were extracting 1,200 bhp from the little 2.5-litre engine after extensive tuning, nearly ten times its original 140 bhp.

But 140 bhp was enough to make the Dart exciting, especially when teamed with its other innovation: a glass-fibre body. Composites were beginning to find a use among specialist sports-car firms like Rochdale, Lotus and Berkeley, but Daimler was the first of the major British marques to adopt it. Even with a cast-iron V8 and a steel ladder chassis, the Dart weighed in at only 1,008 kg. So while the flexible chassis and somewhat vague steering needed improvement, the acceleration and 127-mph top speed were striking.

The car's fate was decided not by the market, but by the sale of Daimler to Jaguar in 1960. William Lyons, Jaguar's boss, was impressed enough by the car's concept and Turner's V8 engine to design a graceful, more understated new body for a 'Mark 2' version of the Dart, called the SP252. Yet even Lyons could see no sense in building it when he discovered the hand-laid glass-fibre meant each one would take twice as long to build as his dramatic new E-type … and potentially compete with it on price and even performance.

So the Dart was allowed to die in 1964, though its influence would be significant. A coupé version by Ogle Design, rejected by Daimler, went on to become the first Reliant Scimitar. The 2.5-litre V8 was used to power the Daimler version of the Jaguar Mk 2 saloon, and the 250 saloon became the best-selling Daimler yet. Drive a Dart today and the excess of power over grip is still thrilling – but is it that muscular engine note or the car's looks that are turning heads?

**TOP:** At home in the English countryside.

**MIDDLE:** A police-issue Dart.

**BOTTOM:** The Dart's best angle? The side profile looks low and lean.

| 1959 Daimler SP250 'Dart' ||
|---|---|
| Length | 4,077 mm |
| Width | 1,664 mm |
| Weight | 1,008 kg |
| Wheelbase | 2,337 mm |
| Suspension | Independent via wishbones, coil springs and hydraulic dampers (front); live axle with semi-elliptic leaf springs and hydraulic dampers (rear) |
| Brakes | Hydraulic discs, front and rear |
| Engine | 2,548 cc V8, overhead valve, water cooled |
| Power | 140 bhp @ 5,800 rpm |
| Torque | 155 lb-ft @ 3,600 rpm |
| Transmission | Four-speed manual, rear-wheel drive |
| 0–60 mph | 9.1 sec. |
| Top speed | 127 mph |
| Cost new | £1,395 |
| Value today | £10,000–£45,000 |

# THE SWINGING SIXTIES
## 1960 TO 1969

# Jaguar E-type

If you had to choose one car, above all others, for the title of 'greatest classic' then the Jaguar E-type would be an excellent candidate.

It has all the key ingredients – great beauty, high performance, advanced construction and even motorsport heritage – while the impact it made on the car market when it arrived in 1961 was a sensation. Yet there was little about the E-type that was genuinely new, as it evolved directly from a decade of Jaguar's success and innovation.

Like all Jaguars of the time, the E-type would be powered by the six-cylinder XK engine. This unit was introduced in the XK120 in 1948, a car whose launch caused a very similar stir to that of of the E-type. The XK120's engine used twin overhead camshafts, a more efficient, high-revving design feature usually found only on racing cars at that time, which provided a top speed beyond 120 mph.

The XK120 evolved into the XK140 and then XK150, but more important in the E-type's ancestry were the racing variants – the C-type and the D-type. The C-type was a re-bodied, streamlined XK120 equipped with a tuned engine and clever changes to the chassis and rear suspension. It won the Le Mans 24-hour race in 1951, only six months after development started, and again in 1953. Its successor, the D-type, did even better – a hat-trick of wins in 1955, 1956 and 1957.

The D-type's major innovation was in the way it was built. It no longer relied on a separate steel chassis beneath the aluminium bodywork; now Jaguar opted for a centre section constructed like an aeroplane fuselage, with a tubular subframe running forward on which the engine, steering and front suspension were mounted. The same approach was used for the E-type. Yet the clever, lightweight construction and race-bred suspension all played second fiddle to the E-type's glorious looks.

Remarkably, the shape is not the result of an inspired moment at an artist's drawing board, but largely down to aerodynamics – a science still in its infancy for car design in the 1950s. Malcolm Sayer, the man responsible for creating the low-drag, high-speed D-type's shape, hated being called a stylist. He was an aerodynamicist, though he insisted a car had to look right as well as perform well aerodynamically. In this, he was led by Jaguar's founder and managing director, Sir William Lyons. This remarkable man was not a trained designer, yet he styled every Jaguar model himself until Sayer's aerodynamic know-how began to contribute.

The E-type was unveiled at the Geneva Motor Show in March 1961. Sir William Lyons was there to show off a beautiful, grey, fixed-head coupé and the roadster version, called Open Top Sports (OTS) by Jaguar, in British Racing Green – registration numbers 9600 HP and 77 RW respectively. Both cars had been late in leaving Coventry and were driven at high speed across Europe to arrive in time for the press launch. It was a huge success. With a nicely timed magazine road test that coaxed 9600 HP past the magic 150 mph mark (thanks

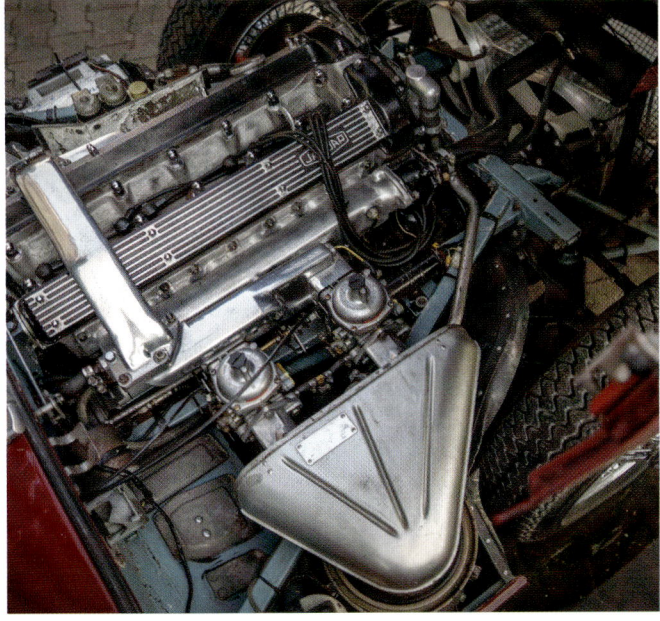

TOP: A Series 1 fixed-head coupé.

BOTTOM: The 4.2-litre straight-six engine of an American-market Series 2.

| 1961 Jaguar E-type coupé | |
|---|---|
| Length | 4,453 mm |
| Width | 1,656 mm |
| Weight | 1,226 kg |
| Wheelbase | 2,438 mm |
| Suspension | Independent via wishbones and torsion bars (front); wishbones, coils and radius arms (rear) |
| Brakes | Power-assisted Girling discs, front and rear |
| Engine | 3,781 cc DOHC in-line four |
| Power | 265 bhp @ 5,500 rpm |
| Torque | 260 lb-ft @ 4,000 rpm |
| Transmission | Four-speed manual |
| 0–60 mph | 6.9 sec. |
| Top speed | 151 mph |
| Cost new | £2,196 |
| Value today | £60,000–£150,000 (much more for earliest 1961 cars) |

to some subtle modifications by the factory), the impact on the car-buying public could not have been greater.

Crucially, the new Jaguar was within reach of many buyers. At just £2,196 for the coupé and £2,097 for the roadster, it was half the price of an Aston Martin DB4 and a quarter the price of a Bentley S2 Continental. It was still expensive compared to a modest family car, but it was an accessible status symbol for anyone with enough salary to cover the recently derestricted hire-purchase agreements offered by dealers. It became a symbol of 1960s Swinging London glamour almost overnight; if chic models in Mary Quant dresses drove Minis, dashing young actors and pop stars bought E-types.

It didn't just look good, it was fabulous to drive. With superb roadholding, high gearing and a sleek shape, the E-type was capable of cruising at speeds far higher than most cars' flat-out maximum. Denis Jenkinson, the motoring journalist and co-driver to Stirling Moss in the 1955 Mille Miglia victory, ran an E-type for several years from 1965. Three-figure speeds on European roads were legal and, for 'Jenks', commonplace – as he recounted in *Motor Sport:* 'The ride and comfort of the E-type was first class … on the Italian Autostrada a leisurely gait was 105 mph. Not unnaturally, one frequently became embroiled in private dices with Ferraris and other fast cars, and on one occasion I ran in company with a 250GT Ferrari at close on 120 mph from Milan to Turin.'

The E-type used a 3.8-litre XK engine until 1964, when the capacity increased to 4.2 litres. This produced no real difference in performance, but the extra mid-range torque and a better gearbox made the car more pleasant to drive. A third body style was introduced in 1966: the 2+2 was a longer, higher-roofed coupé with rear seats. The American market drove the introduction of the Series 2 in 1968 (the USA was always a key source of sales for the E-type), as federal law demanded uncovered headlamps and higher bumpers, but the purity of the E-type's good looks was fading. The Series 3 of 1971 brought in a much larger change: the introduction of Jaguar's 5.3-litre V12 engine to replace the XK six-cylinder unit, with all cars built on the 2+2's longer wheelbase. It transformed the image of the rakish sports car into a more civilised grand tourer, but it was more powerful than ever. Sales remained quite strong until the model was replaced by the XJ-S in 1975.

Today, the Jaguar E-type is almost everyone's idea of a classic British sports car. Values rose strongly in the 2000s and 2010s, with the greatest interest from collectors in the very first 1961 Series 1 examples, marked out by their welded-in bonnet louvres and exterior bonnet locks – they have seen auction results in excess of £250,000. But all E-types have enormous cachet and still turn heads wherever they go. It would be hard to find a more widely admired classic car.

# Nobody's Pussycat.

Of all the sports cars available to you, this is the one—the ultimate cat.

Because it offers what the others can't offer: the Jaguar V-12 engine.

And that changes the discussion from *what* a sports car can do to *how well* it can do it.

That's what the Jaguar E-type V-12 is all about. How well it glides from zero to fifty. How well it accelerates out of a pack and into the clear. Even how well it behaves in downtown traffic at quitting time before a holiday weekend.

In a word, the Jaguar V-12 is smooth. It's smooth going up the scale from zero and it's smooth going from cruising speed to passing speed. It's even smooth waiting for the light to change.

Because, from an engineering viewpoint, the Jaguar V-12 is in perfect balance. Since its 5.3 litres of capacity are divided by twelve—not eight or six—the forces are spread more evenly over the crankshaft by delivering smaller but more frequent pulses of power.

What is the effect like? Well, it's something like a turbine. And it's something like an express elevator. But it's not *exactly* like anything else. That's why you have to drive a Jaguar E-type V-12 before you decide on anybody else's sports car.

Since it is a Jaguar, it has independent front and rear suspension with "anti-dive" control. Power-assisted rack and pinion steering. Power-assisted disc brakes on all four wheels—ventilated in the front. A four-speed manual is standard, an automatic is optional.

So see the Jaguar E-type V-12. It's the only production V-12 sports car in town. And that makes it second to none.

For your dealer's name and for information about overseas delivery, call (800) 447-4700. In Illinois, call (800) 322-4400. Calls are toll free.

BRITISH LEYLAND MOTORS INC., LEONIA, N.J. 07605

Contemporary advertising played on the brand's feline identity, as in this American advert for the Series 3 from 1974.

# AC / Shelby Cobra

Sometimes the most iconic cars are created by years of inspired, ground-breaking innovation … and sometimes by a single good idea. The Cobra was one of the latter, and the idea popped into the head of recently retired racing driver Carroll Shelby some time in 1961. He felt that American manufacturers were missing a trick by failing to offer a potent sports roadster that could be driven to work on a weekday and raced at weekends. The Chevrolet Corvette had the power, but perhaps not the handling to match. He decided to fill the gap.

Shelby realised that some of the British sports cars he had encountered were capable of handling much more power; American power, just like the Cadillac-engined Allards, in which he'd won some of his first races in the early 1950s. Amongst the prettiest and most agile of these was the AC Ace. The Ace was already eight years old, but a relatively sophisticated chassis design and agelessly beautiful body from designer John Tojeiro made it appealing. Shelby persuaded AC to let him have a chassis on credit and did the same with a V8 engine and transmission from Ford in the USA, who were only too keen to create a sports car that would out-do the Corvette.

The result was as dramatic as it was successful. The first prototype was running in February 1962 and, after minimal changes, production began a few months later. AC would build the chassis and bodywork in England and trim the interiors, then send the cars to Shelby in California for engine fitment. The first 75 were fitted with a 4.2-litre (260 cu. in.) Ford V8, but this was soon replaced with the 4.7-litre (298 cu. in.) version. Even with the smaller unit the new car astonished the road testers of *Road & Track* magazine by recording a 0–60 mph time of 4.2 seconds, and a standing quarter mile in 13.8 seconds at 112 mph – 'equal to the best efforts of drag-strip tuned Corvettes', said the magazine, though subsequent testers couldn't get theirs to move quite as fast as that first example prepared by Carroll Shelby.

In 1964 AC and Shelby developed a new, stronger chassis for the 'big block' 7-litre (427 cu. in.) Ford V8, to keep the Cobra winning on track. But this version missed homologation for the 1965 season and was slow to sell either in competition form or as a detuned road car. Once the Cobra started to lose money in 1967, Shelby ceased importing chassis from AC's factory.

Rather like the Lotus Seven, though, the end was also a beginning. Kit-car producers were enticed by the Cobra's shape and its simple recipe of a big V8 in a small roadster, and in 1986 a firm called Autokraft bought AC and put the car back into production as the Cobra Mk VI, with a 427-type body and a small-block V8. Since then, many other new models have been produced by several incarnations of the company, and separately by Shelby. Yes, it began as a 'bitsa' – made from bits of various cars – but sometimes the simplest recipes are the most successful.

**TOP:** A Mk II Cobra, noticeably more slender than the later big-block 427 shape.

**BOTTOM:** The 427, with extra air intakes and bulging wheel arches.

| 1965 AC Cobra | |
|---|---|
| Length | 4,013 mm |
| Width | 1,600 mm |
| Weight | 1,051 kg |
| Wheelbase | 2,286 mm |
| Suspension | Independent via wishbones, transverse leaf spring and hydraulic dampers (front); independent via transverse leaf spring, articulated driveshafts, hydraulic dampers (rear) |
| Brakes | Hydraulic discs, front and rear |
| Engine | 4,727 cc V8, overhead valve, water cooled |
| Power | 300 bhp @ 5,750 rpm |
| Torque | 285 lb-ft @ 4,500 rpm |
| Transmission | Four-speed manual, rear-wheel drive |
| 0–60 mph | 5.5 sec. |
| Top speed | 140 mph |
| Cost new | £2,454 |
| Value today | £600,000–£1 million (authentic 1960s cars) |

# Aston Martin DB5

The DB5 was already a year old and a familiar object of desire to car enthusiasts when it made an appearance in a film that would change the model's – and the marque's – fate for evermore. *Goldfinger*, Sean Connery's third outing as James Bond, opened at the Odeon in London's Leicester Square on 17 September 1964, and one of the most enduring aspects of the Bond franchise was born.

Whether the association with a womanising super-spy actually helped sales of the DB5 is hard to establish, especially as the DB4 and DB6 both sold in slightly greater numbers than Bond's model, though both had longer production runs too. What has become apparent since the DB5 left production in 1965 is that classic-car enthusiasts regard it as the high point of Aston Martin's DB era. The Bond connection is something of a bonus.

The DB models evolved steadily from the first post-war Aston Martin, and by the time Ian Fleming gave Bond a DB Mk III to drive, when *Goldfinger* was first published in 1959, they were amongst the fastest and most desirable sporting cars in Britain. That status took another jump forward the same year when Aston launched the DB4, a glamorous step change in development with a new chassis, new 3.6-litre twin-cam straight-six engine and coachwork by Carrozzeria Touring of Milan. Aston Martin was no longer trying to out-do homegrown rivals; it was taking on Maserati and Ferrari at their own game.

An exciting DB4 variant, the DB4 GT, had a shortened wheelbase, more power and a new nose with sloping fairings over the headlamps. The same look was used for most of the DB4 Vantage models, with greater power but the standard wheelbase, and it was carried over into the DB5 in 1963. This time, the motorsport edge was less important and no lightweight GT version was offered, but the engine size and power outputs were up again, peaking at 325 bhp for the Vantage with its triple Weber carburettors. This put the car's performance ahead of the Jaguar E-type, but so did the equipment level and (perhaps thanks to Bond) the brand image, which it needed to do, as the E-type cost only a third as much.

As well as the famous coupé there were 123 convertibles, which began using the name Volante in 1965 as the model was nearing the end of its run. Convertible Astons have been known by that name ever since, but these DB5 versions (and especially the dozen cars with Vantage engines) have become even more highly valued than the coupés. In the twenty-first century, a boom in the value of all classic Aston Martins carried the prices of the DB models higher than ever, with the DB5 cementing its status alongside the likes of the Ferrari Daytona as one of the most sought-after sporting cars ever made. Appearances in several of the more recent Bond films did no harm either.

| 1964 Aston Martin DB5 | |
|---|---|
| Length | 4,610 mm |
| Width | 1,676 mm |
| Weight | 1,502 kg |
| Wheelbase | 2,489 mm |
| Suspension | Independent via wishbones, coil springs and hydraulic dampers (front); live axle with trailing arms and Watts linkage, coil springs and hydraulic dampers (rear) |
| Brakes | Hydraulic discs, front and rear |
| Engine | 3,995 cc straight-six, DOHC, water cooled |
| Power | 282 bhp @ 5,500 rpm |
| Torque | 280 lb-ft @ 4,500 rpm |
| Transmission | Five-speed manual, rear-wheel drive |
| 0–60 mph | 8.1 sec. |
| Top speed | 142 mph |
| Cost new | £4,249 |
| Value today | £350,000–£650,000 (more for the Volantes) |

TOP: Sleek and elegant, but at the same time oozing power.

BOTTOM: The DB5 has fin-like wings, whereas the DB6 has a full-width lip spoiler.

# FERRARI 250 GTO

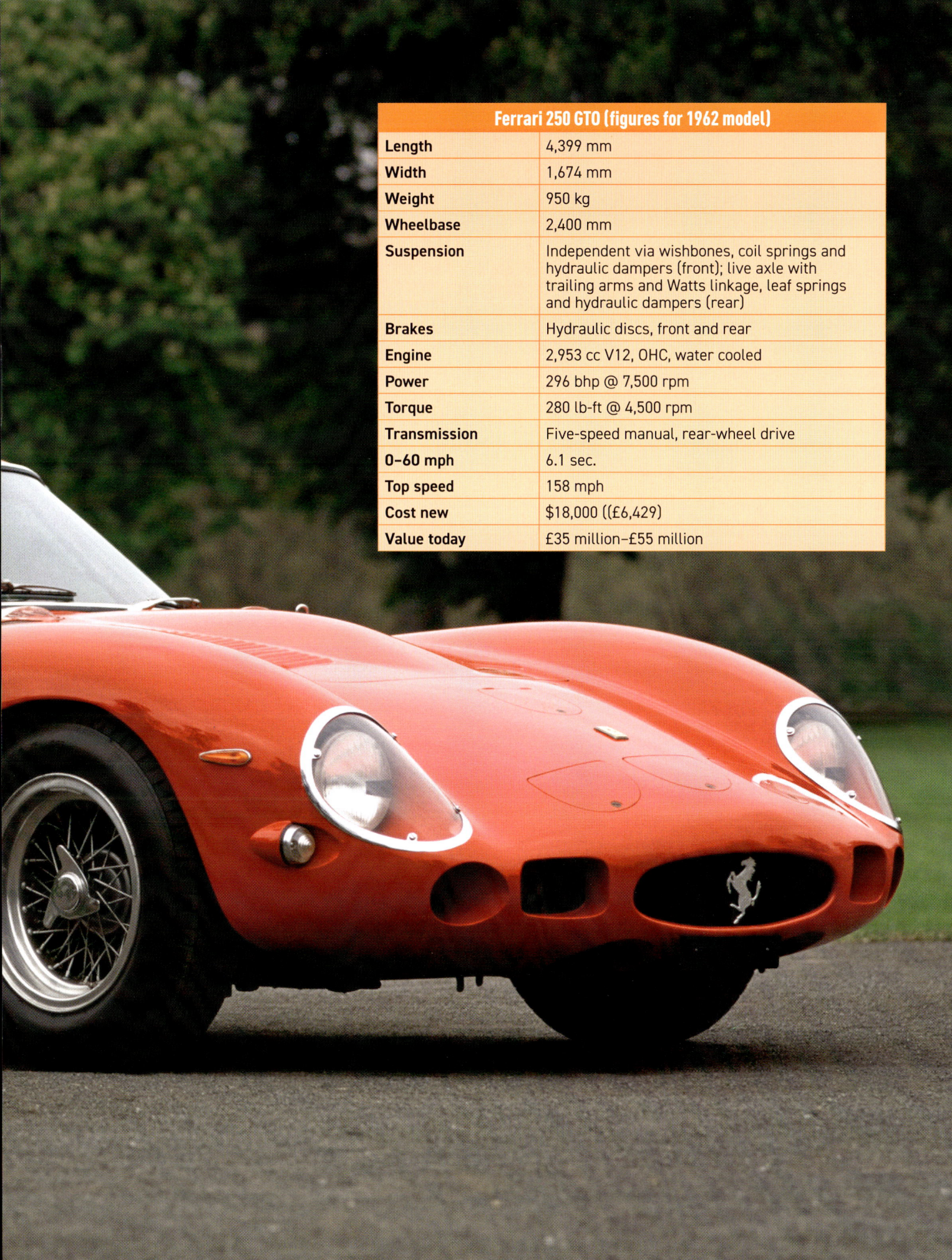

| Ferrari 250 GTO (figures for 1962 model) ||
|---|---|
| Length | 4,399 mm |
| Width | 1,674 mm |
| Weight | 950 kg |
| Wheelbase | 2,400 mm |
| Suspension | Independent via wishbones, coil springs and hydraulic dampers (front); live axle with trailing arms and Watts linkage, leaf springs and hydraulic dampers (rear) |
| Brakes | Hydraulic discs, front and rear |
| Engine | 2,953 cc V12, OHC, water cooled |
| Power | 296 bhp @ 7,500 rpm |
| Torque | 280 lb-ft @ 4,500 rpm |
| Transmission | Five-speed manual, rear-wheel drive |
| 0–60 mph | 6.1 sec. |
| Top speed | 158 mph |
| Cost new | $18,000 ((£6,429) |
| Value today | £35 million–£55 million |

If the Jaguar E-type is the most widely admired classic we can see and enjoy in the real world, the Ferrari 250 GTO is the fantasy – an icon that few of us get to encounter, never mind own or drive. There were just 36 of them built between 1962 and 1964, and most are now locked up in private collections, emerging only for concours shows or special demonstrations. Thankfully, a few owners still allow them to be driven in anger and raced at events such as the Goodwood Revival.

You can't get far in a discussion of the 250 GTO without mentioning values. With the exception of one extraordinary Mercedes racing car, the GTO is the most valuable automobile there is. Certainly, it's the most valuable to have been produced in any number. Depending on history, ownership provenance and competition success, at the time of writing a 250 GTO is valued at nearly £50 million. The graph has been sloping upwards for decades; of the few for which sale prices were released, one sold for £30.8 million in 2014, another for £37.6 million in 2018 and a third for £42.2 million in 2023. What makes it so special?

In short, everything. The 250 GTO has a unique combination of features that no other car has been able to match. First, it was a huge success on the racetrack; combining the V12 engine from the Testarossa with a five-speed gearbox and a lighter body than the 250 GT SWB made it nearly unbeatable. With 300 bhp from the 3-litre engine it could touch 155 mph and out-accelerate and out-handle its rivals, winning the International Championship for GT Manufacturers in 1962, 1963 and 1964.

Second, that bodywork wasn't just light in weight, it was stunningly beautiful. The shape was created by Giotto Bizzarrini and tweaked in a wind tunnel, and the end result was a gorgeous combination of art and science – a trait it had in common with the Jaguar E-type. Third, the number of cars produced was enough to create fame, but nowhere near enough for supply to ever exceed demand. Yes, GTOs spent a few years changing hands for less than their huge $18,000 price new, but by the mid-1970s they were worth twice that. The 250 GTO was a nailed-on classic while other exotic cars of the era were just second-hand.

Finally, there's the name itself. If another manufacturer had built this car and won those races, the model would still have become famous. But with a badge from Jaguar, Maserati, Alfa Romeo or Aston Martin, it would never have become such an icon. That's an over-used word, but here it's apt: Ferrari is almost a religion for its fans, especially the *tifosi* who follow the marque's motorsport exploits. If there's one focus for the worship of the Prancing Horse, it's the 250 GTO.

In some ways it's amazing that the 250 *Gran Turismo Omologato* turned out as well as it did. Enzo Ferrari could be an autocratic employer and late in 1961 eight of his senior engineers, including Giotto Bizzarrini, staged a walk-out in protest over management decisions, with the 250 GTO not yet complete. Rather than cave in to their wishes, Ferrari sacked them all and promoted the young Mauro Forghieri to the position of chief racing engineer.

Because the design was an evolution rather than an innovation, Forghieri and his new team were not faced with any untested concepts. The chassis of the 250 GT SWB, itself a successful car, was modified slightly to sit lower to the ground, lose weight and gain in torsional stiffness. The front suspension consisted of a pair of wishbones each side and the rear set-up was an old-fashioned live axle on leaf springs, with a Watts linkage – two rods locating the differential to the chassis to keep the body from moving side-to-side over the axle in hard cornering. Disc brakes at each corner slowed it effectively. The engine, which was far enough back in the chassis to sit entirely behind the front axle line, was the Tipo 168/62 overhead camshaft V12 evolved from the original Colombo V12 design that reached back to 1947. The gearbox was all new, though, with five forward gears and synchromesh.

Rough prototypes had been running before Forghieri took over and by the end of 1961 production cars were in build. The first race, the 12 Hours of Sebring in March 1962, saw a GTO win its class, as it would go on to do at numerous other events. Outright wins included the Tour de France Automobile, a multi-venue road rally and race event, in both 1963 and 1964, and the Targa Florio in 1965. GTOs were driven by all the famous names of the day, not least Stirling Moss, Phil Hill and John Surtees. Since then, the famous names have become the collectors who own them: Nick Mason of Pink Floyd, Ralph Lauren, Lawrence Stroll and others.

Those lucky enough to take the wheel of a 250 GTO, either in the full commitment of a race or just to taste the car's ability on a public road, tend to agree that the GTO is worthy of all the fuss. The car occupies a sweet spot: perfect handling balance with enough power to overcome the grip of narrow 1960s racing tyres, meaning that the car's attitude through a corner can be set by the accelerator pedal rather than the steering wheel. Powerful brakes and a kerb weight under 950 kg make it an extremely agile competitor. Then there's the noise: whether you're in the car or simply a bystander, a GTO engine howling away at 7,500 rpm really does make the hairs on the back of your neck stand up.

The 250 GTO is a truly great car and a pinnacle of the Ferrari legend, but it's now so valuable and famous it's become the four-wheeled equivalent of an Old Master. Cars as art? Yes, both as an aesthetic achievement and an investment. Try to see one in action before they're locked away forever.

**ABOVE:** 250 GTO chassis 3445 was painted in Sweden's national colours by a Swedish owner in 1963, and it's worn them ever since.

**PREVIOUS PAGE:** A 1962 GTO in the classic shade of *Rosso Cina*.

# MGB

The MGB was the perfect sports car for the everyman – it provided a bit of the Jaguar E-type experience, but at a price most people could afford. It wasn't as fast or as glamorous, but it was cheaper to run, easier to maintain and tough enough to use as a daily driver. Like the E-type, you could buy a two-seat roadster or a fastback GT version with a tailgate, and it too came with the heritage of a much-loved sporting marque.

The initials MG stand for Morris Garages, a sales and service centre in Oxford, and it originated in the 1920s as a project run by Cecil Kimber, the manager. Kimber modified the vintage 'Bullnose' model and sold it as the MG Super Sports. The MG brand was later incorporated into Morris, and in turn into BMC, where it eventually became a division of its own. But the pattern was set from the beginning – take mechanical parts from relatively humble models and use them to build affordable sports cars.

In the post-war years MG started with the TD and TF, nimble little roadsters that harked back to the 1930s, but then took a major step forward with the MGA. Launched in 1955, it featured bang-up-to-date styling and a new engine, the BMC B-series. Its successor was already being planned in 1955, using much of the same driveline and running gear but in a new body that made two important improvements: it was a monocoque structure and so didn't rely on a separate chassis, and in 1965 it introduced the option of the GT version. Both these features gave it something to boast about when compared with its main rivals, the Triumph TR family.

The MGB was also very good looking. This is often overlooked in Britain, where the car is so familiar, but the roadster was as neat as any Italian equivalent, while the GT looked like a baby Aston Martin. The MGB launched as a roadster in 1962 with the 1,798 cc twin-carburettor version of the B-series engine, though two spin-off models, the MGC (1967–69) and the MGB GT V8 (1973–76), used the C-series straight-six and the Rover V8 respectively. Gearboxes were four-speed manuals with optional overdrive, or a less popular three-speed automatic. In 1974 the cars were restyled to introduce large, rubber-covered steel bumpers to comply with American impact regulations. In addition, the headlamps needed to be a certain height from the ground, which British Leyland – by then in charge of the MG brand – chose to achieve by placing blocks in the suspension to raise the car by an inch.

This all harmed the handling, and by the late 1970s the MGB was looking and feeling its age. Born in 1962, it lasted to 1980 when hot hatchbacks were taking over. It achieved the rare feat of being seen as a classic before it left production and it's been a fixture in the classic car scene ever since.

**TOP:** A 1969 MGB GT.

**MIDDLE:** Rubber bumpers appeared in 1974, with other changes.

**BOTTOM:** An MGB roadster on Rostyle wheels, offered from 1970 onwards.

| 1965 MGB roadster | |
|---|---|
| Length | 3,891 mm |
| Width | 1,521 mm |
| Weight | 966 kg |
| Wheelbase | 2,311 mm |
| Suspension | Independent via wishbones, coil springs and hydraulic lever-arm dampers (front); live axle with leaf springs and hydraulic lever-arm dampers (rear) |
| Brakes | Hydraulic via discs (front); drums (rear) |
| Engine | 1,798 cc in-line four, overhead valve, water cooled |
| Power | 95 bhp @ 5,400 rpm |
| Torque | 100 lb-ft @ 3,000 rpm |
| Transmission | Four-speed manual plus overdrive, rear-wheel drive |
| 0–60 mph | 12.9 sec. |
| Top speed | 106 mph |
| Cost new | £847 |
| Value today | £2,000–£14,000 |

# Lotus Elan

Drive a Lotus Elan and you'll understand what all the fuss is about. Its reputation is for perfect handling: the finest, purest cornering experience ever made available to the general public. Most of the time reputations like that are exaggerated, but in this case it's true.

The Elan's predecessor, the Elite, was also wonderful from behind the wheel, but it was never cut out for a long life as a production car. It was an incredibly bold design – a monocoque body structure made entirely of glass-fibre, with running gear and driveline components mounted to it. This made it light and nimble but also rather fragile, especially as it used a race-bred Coventry Climax engine that was never intended for long service intervals and traffic jams.

The Elan, which Lotus introduced in September 1962 in a two-seat roadster form, brought with it a new engine. It was a sturdy, iron-blocked four-cylinder Ford with a new Lotus cylinder head featuring two overhead camshafts. Big valves helped it breathe deeply and it made 106 bhp from 1,588 cc, with the tuning potential for a lot more. That alone would have made a 580 kg car lively, but it was the Elan's layout and chassis design that made it such a delight to steer.

Rather than stick with the glass-fibre monocoque, Lotus chose to use a steel backbone chassis that splayed into a long, narrow Y-shape at the front and a short, wide Y-shape at the back. At the front, the engine and gearbox fitted into the Y with the double-wishbone suspension mounted at the forward ends. At the rear, each end of the Y rose up to carry a long Chapman strut – a coil spring with a telescopic damper – descending to a hub casting. The differential was fixed to the chassis in the centre, and below it a tubular wishbone on each side carried the hubs. As a result, the front and rear wheels were as perfectly located as on any racing car, with the unsprung weight kept to a minimum and most of the chassis mass concentrated near the centre line.

On top of this clever design, Lotus rested a sleek, lightweight glass-fibre body only 3.7 metres long. Through excellent ergonomics, this left room for a driver and passenger to get comfortable, even if both were well over six feet tall. The Elan evolved over eleven years through four series – as power rose steadily, brakes improved, and dashboards and external details changed – and culminated in the 126 bhp big-valve Sprint, with two-tone paint and the option of a five-speed gearbox.

The Elan embodied Colin Chapman's philosophy of simplicity, lightness and high performance, though the actual design work was done mainly by Ron Hickman, who had previously worked on the Elite and later found great success as the creator of the Black & Decker Workmate. As a practical tool to do a job, the Workmate was a roaring success; as a practical sports car to enjoy on Britain's winding roads, the Elan has never been bettered.

| 1963 Lotus Elan | |
|---|---|
| Length | 3,688 mm |
| Width | 1,422 mm |
| Weight | 681 kg |
| Wheelbase | 2,134 mm |
| Suspension | Independent via wishbones, coil springs and telescopic dampers (front); Chapman struts and lower wishbones (rear) |
| Brakes | Hydraulic discs (front and rear) |
| Engine | 1,588 cc in-line four, DOHC, water cooled |
| Power | 105 bhp @ 5,500 rpm |
| Torque | 108 lb-ft @ 4,000 rpm |
| Transmission | Four-speed manual, rear-wheel drive |
| 0–60 mph | 8.5 sec. |
| Top speed | 107 mph |
| Cost new | £1,499 |
| Value today | £12,000–£35,000 |

TOP: Pop-up headlamps were innovative in 1963, but the Elan's cleverest design was hidden under the skin.

MIDDLE: The Sprint was the final version and the fastest; this one is a rare coupé.

BOTTOM: The Elan introduced the fabulous Lotus Twin-Cam engine, they key to its nippy performance.

# Chevrolet Corvette Sting Ray

The Corvette took a long while to find its market. Launched in 1953 as a low-slung roadster with a streamlined glass-fibre body and a six-cylinder engine, it was more boulevard cruiser than sports car. It sold in tiny numbers by American standards – 300 in that first year, when Chevrolet sold more than 630,000 four-door sedans. Sales rose into the low thousands and reached 10,000 in 1960, four years after a V8 engine was introduced to give the Corvette some sports car performance, even if the handling wasn't in the same league. It was a model in need of a reboot, which it certainly received for 1963.

The Sting Ray (two words until the next generation came along in 1968, when it was styled Stingray) was more than a bold new look. It used a heavily revised chassis with a shorter wheelbase and independent rear suspension in place of the heavy old live axle. This set the pattern for future generations of Corvettes and finally gave the model the rear-end grip and handling poise it needed to exploit all that power. And power was available aplenty, with 250 bhp as standard from the 5.4-litre (327-cu. in.) V8 and options rising to 300 bhp, 340 bhp and topping out at 360 bhp from the fearsome fuel-injected L84 engine.

Despite this transformation in driver appeal, the first thing that struck most observers was the car's radical new look. Both convertible and coupé hid four headlamps in two rotating pods that, when resting in their daytime position, allowed the sleek nose to remain uninterrupted. Indeed, you could follow that waist-level crease across the nose, right down each side and across the tail of the car, too. Huge bulges above each wheel did more to give a muscular look than to provide room for wheel travel, all of which was drawn from a car sketched by GM designer Pete Brock and built for his boss Bill Mitchell in 1959. This was a combination of concept car and racer, and though dubbed the XP-87 it was usually known as the Sting Ray.

For the production cars, it was the coupé's rear window that really caught the eye. Here, the sloping roof tapered to a kind of beetle-back shape, with a spine-like feature running the length of the roof and splitting the screen down the middle. It called to mind exotic cars of the past, like the Bugatti Type 57SC Atlantic, but was probably inspired by earlier GM show cars created by Mitchell's predecessor, Harley Earl. This striking feature only lasted one year, with the 1964 Sting Ray doing away with the split and leaving a one-piece rear screen.

That makes the 1963 coupé one of the most sought-after of all Corvettes, while the C2 generation (as the 1963–67 Corvettes are known) are also highly regarded as the models that finally gave America something to rival the powerful GTs and roadsters from Jaguar, Aston Martin, Ferrari and others. Yes, America could build sports cars, and after the Sting Ray it never looked back.

| 1963 Chevrolet Corvette Sting Ray 'L84' ||
|---|---|
| Length | 4,453 mm |
| Width | 1,768 mm |
| Weight | 1,375 kg |
| Wheelbase | 2,489 mm |
| Suspension | Independent via unequal-length wishbones, coil springs and telescopic dampers (front); transverse leaf spring and links, trailing arms and leading links (rear) |
| Brakes | Hydraulic drums (front and rear) |
| Engine | 5,340 cc V8, overhead valve, water cooled, mechanical fuel injection |
| Power | 360 bhp (gross) @ 6,000 rpm |
| Torque | 352 lb-ft @ 4,000 rpm |
| Transmission | Four-speed manual, rear-wheel drive |
| 0–60 mph | 5.9 sec. |
| Top speed | 142 mph |
| Cost new | $4,875 (c.£1,741) |
| Value today | £50,000–£150,000 |

TOP: An 1967 Sting Ray convertible with perforated covers on the side-exit exhausts.

BOTTOM: The Batmobile-esque split rear window of the 1963 Sting Ray coupé. This car's number plate suggests it's a potent fuel-injected version.

# Ford Cortina Lotus

In more recent decades we've become used to collaborations between marques: Ford Escorts and Sierras with engines by Cosworth; Mercedes or Audi Q-cars engineered by Porsche; and modern Aston Martins and Paganis relying on Mercedes power. In the 1960s this was still a novelty. Plenty of small sports-car builders used engines from larger manufacturers, but for a major car builder to look elsewhere for a high-performance engine was unusual. The exception came with a few aftermarket tuning firms given friendly approval by dealers or manufacturers, especially where motorsport was involved.

Motorsport was key to this collaboration. Lotus founder Colin Chapman commissioned his friend Harry Mundy, a talented engine designer and technical editor of *Autocar* magazine, to design a version of the Ford Kent four-cylinder engine with twin overhead camshafts. The intention was to provide Lotus with a capable, tuneable engine for motor racing that could also be used in their new production sports car, the Elan. In a considerable stroke of luck for Chapman, Ford boss Walter Hayes – something of a petrolhead by boardroom standards – got wind of the engine's development and asked Chapman if he could manufacture and fit 1,000 of these engines to Consul-Cortina saloons. This was the magic number that would homologate the model for Group 2 saloon car racing; it was necessary to build and sell 1,000 units to prove the car entered in competition was a true production model. In years to come, it would be the reason behind the creation of some of the most exciting road cars ever seen.

Lotus did much more than fit a twin-cam engine in a standard Cortina. They took delivery of the two-door bodyshells from Ford and replaced the doors, bonnet and boot with lighter aluminium alloy versions, also altering the rear suspension to locate the differential with an A-shaped frame and two trailing arms, and replacing the leaf springs with coil-and-damper struts, rather like an Elan. A close-ratio gearbox and bigger, servo-assisted brakes made the cars instantly competitive on track and very hard to catch on the road, where skilful drivers found they could get away from larger-engined sports cars.

Beating larger opposition became a theme, as the Lotus Cortinas diced with and defeated huge V8 Ford Galaxies and 3.8-litre Jaguar Mk 2 saloons. In his spare time between grands prix, Jim Clark won the 1964 British Saloon Car Championship in a Lotus Cortina and in 1965 Sir John Whitmore won the European Touring Car Championship in a revised version of the model. That early rear suspension had proved troublesome, putting too much strain through parts of the rear axle assembly and bodyshell, and it was simplified to a leaf spring and trailing-arm arrangement after the first couple of years.

The car stayed competitive through 1966 and was selling well too, with 3,301 produced – well up from the original aim of 1,000. It was succeeded by the Mk 2 version in 1967 and remains an object of desire for many fans of fast Fords. In historic motorsport, it's still winning today.

| 1963 Ford Cortina Lotus | |
|---|---|
| Length | 4,216 mm |
| Width | 1,588 mm |
| Weight | 826 kg |
| Wheelbase | 2,502 mm |
| Suspension | Independent via MacPherson struts (front); coil spring and damper units, trailing arms and A-bracket (rear) |
| Brakes | Servo-assisted hydraulic discs (front); drums (rear) |
| Engine | 1,558 cc in-line four, DOHC, water cooled |
| Power | 105 bhp (gross) @ 5,500 rpm |
| Torque | 108 lb-ft @ 4,000 rpm |
| Transmission | Four-speed manual, rear-wheel drive |
| 0–60 mph | 9.9 sec. |
| Top speed | 107 mph |
| Cost new | £1,100 |
| Value today | £40,000–£80,000 |

### 'The most exciting British car since the Jaguar E-type.'

*Motor Sport* magazine, January 1964

A restored example in rally trim.

# Pontiac GTO

It's probably not the most famous American muscle car, but the Pontiac GTO is arguably the most important. It's the car that kicked off something that came to define a decade of American motoring, and which still has an immense following more than 50 years later.

What exactly makes a muscle car? Typically, they were mid-size models fitted with V8 engines from cars a size larger. There had been isolated examples before the GTO, like the Oldsmobile Rocket 88 in 1949, the Chrysler C300 in 1955 and the Rambler Rebel V8 in 1957. But it was more than that. True muscle cars had an image all their own and a marketing strategy that was just as fresh. For the first time, car manufacturers were aiming their products directly at the young – typically men in their twenties. So these cars had to be relatively cheap, even with the generous credit terms that were becoming normal at American car-dealer networks. It was all about who could offer the most performance for the money and the most attractive image to go along with it.

John DeLorean understood this. He was a maverick: the guy with the open shirt collar in an office full of suits and ties. By 1961 he had serious power as Pontiac's engineering chief and he was always looking for new ideas. He met once a week with engine specialist Bill Collins and fellow engineer Russ Gee, and on one occasion they were examining a prototype for the 1964 Pontiac Le Mans – a low-priced, two-door coupé. As standard, it would have a 3.5-litre straight-six making 140 bhp. Collins wondered what it would be like with the 6.4-litre (389-cu. in.) V8 from the full-size Catalina and Bonneville.

This got DeLorean thinking and he pushed the project ahead as fast as possible. It's unclear who thought of 'borrowing' the three letters GTO from Ferrari, but it was an inspired choice. It wasn't a GT, it wasn't a homologation special and it wasn't even a new model. Because of a motorsport ban by General Motors that forbade putting large engines in mid-size bodies, DeLorean and Pontiac's PR chief Jim Wangers only managed to sneak the GTO into production as an option package on the 1964 Tempest Le Mans. Starting at $2,852, the GTO was a clear bargain when a sports car like the Corvette was $4,252, and even the closest Chevrolet two-door coupé equivalent, the Chevelle Malibu SS, was around $2,950 with a less-powerful V8 installed.

Pontiac sold 32,450 GTOs in the first year, the rest of Detroit jumped on the bandwagon, and the muscle car was born. Aggressive model names, loud paint jobs, basic interiors and ever-larger and more powerful engines featured as an arms race of horsepower developed. Today the GTO is respected as the match that lit the whole bonfire. Now just imagine being 21 years old in 1964 and picking up the keys to your new GTO – no wonder it makes a generation of Americans nostalgic.

TOP: The aggressive stance of a 1964 GTO.

BOTTOM: An advert for the GTO in *National Geographic* from 1965.

How to tell a real tiger from a pussycat:

Drive it.  Pontiac Motor Division • General Motors Corporation

| 1964 Pontiac Tempest Le Mans GTO ||
|---|---|
| Length | 5,156 mm |
| Width | 1,862 mm |
| Weight | 1,543 kg |
| Wheelbase | 2,921 mm |
| Suspension | Independent via unequal-length wishbones, anti-roll bar, coil springs and hydraulic dampers (front); live axle with leaf springs and hydraulic dampers (rear) |
| Brakes | Hydraulic drums, front and rear |
| Engine | 6,377 cc V8, overhead valve, water cooled |
| Power | 325 bhp @ 4,800 rpm |
| Torque | 428 lb-ft @ 3,200 rpm |
| Transmission | Four-speed manual, rear-wheel drive |
| 0–60 mph | 6.9 sec. |
| Top speed | 122 mph |
| Cost new | $2,852 (c.£1,018) |
| Value today | £25,000–£75,000 |

# Rover 2000/2200/3500

Rover was one of the oldest and most respectable names in the British car industry, with origins as a bicycle manufacturer in the nineteenth century. It made safe, durable, dependable but not terribly exciting cars, though with occasional bold steps forward like the 'cyclops' styling of their new Rover 75 in 1948, the first of the P4 family. The P5, an enlarged variation on the same theme, arrived in 1958 but fitted into a slot above the P4. The whole range was badly in need of a replacement by the early 1960s.

The P6, as it came to be known, was a rare thing in car production – a true 'clean sheet of paper' design. Even the revolutionary Citroën DS had used a version of the old Traction Avant engine, but the Rover was new from nose to tail. The DS was a strong influence, both to stylist David Bache and to the engineers who created the car underneath those sleek panels and wide, low nose. The panels were mounted on a separate base unit, which was a monocoque structure with high torsional rigidity. Like the Citroën, the Rover offered a remarkable ride – serene high-speed cruising, fine roadholding, decent economy and plenty of interior space – but it achieved all this in a totally different way.

There were none of the Citroën's high-pressure hydraulics powering the brakes or suspension, just four-wheel, servo-assisted discs (inboard at the rear) and sophisticated coil-spring suspension. At the rear there was a de Dion tube with a telescopic section to remove the need for sliding splines in the driveshafts, while at the front the springs were pushed by a bell crank arrangement and sat horizontally, fore and aft, inside each front wing. This was to allow an engine bay wide enough to fit a gas turbine engine, the focus of much Rover research in the 1950s and 1960s.

In the end, of course, gas turbines never quite worked for road cars, and a new overhead-cam four-cylinder unit was developed for the Rover 2000's launch in 1963. In single-carburettor form it gave an acceptable if not dazzling performance, leading to a twin-carb, high-compression version in 1966 with more dashing acceleration. Top of the tree, though, was the Rover 3500 that debuted in 1968 with the Buick-sourced aluminium V8 that first appeared in the P5B a year before. This catapulted the P6 into a new league, leaving four-cylinder rivals like the DS in the dust and also showing a clean pair of heels to the six-cylinder Triumph 2500, even in fuel-injected PI form.

To drive, a P6 can seem more Continental than British. With a restrained, almost minimalist dashboard layout and a minimum of external brightwork, it was nothing like the American-influenced Fords and Vauxhalls of the time. The soft ride and pronounced body roll was rather French, as were the impressively high grip levels and well-insulated cabin. Perhaps it was this cosmopolitan feel that helped the P6 to win the first ever European Car of the Year award in 1964.

| 1964 Rover 2000 | |
|---|---|
| Length | 4,534 mm |
| Width | 1,676 mm |
| Weight | 1,309 kg |
| Wheelbase | 2,629 mm |
| Suspension | Independent via bell cranks, top and bottom links, coil springs and hydraulic dampers (front); de Dion rear axle with Panhard rod, coil springs and hydraulic dampers (rear) |
| Brakes | Hydraulic discs, servo-assisted, front and rear |
| Engine | 1,978 cc in-line four, OHC, water cooled |
| Power | 90 bhp @ 5,000 rpm |
| Torque | 113 lb-ft @ 3,600 rpm |
| Transmission | Four-speed manual, rear-wheel drive |
| 0–60 mph | 15.3 sec. |
| Top speed | 101 mph |
| Cost new | £1,264 |
| Value today | £3,000–£15,000 |

TOP: Inside a 2000: comfortable, well-equipped but not flashy.

BOTTOM: A subtle mid-level crease gives form to the P6's smooth surfaces.

# Aston Martin

If you ever doubt how important motorsport success was to the early days of car manufacture, think of Aston Martin. The firm that built the cars was Bamford & Martin, but part of the name of the Aston Hill Climb ( a speed hill climb on public roads) was borrowed to signify sporting intent. Lionel Martin began production of his own cars in 1922, concentrating on low, lightweight sports machines and focusing on race success right from the beginning. This gave the firm a famous name – and little profit.

Even by the standards of small-scale British sports-car makers, Aston Martin had a shaky financial history, suffering several bankruptcies and changes of ownership through the 1920s and 1930s. Nonetheless, they continued to find success on the track thanks to an advanced overhead-camshaft four-cylinder engine, available to customers in dry-sumped racing configuration. By 1936 the penny dropped and Aston Martin concentrated on road cars. Then came war and production shifted to aircraft components. When peace came the company soon changed hands once again, this time to David Brown Ltd.

A tractor manufacturer from Huddersfield might not seem the likeliest owner for a prestigious sports-car marque, but Aston Martin thrived as never before under David Brown's ownership. This was in part down to the 2.6-litre engine that Brown had acquired when he bought Lagonda, which also struggled after the war. This was a double overhead-camshaft straight-six, rather like the Jaguar XK engine but designed by W. O. Bentley. It transformed the company's products: the DB1 used a pushrod, four-cylinder, 2-litre engine while the Bentley-designed engine in a streamlined new body gave 120 mph and became the DB2. The DB 2/4 and DB Mk III followed, and Aston's reputation for fast, handsome and desirable GT cars grew rapidly.

Always more expensive and exclusive than Jaguars, and faster than Bristols, the DB Aston Martins took another leap forward in 1958, when the DB4 launched with styling and *Superleggera* construction by Touring of Milan. Meanwhile, racing derivations had been challenging the C-types and D-types, culminating in a Le Mans victory for the DBR1 in 1959. Exotic, lightweight versions of the DB4 GT by Zagato would find more race success in the early 1960s. But it was production designer Ken Adam's decision to use the new DB5 as James Bond's steed in *Goldfinger* (1964) that defined the company's image forever after.

Bond returned to Aston Martin in *Thunderball*, *On Her Majesty's Secret Service*, *The Living Daylights*, *Goldeneye*, and every movie since then. It's difficult to think of another car brand so closely identified with one character, especially one so helpful for marketing purposes. Away from the fictional universe, Aston Martin saw further financial troubles in the 1970s and 1980s, despite launching the long-lived and desirable V8 family. Ford took over in 1987 and for 20 years helped fund the creation of cars like the DB7, DB9, V8 Vantage and Vanquish, securing a future for the brand. After an engineering partnership with Mercedes and another change of control to Canadian billionaire Lawrence Stroll, who renamed his Formula One team as Aston Martin, it looks ready to move forward again.

# THROUGH THE YEARS

**CLOCKWISE FROM TOP LEFT:** An Aston Martin Ulster; DB1; DB4 GT Zagato; Bulldog concept car; V8 Vantage.

# Mercedes-Benz SL 'Pagoda'

While the 300SL Gullwing and its roadster sibling raised Mercedes's profile, they made far less money for the firm than the smaller, slower 190 SL. This showed the way forward – halo models were all very well, but it was important to make cars people could afford. And Mercedes products were expensive anyway, especially with the import duties applied in many countries in the early 1960s. By 1964, the new 230 SL cost £3,595 in the UK when a Porsche 356 cabriolet was £2,527 and even a Zagato-bodied Alfa Romeo 2600 Sprint was only £2,899. A homegrown rival, the Jaguar E-type, was famously good value at £1,829. So why was the SL a worldwide success? Quality speaks for itself, in the end, and nothing else was quite as well built, durable or delightful to live with as the Mercedes. If you could afford one, you bought one.

The W114 model was created by a mix of long-established wisdom and young talent. The styling team was led by Friedrich Geiger, who had masterminded not only the 300SLs but the 500K and 540K of the 1930s. The design work was largely carried out by French-born Paul Bracq and Hungarian Béla Barényi. The Pagoda nickname came from the hard-top roof with its slightly concave top surface, thought to resemble the roof of an East Asian temple. The car's lines were clean, simple and not particularly fashion conscious, which made it slow to age. But what was concealed under that pretty exterior was also important.

The old 190 SL sold well, but it couldn't outrun many cheaper sports roadsters. Mercedes was determined to give its replacement some credibility, which meant using a six-cylinder engine. With fuel injection as standard, the 230 SL arrived with 150 bhp and a choice of manual and automatic transmissions. It could make use of the power too, thanks to a shorter, wider chassis with low-pivot swing-axle rear suspension, excellent brakes and relatively wide radial tyres. The brakes were part of an unusual element of the design mission, at least for the era: an emphasis on safety. Designed more than 60 years ago, the SL had built-in crumple zones and a collapsible steering column before other manufacturers even paid lip service to collision protection.

The W114 developed gradually as the torquier 250 SL came along in 1966, then the final 280 SL a year later, offering 168 bhp and selling better than ever, with 23,885 sales contributing to a total figure of 48,912 by the time production ended in 1971. Today, the SL is an expensive car once again, its combination of chic 1960s looks, capability in modern traffic and badge prestige persuading owners to invest. The 230 SL is even sought-after as an endurance rally car, echoing the success it had when new by winning the Spa-Sofia-Liege Rally. In the end, it's the SL's glamour that appeals. When new, it was the choice of Sofia Loren, Stirling Moss, Juan Manuel Fangio and Charlton Heston, and the celebrities are still buying them today. Where they lead, many of us follow.

TOP: Pure German elegance personified in Mercedes roadster form.

MIDDLE: W114 SLs make excellent historic rally cars.

BOTTOM: Paul Bracq's superb proportions revealed with the hard top in place.

| 1964 Mercedes-Benz 230 SL | |
|---|---|
| Length | 4,293 mm |
| Width | 1,758 mm |
| Weight | 1,331 kg |
| Wheelbase | 2,400 mm |
| Suspension | Independent via unequal-length wishbones, coil springs and hydraulic dampers (front); low-pivot swing axles, semi-trailing arms, coil springs and hydraulic dampers (rear) |
| Brakes | Hydraulic discs (front); drums (rear), servo-assisted |
| Engine | 2,306 cc in-line six, OHC, mechanical fuel injection |
| Power | 150 bhp @ 5,500 rpm |
| Torque | 159 lb-ft @ 4,500 rpm |
| Transmission | Four-speed manual, rear-wheel drive |
| 0–60 mph | 10.7 sec. |
| Top speed | 121 mph |
| Cost new | £3,595 |
| Value today | £40,000–£150,000 |

# Porsche 911

The Porsche 911 is an extraordinary survivor, seemingly fighting an uphill battle against its own basic design from day one. Yet it's been in continuous production since 1964 and over the last 60-odd years has built the Porsche brand ever higher, creating a worldwide following that now outstrips any other sports car.

Porsche's Volkswagen origins were pretty obvious with the 356: a rear-mounted, air-cooled flat-four with Beetle-esque styling. By the early 1960s the company needed a replacement and F. A. 'Butzi' Porsche, grandson of Ferdinand Porsche, led the design direction. The rear-engined layout remained, with the engine growing from four cylinders to six and still air cooled, and the body stretching to a sleek fastback shape with more room in the cabin and better luggage capacity. Porsche launched it as the 901 on 12 September 1963, but a protest from Peugeot about model names ending in '01' meant the name changed to 911 before production began. The first 911 used a 2-litre engine and although it was nearly 12 cm longer in wheelbase than the 356, the extra weight of that six-cylinder engine hanging behind the rear wheels made the cars tricky in fast corners – lift off the throttle halfway round and the rear end would go light, lose traction and spin the car.

This was partially cured by adding another 6 cm to the wheelbase from late 1968, but the same challenge would continue across future generations of 911s as power rose ever higher. Yet Porsche kept overcoming that challenge, maintaining the 911's unique niche: it was as useable every day as a VW Beetle or Golf but with true sports-car performance, and once the 911/930 Turbo arrived in 1974 it had a model that could match Ferrari and Lamborghini supercars. Some of the most celebrated 911 models are the quickest variants, such as the 911S of the 1960s and early 1970s, and the 1973 RS Carrera, a lightweight homologation special with a howling 2.7-litre engine and a duck-tail spoiler.

As the generations progressed from 2 litres to 2.2, 2.7, 3.0 and 3.2, the design remained remarkably consistent and outsold the faster, more advanced front-engined 928 that Porsche thought might replace the 911. With the 964 generation in 1989, the 911 gained a thorough redesign – though with the same basic layout – and four-wheel drive became an option. In 1999, the 996 generation heralded the arrival of the first water-cooled engine, to help the 911 pass twenty-first century emissions standards, and now, three further generations on, the 911 is as popular as ever.

Driving a classic 911 is a unique experience, not least because of the rear-engine layout. The steering is always light but informative, the pedals are offset to the middle of the car and the engine needs revs to deliver performance. However, guiding one down a fast road, using those excellent brakes and learning to balance the car on the throttle through corners soon becomes addictive. Whichever variant you're in, it's easy to understand why 911 owners think it's the greatest sporting all-rounder of all time.

| 1965 Porsche 911 ||
|---|---|
| Length | 4,178 mm |
| Width | 1,615 mm |
| Weight | 1,071 kg |
| Wheelbase | 2,210 mm |
| Suspension | Independent via wishbones, longitudinal torsion bars and hydraulic dampers (front); swing axles, semi-trailing arms, transverse torsion bar and hydraulic dampers (rear) |
| Brakes | Hydraulic discs (front and rear), servo-assisted |
| Engine | 1,991 cc flat-six, OHC, two triple-choke carburettors |
| Power | 145 bhp @ 6,100 rpm |
| Torque | 143 lb-ft @ 4,200 rpm |
| Transmission | Five-speed manual, rear-wheel drive |
| 0–60 mph | 9 sec. |
| Top speed | 132 mph |
| Cost new | £2,745 |
| Value today | £60,000–£200,000 (1960s models) |

**TOP:** The unmistakable muscle of a 930 Turbo: wider arches, huge spoiler.

**MIDDLE:** A Carrera 2.7 RS.

**BOTTOM:** The first and purest 911, in original 2-litre form.

# Ford Mustang

Launched in the same year as the Porsche 911, the Ford Mustang similarly created a niche and following all of its own: the 'Pony Car'. This came to mean a smallish two-door model, offering younger buyers a mixture of affordability, style and sportiness. The Mustang existed alongside the muscle-car boom, but muscle cars were all about a big engine in a cheap mid-size car, while the Mustang had its own individuality from the start.

That individuality was the key to its almost unbelievable success, and it was very carefully judged. Seeking to compete with the Chevrolet Corvair, Ford demonstrated a running concept car called the Mustang I at Watkins Glen racetrack in 1962, where it received a rapturous reception. A sleek two-seat open roadster with concealed headlamps and a 1.5-litre V4 engine mounted behind the driver, it was bold, but unsuitable for large-scale production.

Instead, Ford began with what they were already building, namely a compact car called the Falcon: rather dull but a strong seller. Could that be used as a basis? Sales director Lee Iacocca brought matters to a head by getting the various Ford design teams to compete with proposals of their own, and the winner was a design by Joe Oros and Dave Ash called the Cougar. Changing little as it made its way from paper to a clay model to a running prototype, it was eventually renamed the Mustang.

Using the Falcon's underpinnings would be essential to the Mustang's success. Cost-added extras were a key sales tool for American car-makers, but the Mustang would take this approach further than ever. From a low base price of $2,368 for the hard-top and $2,614 for the convertible, buyers could add an almost endless range of engines, gearboxes, brakes, body kits and interior upgrades from across Ford's range, which the Corvair could never match.

As the launch date approached, Iacocca became more and more confident of the Mustang's success and eventually committed much of Ford's Dearborn factory to Mustang production. He was on the right track – the car sold nearly 130,000 units in the half-year of production to autumn 1964, and production was soon extended to San Jose, California and Metuchen, New Jersey. By the end of December 1964, 263,434 Mustangs had been sold. By 17 April 1965, the first birthday of the day the car went on sale, more than 418,000 had been sold – a new record for Detroit, and indeed the world.

From this extraordinary beginning, Ford worked hard to keep the Mustang on top through successive restyles in 1967, 1969 and 1971. Ford redesigned it completely for 1974, using the Pinto as a platform to create the Mustang II. Third, fourth, fifth, sixth and seventh generations have kept the Mustang galloping hard, though it would be interesting to know what Lee Iacocca would have made of the four-door electric SUV, the Mustang Mach E, launched in 2019.

The Mustang is one of the great automotive success stories and has an immense following as a classic, with a large aftermarket industry supporting every model since 1964. A great car, yes, but an even greater bit of product planning.

TOP: The fastback, seen here, was one of three body styles offered, along with the convertible and 'notchback' coupé.

BOTTOM: The interior of a red-on-red 1965 Mustang convertible.

| 1965 Ford Mustang coupé ||
|---|---|
| Length | 4,613 mm |
| Width | 1,727 mm |
| Weight | 1,330 kg |
| Wheelbase | 2,743 mm |
| Suspension | Independent via wishbones, coil springs and hydraulic dampers (front); live axle, leaf springs and hydraulic dampers (rear) |
| Brakes | Hydraulic drums (front and rear) |
| Engine | 4,737 cc V8, overhead valve, one two-barrel carburettor |
| Power | 200 bhp @ 4,400 rpm |
| Torque | 282 lb-ft @ 2,400 rpm |
| Transmission | Four-speed manual, rear-wheel drive |
| 0–60 mph | 9 sec. |
| Top speed | 109 mph |
| Cost new | $2,688 (c.£960) |
| Value today | £15,000–£60,000 (1965 models) |

# Jensen FF

Fourteen years before the Audi Quattro, the small British firm of Jensen introduced the world's first four-wheel drive road car. The letters 'FF' stood for Ferguson Formula, in honour of the Ferguson Research company. Harry Ferguson's name is probably best remembered in connection with the Ferguson tractor, but his work on four-wheel drive systems for road cars went back to 1950, when he formed his own research company. He produced a prototype saloon car in 1959 but sadly did not live to see his ideas taken up, though the entry of the one-off Ferguson P99 Formula One car in a couple of races in 1961 raised the profile of the idea just months after Ferguson's death.

His son-in-law Tony Sheldon refocused the business on selling four-wheel drive systems that manufacturers could adopt for their models, which Jensen duly did. They were developing a new model to replace the C-V8, so used a C-V8 as a trial installation for the FF system and found it could be made to fit. Indeed, they produced a brochure for the FF with the C-V8 version pictured, but when it came to production it would be the new Interceptor-based FF that went on sale. The Interceptor was another bold step for Jensen, with a body styled by Carrozzeria Touring in Milan but built by another Italian coachbuilder, Vignale, until Jensen tooled up to build them at their own factory in West Bromwich.

Though the FF was already a large car with a powerful Chrysler V8 engine, Jensen found they needed to extend the structure by 12.7 cm to fit the bulky four-wheel drive arrangement. In addition, the front passenger seat had to be narrower than the driver's seat, as the transmission tunnel grew to immense proportions to cover the transfer case and the propeller shafts. This had a serious repercussion: there could be no left-hand drive version, as there was no room for the steering gear and brake servo on the already overcrowded left side of the car. In an era when American sales meant a huge amount for luxury and sports-car sales, it was almost enough to condemn the FF to commercial failure before it began.

Jensen sold 320 of them over five years and it was recognised in its time as a technical tour de force. Not only did the four-wheel drive system work perfectly well on the road, the FF also introduced anti-lock braking. This was the Dunlop Maxaret system that had its origins in aircraft technology. It was a mechanical rather than electronic system and worked a little less well in car installations, as the brake pedal gave a disconcerting shove back towards the user's foot. Although the car avoided a skid, it did not necessarily allow shorter overall braking distances.

Nonetheless, the FF was declared the safest car in the world by an American magazine, and driving one is a memorable experience. Being able to floor the throttle in a 325 bhp GT car in the middle of a damp corner, to find it does nothing more alarming than squat down and charge round on your chosen line, is deeply impressive.

**TOP:** The roomy driver's side in the Jensen FF; the transmission tunnel made the passenger side much more cramped.

**BOTTOM:** You can tell an FF from an Interceptor by the side vents: an FF like this has two, whereas an Interceptor has one.

| 1968 Jensen FF | |
|---|---|
| Length | 4,581 mm |
| Width | 1,778 mm |
| Weight | 1,807 kg |
| Wheelbase | 2,769 mm |
| Suspension | Independent via upper and lower wishbones, twinned coil springs and hydraulic dampers (front); live axle, leaf springs and hydraulic dampers (rear) |
| Brakes | Hydraulic discs (front and rear), Dunlop Maxaret ABS control |
| Engine | 6,276 cc V8, overhead valve, one four-barrel carburettor |
| Power | 325 bhp @ 4,600 rpm |
| Torque | 425 lb-ft @ 2,800 rpm |
| Transmission | Three-speed automatic, rear-wheel drive |
| 0–60 mph | 8.4 sec. |
| Top speed | 130 mph |
| Cost new | £5,340 |
| Value today | £40,000–£140,000 |

# Lamborghini Miura

If you had to pick the first true supercar, this is the one that set the pattern. We'd had fabulously fast, glamorous and expensive sports cars before, but Lamborghini's bold placement of the V12 engine behind the cabin in a transverse installation set it apart.

Lamborghini was still a young company when they launched the Miura. They introduced the 350 GT in 1964 and sprang the Miura on an unsuspecting world just a year later at the 1965 Turin Motor Show. Ferruccio Lamborghini was wise or lucky in his choice of senior engineers for the car-building arm of his tractor-manufacturing empire. Giampaolo Dallara, Paolo Stanzani and test driver Bob Wallace went ahead and developed a mid-engined prototype, even though the boss didn't fancy the idea, and when Lamborghini saw it he could only concede that it was an impressive piece of work. At the very least they would get some marketing value out of it, so he gave the design team free rein and told them to get on with it.

This they did, working with Marcello Gandini of Bertone to style the body. The rolling structure of the new car was ready just days before the Turin show, but rumour has it that no one checked that the V12 would actually fit in the engine bay, so the back of the P400 show car was filled with ballast and the rear clamshell of the bodywork kept firmly shut. Lamborghini's sales manager must have been fighting back the tears as he refused those who wanted to place orders, but no one knew if the car could be built.

They did make the engine fit, of course. The gearbox was sited underneath and behind the engine, sharing its oil rather like a Mini did, to create an impressively compact installation in a car needing a wheelbase only 6 cm longer than a Ferrari 250 GTO. Unlike contemporary Ferraris, the Miura did without a separate chassis, using a central tub for the passenger compartment with front and rear cradle-like structures emerging from it to carry the engine and transmission behind, and the front suspension and steering in front. Early cars were criticised for not being stiff enough, something that was addressed in 1968 in the P400S, which saw some chassis revisions and a rise from 350 bhp to 375 bhp. The SV of 1971 raised that to 385 bhp. Getting anywhere near the Miura's claimed top speed of 170–180 mph could be an alarming experience thanks to a front end capable of generating lift, but this didn't put off the celebrity buyers.

French pop star Johnny Hallyday lost control of his and uprooted a tree; jazz trumpeter Miles Davis crashed one and bought another; Rod Stewart seemed made for Lamborghinis and started a long association with the marque when he bought his first Miura; while other owners of note range from Peter Sellers to the Shah of Iran. Miuras always feel intimidating to drive yet only reveal what they can do if pushed hard. Swallow a bravery pill, put on your 1960s sunglasses and go for it.

| 1967 Lamborghini Miura P400 | |
|---|---|
| Length | 4,348 mm |
| Width | 1,763 mm |
| Weight | 1,289 kg |
| Wheelbase | 2,466 mm |
| Suspension | Independent via double wishbones, coil springs and hydraulic dampers (front and rear) |
| Brakes | Hydraulic discs (front and rear), servo-assisted |
| Engine | 3,929 cc V12, DOHC, four three-barrel carburettors |
| Power | 350 bhp @ 7,000 rpm |
| Torque | 286 lb-ft @ 5,500 rpm |
| Transmission | Five-speed manual, rear-wheel drive |
| 0–60 mph | 5.5 sec. |
| Top speed | 180 mph |
| Cost new | £8,050 |
| Value today | £800,000–£2 million |

TOP: The wider rear wheels and more aggressive wheel arches of a Miura SV.

MIDDLE: The front of the Miura, with 'eyelashes' seen on the P400 and P400S but dropped for the SV.

BOTTOM: The orange Miura that appeared in the opening sequences of the film *The Italian Job*.

# Alfa Romeo 'Duetto' Spider

Alfa Romeo held a contest to suggest a name for its new two-seat roadster and win a car, and *Duetto* (translating simply as Duet) won out. When you consider some of the other entries amongst the 140,000 submitted – Acapulco, Lollobrigida, Michaelangelo, Edelweiss, Gin, Pizza – you can only conclude Alfa chose well. Or rather they would have, had there not been a copyright dispute that prevented the name being used after the first 18 months.

None of this did much damage to the new Spider's sales, even when the car's rounded nose and tail led Italians to give it yet another name – *Osso di Sepia,* or Cuttlefish Bone. Alfa Romeo brought in the Duetto to replace both the pretty little Giulietta/Giulia Spider, as driven by Edward Fox in *The Day of the Jackal,* and also the open-topped version of the Giulia Sprint coupé, called the GTC, which never sold strongly despite having four seats. The Duetto soon had a starring movie role of its own in *The Graduate*, providing transport for Dustin Hoffman.

When the Duetto reverted to the Spider badge in 1967, the engine size increased from 1,570 to 1,779 cc. It was known as the 1750 Spider Veloce, which was then joined a year later by a cut-price 1,290 cc version called the Spider Junior. In 1970 that rounded tail was chopped off square, and the year after the 1750 became the 2000 Spider. Factory imports to the UK stopped after 1977, so right-hand drive examples made after that date are usually aftermarket conversions. The looks were spoiled somewhat by large impact bumpers for the American market and a raised ride height, just like the MGB.

The Series 3 Spider grew a little black rubber boot spoiler and the Series 4, a run-out model from 1990 to 1993, used body-coloured bumpers, side skirts and smoothed-in rear lights as a not-entirely-successful attempt to make Pininfarina's classic 1960s shape look current in the 1990s. By then, though, the Spider had passed through the second-hand market and straight towards classic status, where it has remained a firm favourite ever since.

The Spider is a very appealing car to drive and to live with, if you can keep the rust at bay. The twin-cam engines provide a useful bit of zip in all sizes and often sound more powerful than they really are. Neat handling and good brakes (discs all round) allow high average speeds on the twisty country roads the Spider loves, but there are small touches that set it apart too. The gearstick emerges diagonally from under the middle of the dashboard and is only a handspan from the steering wheel, and the dashboard is a delight with those two main dials – speedometer and rev counter – telling you all you need to know. For uncertain British climates the folding roof is a godsend, as the driver can reach behind and flip it up with one hand, fastening it easily via two clips. All Spiders are deservedly beloved.

Italian chic personified.

| 1967 Alfa Romeo 'Duetto' Spider | |
|---|---|
| Length | 4,249 mm |
| Width | 1,631 mm |
| Weight | 996 kg |
| Wheelbase | 2,250 mm |
| Suspension | Independent via lower wishbones, upper links, coil springs and hydraulic dampers (front); de Dion tube, trailing arms, coil springs and telescopic dampers (rear) |
| Brakes | Hydraulic discs (front and rear), servo-assisted |
| Engine | 1,567 cc in-line 4, DOHC, two twin-choke carburettors |
| Power | 125 bhp @ 6,000 rpm |
| Torque | 115 lb-ft @ 2,800 rpm |
| Transmission | Five-speed manual, rear-wheel drive |
| 0–60 mph | 11.3 sec. |
| Top speed | 113 mph |
| Cost new | £1,749 |
| Value today | £20,000–£45,000 |

'A true sports car of impeccable manners and considerable performance.'

*Motor Sport* magazine, February 1967

# Oldsmobile Toronado

American car-makers had flirted with front-wheel drive long before the 1960s, notably with the Cord L-29 in the 1930s, but the pattern for success seemed so fixed by then that a return to the idea was decidedly left field. Throughout the 1950s, the formula of overhead-valve V8, a ladder chassis with a separate body structure and a lazy automatic transmission driving the rear wheels became more and more standardised. It would, in fact, remain the standard until well into the 1990s, when Detroit's car-makers abandoned it. But not Oldsmobile.

It made sense for General Motors to try new ideas via Oldsmobile rather than risk the reputation of their top division, Cadillac. It had happened before with the Hydramatic transmission in 1940, which was a major success, and the turbocharged Jetfire in 1962, which was not. Oldsmobile's innovative chief engineer, John Beltz, became general manager of the division in this era and brave ideas were allowed to flourish. One important emerging market segment was that of the personal luxury car, a niche Ford could probably claim to have invented with the Lincoln Continental and Ford Thunderbird. Buick, Oldsmobile's GM stablemate, joined in with the excellent Riviera in 1963, around the time Oldsmobile was given the green light to compete.

The Toronado was the result of mating a design by stylist David North called the Flame Red Car with a front-wheel-drive project that John Beltz had been working on since 1958. This was the Unitised Power Package (UPP), which featured a three-speed automatic transmission hugging the left underside (as viewed from the driver's seat) of a large V8 engine, driven by a multi-row chain off a torque converter on the rear of the crankshaft. This was hidden behind a cover and the whole lot fitted neatly into an engine bay no bigger than that of a rear-wheel-drive car. Oldsmobile even dispensed with a conventional ladder chassis, using a subframe that carried the engine and transmission unit and front suspension, extending to the front end of the rear leaf springs.

It was important for the Toronado to look different so it could drive home its innovations, but not so different that it put people off. Perhaps Oldsmobile went a little too far down that path, with headlamps hidden by covers that gave a sinister, narrow-eyed look. No Coke-bottle hips or fins here – just a clean fastback shape with exaggerated wheel arches. In the cabin there was a different feel to most rivals, with a deep-dish steering wheel, like something from a custom car, and an inclined cliff of dash instruments that featured a speedometer on a roller, like the later Citroën CX.

As a personal luxury coupé it was a brave, attractive statement, and though sales were strong in the first year at 40,000, they didn't ever grow to match expectations. Still, the Toronado lasted an amazing four generations, right up to 1992, and the UPP front-wheel-drive system was used successfully on the related Cadillac Eldorado and the amazing six-wheeled GMC motorhome. With a small but dedicated following, the original Toronado is an underappreciated oddity.

| 1966 Oldsmobile Toronado | |
|---|---|
| Length | 5,359 mm |
| Width | 1,943 mm |
| Weight | 2,074 kg |
| Wheelbase | 3,023 mm |
| Suspension | Independent via double wishbones, torsion bars and hydraulic dampers (front); live axle, leaf springs and telescopic dampers (rear) |
| Brakes | Hydraulic drums (front and rear), servo-assisted |
| Engine | 6,965 cc V8, overhead valve, one four-barrel carburettors |
| Power | 385 bhp @ 4,800 rpm |
| Torque | 475 lb-ft @ 3,200 rpm |
| Transmission | Three-speed automatic, front-wheel drive |
| 0–60 mph | 8.7 sec. |
| Top speed | 127 mph |
| Cost new | $4,779 (c.£1,713, deluxe version) |
| Value today | £10,000–£35,000 |

## 'Toronado. Built for leaders, not for followers.'
### 1968 Oldsmobile slogan

The Toronado looked unlike other American cars of the mid-1960s, quite deliberately – it was born to be different.

# NSU Ro80

Pronounce this 'Row Eighty', not 'R. O. Eighty', because the 'Ro' is short for rotary engine, which was the key selling point of this advanced, exciting car. Felix Wankel first developed his engine as an air compressor or supercharger in the 1920s, but by 1934 he realised it could feature an inlet and exhaust port and work as an internal combustion engine too. It's hard to visualise, but imagine it this way: instead of a piston rising and falling in a cylinder, there is a triangle-shaped rotor with bulging sides that rotates inside a chamber shaped like a very fat figure of eight. But the rotor rotates on an eccentric shaft, so the tips of the triangle are always in contact with the edge of the chamber. This creates gaps between the sides of the rotor and the chamber that widen (like a piston going down a cylinder) and then tighten again, like a piston rising up.

German car- and motorcycle-maker NSU developed the first Wankel gasoline engines and got there first with a production car too – the NSU Spider, launched in 1963. But while the power output and smoothness of the tiny 497 cc rotary engine were impressive, there were reliability problems. Nonetheless, it was seen as the design of the future by NSU's board, who approved the development of a large saloon car to take on the Citroën DS, Rover 2000 and even the Mercedes 200.

As often seems to be the way with bravely innovative cars, just one major revolution wasn't enough. The styling by Claus Luthe paid no heed to fashion and it was deceptively slippery to reduce drag at high cruising speeds. That rear wheel looked too far back, because the designers didn't want it to encroach into a roomy cabin. The gearbox was a three-speed manual, but an unconventional one. It featured a torque converter and an automatic clutch; move the lever and the clutch dipped for you. The gearbox drove the front wheels, meaning the rear suspension could be a space-saving independent design. Brakes, discs all round, were inboard at the front to reduce unsprung weight. The steering was power-assisted as standard and used a precise rack-and-pinion system.

It was all hugely impressive and praised to the hilt by contemporary road tests, achieving 112 mph from an engine that displaced less than 1,000 cc, riding and steering almost as well as the Citroën. Yet the unique selling point, that rotary engine, could not overcome two fatal shortcomings: high fuel consumption and rotor-tip wear. If the tip seals on the rotors failed, you gradually lost compression and power to the point where the engine was impossible to start when hot. This could happen when the cars were still in their first year or two, and warranty claims on top of the huge development cost left NSU vulnerable to takeover by VW-Audi. Still, the Ro80 lasted from 1967–77 and sold more than 37,000 units, and these days the engine problems can be managed. A fascinating 'what if?', and still a delight to drive.

**TOP:** The NSU Ro80's understated looks belied its technological advancement.

**BOTTOM:** The dash of the Ro80. Note there are two pedals, like an automatic, but a manual gear lever!

| 1968 NSU Ro80 | |
|---|---|
| Length | 4,826 mm |
| Width | 1,765 mm |
| Weight | 1,211 kg |
| Wheelbase | 2,863 mm |
| Suspension | Independent via MacPherson struts and lower links (front); trailing arms and MacPherson struts (rear) |
| Brakes | Hydraulic discs (front and rear), servo-assisted |
| Engine | 995 cc twin-rotor Wankel |
| Power | 113 bhp @ 5,500 rpm |
| Torque | 117 lb-ft @ 4,500 rpm |
| Transmission | Three-speed semi-automatic manual, front-wheel drive |
| 0–60 mph | 13.9 sec. |
| Top speed | 112 mph |
| Cost new | £2,249 |
| Value today | £5,000–£20,000 |

# Reliant Scimitar GTE

We think of the Scimitar only with this distinctive sports-estate body, but it began life as a two-door 'notchback' coupé. The body was a proposal by Ogle Design called the SX 250 on a Daimler Dart chassis (see p. 84), which wasn't used as new owners Jaguar had no intention of keeping the Dart in production. Reliant, though, liked the idea and bought the rights.

The timing was ideal: Reliant had quite recently diversified from decades of making small three-wheeled runabouts into being a sports-car-maker, which had come about when they were asked to develop a sports coupé called the Sabra for the Israeli market. They productionised it for the UK, calling it the Sabre when in a four-cylinder, Ford Consul engined form, and the Sabre Six for the restyled version with Ford Zephyr six-cylinder power. It wasn't a huge hit, but interest was strong enough to persuade Reliant to keep trying.

The replacement, called the Scimitar GT, used the SX 250 body on the Sabre Six chassis, which kept evolving and improving from 1964 to 1967, changing from a straight-six to the Ford Essex V6 and gaining chassis bracing and trailing-arm rear suspension for better handling. The big step forward came when the GTE arrived. Ogle Design's managing director and chief designer Tom Karen had created a sporting estate or shooting brake based on the Scimitar GT back in 1965, and a couple of years later, Reliant's management asked him to work up some body designs to put something similar into production. Like the GT, the GTE would be bodied in glass-fibre and based on a sturdy steel ladder chassis, using the same Ford mechanicals but with the chassis design heavily revised and improved.

Karen was a remarkably original and versatile designer, responsible for such disparate items as the Bush TR130 transistor radio and the Marble Run children's game, also directing the design of the Raleigh Chopper and the freakish three-wheeled Bond Bug. These last two echoed Karen's love of wedge-shaped forms, which can also be seen in the side profile of the Scimitar GTE. But it was the sheer practicality of the GTE that made it so popular. It mixed 120 mph performance and fine roadholding with good economy (thanks to an overdrive gearbox, compact size and modest weight), plus four seats, a large boot reached through a glass tailgate and an excellent ability as a tow car.

Throughout the 1970s and 1980s they were a common sight in front of boat trailers, racing-car trailers and horseboxes, not least when driven by Princess Anne, who owned nine GTEs over the years. It proved a very long-lived model, growing in size in 1975 when the SE6 generation arrived but staying true to the same form. Production lasted to 1986 with a convertible GTC joining the range in 1980. The Scimitar was revived with an emphasis on luxury by a firm called Middlebridge in 1988, when a further 77 were built. Always rather undervalued as classics, they remain a little bit under the radar – but those who know them, love them.

| 1968 Reliant Scimitar GTE | |
|---|---|
| Length | 4,318 mm |
| Width | 1,676 mm |
| Weight | 1,107 kg |
| Wheelbase | 2,515 mm |
| Suspension | Independent via double wishbones, coil springs and telescopic dampers (front); live axle with upper and lower trailing arms and Watts linkage, coil springs, telescopic dampers (rear) |
| Brakes | Hydraulic discs (front); drums (rear), servo-assisted |
| Engine | 2,994 cc V6, overhead valve, one twin-choke carburettor |
| Power | 138 bhp @ 5,000 rpm |
| Torque | 172 lb-ft @ 3,000 rpm |
| Transmission | Four-speed manual plus overdrive, rear-wheel drive |
| 0–60 mph | 8.9 sec. |
| Top speed | 121 mph |
| Cost new | £1,759 |
| Value today | £3,000–£12,000 |

TOP: A practical four-seat estate that's also a sports car? It's possible for the Scimitar, like this 1973 SE5A model.

BOTTOM: A 1984 Scimitar SE6B, showing the changes to styling over the years.

# Ford Capri

Without the Ford Mustang there would have been no Ford Capri. Indeed, it was named the Colt during its development phase, as a nod to the larger horse on the other side of the Atlantic. Unusually for the 1960s, it was created as a joint effort across two different divisions: Ford of Britain and the German arm of the company. Work began as early as 1965, when it became plain that the Mustang's roaring success was going to last and it would be madness not to try to imitate that in the European market.

Just as the Mustang was based on the Falcon, the Capri was based on the Mk 2 Cortina. The styling was a good approximation of an American pony car reimagined for the Cortina's wheelbase, but rather than offering notchback, fastback and convertible bodies as the Mustang was doing, only the fastback shape went forward for production. Even then, one of its most distinctive features – that curve to the C-pillar around the rear quarter window – was a last-minute afterthought.

The new model was launched in 1969, but the Colt name disappeared after Ford lost a lawsuit with Mitsubishi, who owned the rights to the nameplate. The Capri badge was revived from a short-lived previous model called the Consul Capri coupé, which had ceased production in 1964. With the new Capri came one of the most memorable advertising slogans: 'The car you always promised yourself.' Like the Mustang, it was offered with a wide range of engines, in this case starting at a 1.3-litre four-cylinder with a barely adequate 61 bhp, rising through 1.6-litre, 2-litre V4 and 3-litre V6 versions. And just like the Mustang, it sold very well in the UK and Europe.

Four seats and sensible running costs made it just about plausible as a family car, as thousands of Britons raised in the 1970s will remember, even if you couldn't see out properly from the back seat or fit quite enough in the boot for a week's camping holiday. But that was never the image that owners (or advertisers) aspired to. The Capri's impressive success in motorsport led to thrilling homologation versions – the RS2600 and RS3100 in 1970 and 1973 respectively, the first being German-built and the second British. In 1974, the Mk 2 Capri arrived with a smoother look and a practical hatchback tailgate. This was an era of ever-expanding trim options, so now you could choose a Ghia version with alloy wheels, a vinyl roof and a plush interior.

Ford spent less than £500,000 revising the Mk 2 Capri into the Mk 3 – peanuts by car-manufacturing standards – yet they got fantastic value for money. Here was a fresher, four-headlamp look that allowed the Capri to carry on to 1986, revived by a fuel-injected 2.8-litre V6 in 1981 that gave the car near-130 mph performance. All Capris now have a huge following and some wild prices have been seen for low-mileage survivors.

| 1968 Ford Capri 3000 GT XLR | |
|---|---|
| Length | 4,280 mm |
| Width | 1,646 mm |
| Weight | 1,047 kg |
| Wheelbase | 2,560 mm |
| Suspension | Independent via MacPherson struts and lower wishbone (front); live axle with leaf springs, anti-roll bar, telescopic dampers (rear) |
| Brakes | Hydraulic discs (front); drums (rear), servo-assisted |
| Engine | 2,994 cc V6, overhead valve, one twin-choke carburettor |
| Power | 136 bhp @ 4,750 rpm |
| Torque | 181 lb-ft @ 3,000 rpm |
| Transmission | Four-speed manual, rear-wheel drive |
| 0–60 mph | 10.3 sec. |
| Top speed | 115 mph |
| Cost new | £1,759 |
| Value today | £15,000–£60,000 (3-litre Mk 1) |

TOP: A 1970s Ford Capri magazine advert.

BOTTOM: A Mk 1 Capri 1600 GT.

# Ferrari 365 GTB/4 'Daytona'

The name trips off the tongue – 'Ferrari Daytona' sounds exciting before you even see one. The looks, of course, did not disappoint, and neither did the performance and dynamics. The Daytona used the chassis from the 275 GTB with minor changes, but the important benefits were there: all-independent suspension and a rear transaxle; a gearbox integral with the back axle. This gave better handling balance and allowed the quad-cam V12 engine to sit back in the chassis, leaving room for a snug but stylish two-seater cabin. As potent and capable as it was underneath, it was the bodywork that made the Daytona turn heads.

Pininfarina's Leonardo Fioravanti was responsible for the shape, which still stands out among older and younger Ferraris as having an identity all its own. The wraparound front lights and indicators, teamed with the headlamps at first hidden behind plexiglass and later behind pop-up covers, remained contemporary well into the 1970s and inspired some obvious imitation when Rover launched their new SD1 3500 saloon in June 1976. It was a slippery shape that allowed the Daytona to hit impressive top speeds, even though the gearing also produced eye-catching 0–60 mph times below six seconds.

The name is something of a mystery. Ferrari almost always referred to it by its clumsy number designation: '365' for the capacity in cubic centimetres of one of the 12 cylinders; 'GTB' for *Gran Turismo Berlinetta*; and '4' for the four camshafts. The Daytona nickname is supposed to have come from Ferrari's first-, second- and third-place finishes at the 1967 24 Hours of Daytona, which somehow inspired the press to apply the word to a new Ferrari launched at the Paris Motor Show 18 months later. Perhaps someone at Maranello encouraged the idea.

The classic appeal of the Daytona stems not only from its looks and exciting performance, but from its status as the last of its line. After this, two-seat, front-engined V12 Ferraris were extinct until 1996, when the 550 Maranello was introduced. The Daytona, therefore, represents everything that Ferrari had learned about building exciting road cars like the 250 GT Lusso, the 275 GTB/4 and the 365 GTC. This has guaranteed a strong image and stronger values ever since, with the price of a good Daytona peaking well above £500,000 around 2015–17. That's for a relatively large production run of 1,285 cars, so the jump up in price to the Daytona Spider – of which just 123 were built – is considerable. Think £2.5 million for a perfect example.

Rarer still are the competition versions – only 15 were built to compete in sports-car racing. The 365 GTB/4 *Competizione* took class wins at Le Mans in 1972–74. Such results did no harm to the Daytona's sales, though it remained in production only up to 1974. Then came a generational change in Ferrari road cars and their engines, when the mid-engined 365 GT4 Berlinetta Boxer was launched, and this just served to underline the Daytona's status as the last of its line. Tricky to drive fast, heavy to drive at all speeds, the Daytona is a glorious challenge that buyers continue to lust after.

| 1970 Ferrari 365 GTB/4 'Daytona' ||
|---|---|
| Length | 4,425 mm |
| Width | 1,760 mm |
| Weight | 1,634 kg |
| Wheelbase | 2,400 mm |
| Suspension | Independent via double wishbones, coil springs and telescopic dampers (front); independent via double wishbones and coil/damper struts (rear) |
| Brakes | Hydraulic discs (front and rear), servo-assisted |
| Engine | 4,390 cc V12, DOHC per bank, six twin-choke carburettors |
| Power | 352 bhp @ 7,500 rpm |
| Torque | 318 lb-ft @ 5,500 rpm |
| Transmission | Five-speed manual, rear-wheel drive |
| 0–60 mph | 5.4 sec. |
| Top speed | 175 mph |
| Cost new | £9,167 |
| Value today | £300,000–£650,000 (The Spider perhaps four times as much) |

TOP: The clean lines of the Daytona can be confused with no other Ferrari.

BOTTOM: A rare *Competizione* version displaying its muscular haunches.

# Triumph TR6

If the Austin-Healey 3000 was looking a bit long in the tooth when it left production in 1968, Triumph refused to admit the same was true of their TR series. All they did was offer the TR5 to German coachbuilder Karmann, who restyled the front and rear of the bodywork to give the model a credible freshness. To be fair, the TR6 was launched in 1968 with two features inherited from the TR5 that placed it firmly ahead of anything Austin-Healey could offer – independent rear suspension, introduced back in 1964 for the TR4A, and fuel injection.

The Lucas Petrol Injection system transformed the Triumph six-cylinder engine from a smooth but unexciting unit into a 150 bhp sporting classic … or it did when it was working properly. Triumph and its customers, especially those a long way from a Lucas service agent, sometimes wished for a pair of carburettors instead, even if this meant a large drop in performance. That is all American buyers were offered, both with the TR5 and TR6 – two Stromberg carburettors and only 104 bhp.

Lucky British and European buyers who could enjoy the 'full-fat' version of the latest TR found it a persuasive package. A front anti-roll bar tightened up the car's cornering behaviour but the ride was still uncompromisingly firm in the true sporting manner. For a price in 1969 of just £1,314 (or £1,380 with a removable steel hard-top) you could become the owner of a brawny sports car with a genuine 120 mph under your right foot. Its acceleration times would put a lot of much costlier glamour-wagons from the likes of Mercedes and BMW to shame; even the famously under-priced Jaguar E-type cost £1,000 more than a TR6.

True, there were a few traditional sports-car rivals left to compete with the Triumph – such as the even faster and more primitive Morgan Plus 8 at £1,508 and the slightly cheaper and more ponderous MGC at £1,226 – but they were a dying breed, and it's really this factor as much as good looks, performance, practicality and heritage that kept the TR6 selling strongly for as long as it did. More than 95,000 had been built by the time the last twin-carb American market car left the factory in 1976 and by then the TR6's replacement had arrived. The TR7 had been compromised by threatened American legislation outlawing convertibles and by a lack of commitment to a V8 version until the car had been on sale for five years. Triumph found itself in the awkward position of selling a TR6 successor with challenging styling that was slower and less exciting to drive than the car it replaced.

This only served to speed the TR6's passage from the second-hand market to classic status. Large numbers of them survive in the UK and values have remained very stable without ever rising beyond the means of most enthusiasts. For wind-in-the-hair motoring with a stirring straight-six soundtrack, the TR6 is still a great choice. Just remember to steer round the bumps!

| 1969 Triumph TR6 ||
|---|---|
| Length | 3,848 mm |
| Width | 1,549 mm |
| Weight | 1,122 kg |
| Wheelbase | 2,235 mm |
| Suspension | Independent via double wishbones, coil springs and telescopic dampers (front); independent via fixed differential, trailing arms, coil springs, telescopic dampers (rear) |
| Brakes | Hydraulic discs (front); drums (rear), servo-assisted |
| Engine | 2,498 cc in-line six, overhead valve, Lucas mechanical fuel injection |
| Power | 150 bhp @ 5,700 rpm |
| Torque | 149 lb-ft @ 3,000 rpm |
| Transmission | Four-speed manual plus overdrive, rear-wheel drive |
| 0–60 mph | 8.2 sec. |
| Top speed | 121 mph |
| Cost new | £1,314 |
| Value today | £10,000–£30,000 |

TOP: Still looking sporty with the roof up.

MIDDLE: The driver's view.

BOTTOM: Sunshine, seaside and a Mimosa Yellow TR6 make for a delightful day out.

# Datsun 240Z

Perhaps the worldwide rise of the Japanese car industry truly began here. Datsun (the brand name under which Nissan sold their exported cars until 1986) had been selling the little Fairlady roadster in America since 1962 with decent success, but the 240Z was a huge step forward.

With great humility, Nissan's senior management had spent a lot of time on market research to identify what consumers in America and Europe admired from the sports car or GT, and it seems likely the Jaguar E-type was mentioned often. Certainly, that seemed to be the main influence in the body styling, for which some credit was claimed by Albrecht von Goertz, who created the BMW 503 and 507. More likely, it was an in-house job by Nissan's own team, led by Yoshihiko Matsuo.

Careful attention to every aspect of the car, from styling to handling, performance, layout, build quality and ease of driving, contributed to a package that must have filled rival car-makers with dismay. In the key American market it cost the same as the smaller, slower Triumph GT6 and only $200 more than the MGB, which was already seven years old when the 240Z arrived in 1969, and which made do with a 1.8-litre four-cylinder engine. The 240Z used a straight-six of 2.4 litres with an overhead camshaft. The 150 bhp it produced via two Hitachi carburettors (modelled after the British SU type) was the same as the fuel-injected Triumph TR6 could muster from its 2.5-litre engine. In short, it was a grown-up six-cylinder GT priced like a small four-cylinder sports car.

It sold quickly, racking up 150,000 units in four years, the vast majority of them in the USA. A successor arrived in the form of the 260Z, with a larger engine designed to maintain the power output of the 240Z in the face of tighter emissions controls, and at the same time Nissan introduced a 2+2 version with a longer body and small rear seats … very much as Jaguar had done with the E-type. In 1978 the larger, longer 280Z was launched with a 2.8-litre engine and a softer image – more cruiser than sports car. But America lapped it up and sales dwarfed those of the 240Z and 260Z combined: 440,059 in just five years.

The 240Z wasn't the first good Japanese car. Toyota had been selling plenty of Corona saloons in the USA and Europe since the mid-1960s, but the difference with the Datsun was that it showed Japan could make cars that were fast, exciting and fun. You no longer bought Japanese because you couldn't afford anything bigger; you bought one because it was more desirable than anything else in that price range, or indeed a few steps beyond that. That's still the appeal today, too. Lightweight controls, nimble handling and, above all, that wonderful straight-six engine make for a thrilling drive, with one of the best engine notes you can buy at any price. Rust claimed many of them, leaving the survivors highly desirable.

| 1970 Datsun 240Z | |
|---|---|
| Length | 4,135 mm |
| Width | 1,628 mm |
| Weight | 1,069 kg |
| Wheelbase | 2,304 mm |
| Suspension | Independent via MacPherson struts and lower links (front); independent via Chapman struts and lower wishbones (rear) |
| Brakes | Hydraulic discs (front); drums (rear), servo-assisted |
| Engine | 2,393 cc in-line six, OHC, two single-choke carburettors |
| Power | 150 bhp @ 6,000 rpm |
| Torque | 148 lb-ft @ 4,400 rpm |
| Transmission | Four-speed manual, rear-wheel drive |
| 0–60 mph | 8.7 sec. |
| Top speed | 122 mph |
| Cost new | £2,288 |
| Value today | £8,000–£35,000 |

TOP: The 240Z, like this left-hand drive example, convinced America to take Japanese cars seriously.

BOTTOM: The Jaguar-inspired styling is evident in this side-on view.

# OIL CRISIS
## AND UNREST
### 1970 TO 1979

# Range Rover

There are those who like to point out that the Range Rover was not the first comfortable, well-equipped, dual-purpose 4x4. What we now call the Sports Utility Vehicle (SUV) was originated by the Jeep Wagoneer in 1963, when Kaiser Jeep introduced a station wagon/estate car body on a Jeep Gladiator chassis with selectable four-wheel drive and optional luxuries such as power steering, automatic transmission and even air conditioning. Yet, back in the UK, Rover had been looking for a way to make a softer, more road-friendly Land Rover since 1948.

Their first effort was not a success, though this was largely to do with the tax regime of the time. A standard Land Rover could be sold as an agricultural or light industrial vehicle and so avoided purchase tax; however, the first station wagon version, with an all-enclosed seven-seat, two-door body, had to be sold as a road car and immediately looked too expensive. Rover tried again with the Road Rover, attacking the problem from a different angle and using the chassis from their P4 road car and clothing it with a tall, flat-sided utility estate body. After much development over several years, Rover backed out of launching it and concentrated its efforts elsewhere.

By the mid-1960s, the idea was alive again and in the hands of Rover's Gordon Bashford and Spencer King. They moved back to a proper four-wheel drive off-road chassis as a basis, with long-travel coil-sprung suspension to give a better on-road ride than the Land Rover. The obvious engine choice was the Buick-sourced 3.5-litre V8 that Rover was starting to fit to the P5 and P6 saloons. The body, like the Land Rover's, would be almost-flat aluminium panels bolted to a steel structure. By September 1968, a running prototype convinced everyone they were onto something.

Pre-production Range Rovers underwent extensive testing (badged as VELARs to maintain a touch of mystery) before launch on 17 June 1970. It was an instant hit, both with road testers and customers, and it soon became apparent that buyers loved it not just for its unique blend of abilities, but for a more subtle reason. There was status attached to it: that high driving position, the V8 power, the implication that a Range Rover owner might need to commute between their grand country estate and their flat in Knightsbridge.

In the troubled times of the 1970s, a whole decade went by without any real change to or investment in the Range Rover. A four-door model – an obvious next step – and an automatic gearbox option took until 1981 and 1982 to arrive, while sales in the most obvious export market, the USA, didn't begin until 1987, where the association with upper-crust Britishness was indelible and it sold well straight away. The original Range Rover, now known as the Classic, lasted all the way to 1995 before a new Range Rover replaced it. By then it had defined a market niche and inspired countless imitators, which reflects the huge kudos and high values of original two-door models today.

TOP: A 1970 Range Rover, the first year of production and now highly valued.

BOTTOM: A 1975 advert showcasing the Range Rover's versatility.

| | 1970 Range Rover |
|---|---|
| Length | 4,470 mm |
| Width | 1,778 mm |
| Weight | 1,761 kg |
| Wheelbase | 2,540 mm |
| Suspension | Live axle, control arms, coil springs and telescopic dampers (front and rear) |
| Brakes | Hydraulic discs, servo-assisted (front and rear) |
| Engine | 3,528 cc V8, overhead valve, two SU carburettors |
| Power | 135 bhp @ 4,750 rpm |
| Torque | 205 lb-ft @ 3,000 rpm |
| Transmission | Four-speed manual, four-wheel drive |
| 0–60 mph | 13.9 sec. |
| Top speed | 92 mph |
| Cost new | £1,998 |
| Value today | £10,000–£100,000 |

# De Tomaso Pantera

For a few years, the Pantera achieved something rarely tried before or since: the sale of a true supercar through a mass-market dealer network. Ford sold it in the USA through Lincoln-Mercury outlets and it's still known to many in America as the Ford Pantera. Its origins, though, were Italian.

Alejandro de Tomaso was born in Argentina, moved to Italy in 1955 and founded his own company in 1959 to build racing cars and sports cars. After the small four-cylinder Vallelunga in 1963 he developed the beautiful, fast and tricky Mangusta in 1966. Both these cars were mid-engined, the latter with a powerful American V8, and it's this pattern that de Tomaso developed into the Pantera – meaning Panther – for launch in 1970.

American-born designer Tom Tjaarda of Carrozzeria Ghia provided the styling, while the engine came from Ford: a 5.8-litre (351-cu. in.) V8. De Tomaso's great coup came soon after the Pantera's appearance at the New York Motor Show, when Ford offered to buy the rights to the Pantera for the USA, perhaps feeling the lack of a Corvette-beating, Ford-powered sports car since the Cobra left production in 1967. Worryingly, the first cars that arrived from Italy were hand-built in the old style: fit and finish were poor, with lavish use of lead solder to hide some of the flaws.

Ford soon took much closer control of body production. It worked, and they sold more than 1,000 Panteras a year until the middle of 1975. This was production on a scale undreamt of by the likes of Lamborghini, Maserati and Ferrari, who couldn't hope to compete with the Pantera's low price in America – about half that of any Italian rival – and never tried. But Ford found the warranty claims on the Pantera tiresome and the V8-powered supercar was always an anomaly. It had nothing whatsoever to do with the rest of Ford's range, and in the wake of the 1973 oil crisis and rising fuel costs, Ford had no intention of evolving or replacing it.

Back home in Modena, de Tomaso was far from finished with the Pantera. He sourced the Ford V8 from the Australian arm of the company after it was discontinued in the USA and redeveloped the Pantera's chassis for 1980. Tuning efforts kept power outputs rising, as more aggressive wheel arches, wings and front spoilers kept the looks contemporary in much the same way as the Lamborghini Countach grew its own body kit of dubious aero add-ons. Production of the base GTS model continued in small numbers alongside the wide-bodied Pantera GT5, which lasted to 1985 and was replaced by the GT5-S. In 1990, the final look for the Pantera appeared in the form of the 90 Si, with a restyle by the Countach's creator, Marcello Gandini, lasting to the end of production in 1993.

Driving a Pantera is still a thrilling experience. The offset pedals and cramped cabin are soon forgotten as you unleash the volcanic V8 power behind your head. For a while, this was the greatest performance bargain on the planet.

| 1972 De Tomaso Pantera | |
|---|---|
| Length | 4,255 mm |
| Width | 1,829 mm |
| Weight | 1,412 kg |
| Wheelbase | 2,5415 mm |
| Suspension | Independent via double wishbones, coil-and-damper units and anti-roll bars (front and rear) |
| Brakes | Hydraulic discs, servo-assisted |
| Engine | 5,763 cc V8, overhead valve, one four-barrel carburettor |
| Power | 330 bhp @ 5,400 rpm |
| Torque | 325 lb-ft @ 3,600 rpm |
| Transmission | Five-speed manual, rear-wheel drive |
| 0–60 mph | 6.2 sec. |
| Top speed | 159 mph |
| Cost new | $10,295 (c.£4,118) |
| Value today | £40,000–£90,000 |

TOP: A later 1980s model, showing the wider wheel arches and large rear spoiler.

BOTTOM: A 1974 Pantera showing the early model's pure lines.

# Alfa Romeo Alfasud

It says something for the spirit of a car company like Alfa Romeo when its identity can survive such a huge change. Not only was the Alfasud the first Alfa Romeo with front-wheel drive – then thought to be anathema to an entertaining, sporting drive – it was the first built away from Alfa's home in Milan. As part of a deal to secure government money to help with development, and to boost employment levels in southern Italy, the car had to be built in a factory near Naples, hence the 'sud' (south) part of the name.

It was an all-new design, created by an impressive team run by the hugely experienced Austrian design engineer Rudolf Hruska and including ex-Ferrari Formula One designer Carlo Chiti, among others. The team settled on a sloping-back design that looked like a hatchback but wasn't – not until nine years after it was launched. Front-wheel drive was bold, but so was a departure from the Alfa and Fiat norm of an in-line four with overhead camshafts. Instead, Carlo Bossaglia's water-cooled flat-four engine seemed inspired by what Lancia had been offering in the Flavia since 1960.

Giorgetto Giugiaro perfected the exterior shape, which concealed an engine that sat forward of the front axle line, but low enough to not upset the car's finely judged handling. This was further improved by a beam rear axle, secured in place by a Watt's linkage, which was a step beyond what most manufacturers would bother with for a small family car. With the free-revving, lively engine and easy gear change, it added up to a delightful driving experience. Car magazines raved about it, orders came in … and the problems began.

Getting it into production was the first challenge and took almost a year after its triumphant launch at the 1971 Turin Motor Show. The area on the outskirts of Naples where the new production lines were built had no history of car production, and training up 15,000 unskilled but heavily unionised workers proved challenging. Once production began, strikes often slowed it almost to a halt. Worst of all, the poor-quality steel and indifferent attempts at rustproofing allowed new Alfasuds to bloom with serious corrosion as soon as they saw their first British winter, and they acquired a 'rot-box' reputation they've never shaken off.

Yet it's now much loved as a classic – why? In the first place, any Alfasud is unmistakably an Alfa to drive, producing a grin on the face of even the grumpiest motorist. Secondly, it helped invent the hot-hatch concept before Alfa Romeo's bosses got round to redesigning it with a hatchback tailgate. The Ti version, launched in 1973, beat the Golf GTI by three years. Better still was the exciting Alfasud Sprint of 1976 with a low-slung coupé body and 75 bhp, giving 100 mph performance.

The Sud was facelifted and revised a couple of times before replacement by the boxier Alfa Romeo 33, which retained the same engine and layout but lost some of the character. Nowadays, the Alfasud has huge appeal as a sporting Alfa with the practicality of an everyday runabout.

| 1972 Alfa Romeo Alfasud | |
|---|---|
| Length | 3,891 mm |
| Width | 1,590 mm |
| Weight | 828.5 kg |
| Wheelbase | 2,456 mm |
| Suspension | Independent via MacPherson struts and lower links (front); beam axle and Watts linkage (rear) |
| Brakes | Hydraulic discs (front and rear) |
| Engine | 1,186 cc flat-four, DOHC per bank, twin carburettors |
| Power | 63 bhp @ 6,000 rpm |
| Torque | 62 lb-ft @ 3,500 rpm |
| Transmission | Four-speed manual, front-wheel drive |
| 0–60 mph | 13.5 sec. |
| Top speed | 96 mph |
| Cost new | £1,423 |
| Value today | £5,000–£15,000 |

**TOP:** The four-door option made the Alfasud as practical as it was enjoyable.

**BOTTOM:** The Sprint featured a sleeker coupé body.

# Maserati Bora

The late 1960s and early 1970s saw the emergence of a new kind of exotic sports car. If the Lamborghini Miura was the first supercar it certainly wasn't the only one, as other manufacturers launched ever more eye-catching designs with top speeds few drivers would ever dare to reach. Maserati was an older name than either Ferrari or Lamborghini, with a long heritage of grand prix success and a more recent history of upscale sporting coupés and grand tourers. Their six-cylinder cars like the Sebring, and especially the Mistral, were E-type rivals, albeit with much increased price and exclusivity, but the V8-engined models were in a higher division.

This engine had its origin in the 450S racer of the late 1950s, and it made a dramatic road car in the form of the 5000GT. Less exciting were the Quattroporte (literally, four-door) and Mexico, a four-seat coupé, but in 1966 Maserati gave the fantastic four-cam V8 engine a home it deserved in the rakish fastback Ghibli. However, after the Miura there was pressure to offer a mid-engined car. It took Maserati until 1971 to deliver the Bora, but it was worth the wait. Like the Ghibli, it was a Giorgetto Giugiaro design, and it followed the Maserati convention of using names from seasonal winds – Mistral, Ghibli, Bora and, later on, Khamsin.

The quad-cam V8 was mounted longitudinally on a subframe that also supported the independent rear suspension. One somewhat surprising change that followed directly from Maserati's takeover by Citroën was the use of high-pressure hydraulics for the brakes, so there was no longer a brake pedal with traditional travel and feel, but the almost on-off sensation of the Citroën system. This wasn't enough to put off buyers, who found the huge stopping power a reassuring feature of a car with 310 bhp (eventually 335 bhp) and a top speed as high as 165 mph.

Fast and daring as the Bora was, its appeal was different to that of the Miura. Rather than the oranges, yellows and acid greens in which Miura customers bought their cars, the Bora was more often seen in burgundy, black or blue … though that bare stainless-steel roof always stood out. Nonetheless, its image was that of a fast grand tourer, despite the strictly limited luggage space in the front compartment.

The Bora was unusually well-equipped inside, with a dashboard featuring every dial and readout drivers could wish for, giving a feel rather like an aeroplane cockpit, especially when ordered in sober black leather. The oleo-pneumatic system was also used to adjust the seats and headlamps, and even the pedals, which provided novelty and headaches in equal measure, at least once the cars began to age.

With the benefit of hindsight, the Bora could look like a misstep from Maserati, as they didn't make another mid-engined car until the MC12 of 2004, which only existed because of the chance to base a new halo model on the Ferrari Enzo. Next to the Miura's stunning replacement, the Countach, the Bora looked unadventurous, although it was anything but. One of the most beautiful of the first-gen supercars is also the most sophisticated.

A 1973 Bora, oozing prestige and power.

'Taut, responsive and yet undeniably luxurious.'

*Car* magazine, January 1972

| 1973 Maserati Bora | |
|---|---|
| Length | 4,343 mm |
| Width | 1,778 mm |
| Weight | 1,591 kg |
| Wheelbase | 2,598 mm |
| Suspension | Independent via double wishbones, coil springs and telescopic dampers (front and rear) |
| Brakes | High-pressure hydraulic discs (front and rear) |
| Engine | 4,719 cc V8, DOHC per bank, four twin-choke carburettors |
| Power | 310 bhp @ 6,000 rpm |
| Torque | 340 lb-ft @ 4,200 rpm |
| Transmission | Five-speed manual, rear-wheel drive |
| 0–60 mph | 6.5 sec. |
| Top speed | 162 mph |
| Cost new | £11,451 |
| Value today | £50,000–£170,000 |

# Ford Escort RS2000

In November 1969, Ford of Britain approved the founding of a business within a business: Advanced Vehicle Operation, or AVO. This was created to design, develop and build a range of low-production sporting derivatives of standard models, for sale through Ford Rallye Sport dealers around the UK and Europe. Crucially, it would support Ford's competition efforts by building enough cars of the chosen type to homologate them for race or rally use.

Ford already had some performance 'specials' in production at this point, namely the Ford Cortina Lotus Mk 2 and the Escort Twin-Cam, which used the same Lotus engine. Just coming on stream was the even quicker Escort RS1600, with its Cosworth-designed BDA engine, which was being built at Halewood, Merseyside, but which would soon move to the new AVO plant in Aveley, Essex. Alongside it in the new Essex factory was the first fast Ford aimed at the everyman – the Escort Mexico, direct predecessor of the RS2000.

AVO could not maintain the volume it needed to fill the factory and break even by building high-cost, high-performance specials alone. So the Mexico offered a dashing side stripe, a long options list for jazzing up the interior and a modest, affordable, but sprightly 1,600-cc engine. It was fun to drive, it looked the part and it sold well, cracking the 10,000 mark by 1975, but it was nippy rather than fast. Ford dealers felt their customers wanted something that was nearly as quick as the exotic Cosworth-engined RS1600 but at a more affordable price, and they said so to Ford.

The result was the RS2000. The Mexico approach of distinctive graphics, some tempting trim options and a regular Ford driveline was repeated, but with the new 2-litre 'Pinto' overhead-cam engine. AVO was shooting for a 110 mph top speed and nearly got there, endowing the new Escort with a pleasing ability for civilised fast cruising as well as exciting B-road blasts. Acceleration from 0–60 mph was only a tenth of a second down on the RS1600, and the firmer front suspension and softer rear springs than the Mexico's specification allowed it to cope with the heavier Pinto engine without losing its poise through corners. It was only in production for 18 months but sold over 5,000 units and clearly deserved a successor when the Escort Mk 2 arrived.

This came along in 1976 when the RS2000 Mk 2 was launched, sporting a different 'beaky' front end with four headlamps to distinguish it from other Mk 2 Escorts. The formula was just the same, though: a 2-litre Pinto in a two-door bodyshell, with nice alloy wheels and a distinctive look. Despite price rises two or three times a year to keep pace with steep inflation, it sold consistently well until it was phased out in 1980. It's now one of the best-loved of all classic fast Fords and prices have shot up as those who once watched on in envy as small boys can now compete at auctions to buy the best. A sporting car for the people, then and now.

| 1974 Ford Escort RS2000 ||
|---|---|
| Length | 4,064 mm |
| Width | 1,570 mm |
| Weight | 898 kg |
| Wheelbase | 2,400 mm |
| Suspension | Independent via MacPherson struts and lower links (front); live axle with leaf springs and telescopic dampers (rear) |
| Brakes | Hydraulic discs (front); drums (rear) |
| Engine | 1,993 cc in-line four, OHC, one twin-choke carburettor |
| Power | 100 bhp @ 5,750 rpm |
| Torque | 108 lb-ft @ 3,500 rpm |
| Transmission | Four-speed manual, rear-wheel drive |
| 0–60 mph | 9.0 sec. |
| Top speed | 108 mph |
| Cost new | £1,965 |
| Value today | £10,000–£45,000 |

TOP: The Mk 2 RS2000 is easy to spot thanks to its sloping, 'beaky' nose.

BOTTOM: A Mk 1 RS2000 enjoying the open country roads it was built for.

# Jaguar XJ12

Replacing three models with one was a masterstroke for Jaguar. Its range in the second half of the 1960s looked unwieldy – one fantastic sports car and four different saloons covering a tightly packed price range, and all using versions of the same engine. The XJ6 solved that at a stroke, doing away with the old Mk 2/340 model, the S-type and the 420, leaving only the immense 420G to hang around a year or two longer in a limousine role. The XJ6 was better than all of them, with class-leading ride and handling thanks to an improved version of Jaguar's all-independent suspension, now with anti-dive geometry. It was a clear step forward but still used the same twin-cam XK engine; the already venerable straight-six was now available as an underpowered 2.8-litre version or a well-proven 4.2. A newer, more exciting engine would make the XJ a challenge for any car in the world, Mercedes and Rolls-Royce included.

A new engine was exactly what it received in 1972, when the XJ12 was launched with the 5.3-litre overhead-cam V12 that had made its debut in the E-type Series 3 the year before. The changes were subtle – slightly wider wheels and tyres, slightly higher-rate springs, and ventilated disc brakes to shed heat after repeated stops from three-figure speeds. Here was a near-silent luxury saloon that *Autocar* magazine tested at 146 mph, with a 0–60 mph time of just 7.4 seconds – only a fifth of a second slower than the E-type V12, and the top speed was actually 3 mph higher. What would compete with this? Very little.

By 1974, when the opposition had had a couple of years to catch up, BMW's top-of-the-range 3.3-litre saloon was still trailing badly in top speed and acceleration, yet it cost £8,400 when the XJ12 cost £5,500. The big Mercedes 450 SEL was a little faster than the BMW but cost even more at £9,400. The Rolls-Royce Silver Shadow still had the edge on ride quality and silence but would be left behind in corners even more surely than it was on the straights. At £13,116 it was also in a different league, even from the expensive Mercedes.

The closest you could get to the Jaguar in performance terms, while still claiming luxurious ride comfort and seating for four adults, was probably another British car: the Bristol 411. However, this cost nearly £10,000, just about bang on the UK's average house price that year. Whichever way you looked at it, the Jaguar XJ12 was peerless at its price. Those who tried one frequently decided it was the best luxury car you could buy at *any* price. Sorry, Rolls-Royce!

It wasn't all wonderful. Industrial unrest and shaky supply lines led to the Series 2 XJ gaining a reputation for poor build quality and rust, but this was shaken off by the sleek, subtly modernised Series 3 from 1979. The XJ12 is still a great bargain among luxury cars and only the fuel consumption (12 mpg!) spoils the fun.

| 1972 Jaguar XJ12 ||
|---|---|
| Length | 4,813 mm |
| Width | 1,768 mm |
| Weight | 1,793 kg |
| Wheelbase | 2,764 mm |
| Suspension | Independent via double wishbones, coil springs and telescopic dampers (front); independent via lower links, twinned coil springs, trailing arms and telescopic dampers (rear) |
| Brakes | Hydraulic discs (front and rear) |
| Engine | 5,340 cc V12, OHC, four single-choke carburettors |
| Power | 265 bhp @ 6,000 rpm |
| Torque | 301 lb-ft @ 3,500 rpm |
| Transmission | Three-speed automatic, rear-wheel drive |
| 0–60 mph | 7.4 sec. |
| Top speed | 146 mph |
| Cost new | £3,726 |
| Value today | £8,000–£25,000 |

TOP: A Series 1 XJ12 looking very 1970s in Carriage Brown with a vinyl roof.

BOTTOM: The 5.3-litre V12, here in later fuel-injected form, is whisper-quiet.

# Triumph Dolomite Sprint

Even in the darkest days of British Leyland's labour problems and mystifying management blunders, there were many good ideas flying about. Some were never built, like the fastback Triumph Lynx that could have given the company a V8 fastback coupé to replace the MGB GT V8 in the mid-1970s, but some did make it to production, like the Dolomite Sprint. Even this excellent sporting saloon had its origins in some British Leyland decision-making that seems hard to credit now.

Triumph launched the 1300 as a replacement for the ageing Herald in 1965, and this small, front-wheel-drive saloon with neat styling by Giovanni Michelotti was revised into the larger-engined 1500 in 1970, which was seven inches longer with a four-headlamp nose. At the same time, Triumph launched the Toledo as a cheaper alternative, which used the same bodyshell with a shorter boot and a rear-wheel-drive layout. An upscale Toledo, called the Dolomite, arrived in 1972 with a new 1,850 cc slant-four engine. So, until 1973, Triumph offered a modern front-wheel-drive saloon car with both a cheaper rear-wheel-drive alternative and a more expensive rear-wheel-drive superior model, all in the same bodyshell.

Whatever the logic of this product planning, there was a chance to produce a more sporting Dolomite as a basis for a competition car and to compete with some of the more dashing saloons in the market. Spencer King, who was working across projects with the Rover-Triumph group within British Leyland, led a team to develop this new model. They worked with Harry Mundy (the man behind the Lotus twin-cam engine) and engineers at Coventry Climax to create a 16-valve cylinder head for the slant-four engine, increased in capacity to 2-litres. This time Mundy didn't use two camshafts but one, using long rockers across the cylinder head to actuate the other bank of valves. Cheaper to build than a twin-cam, it retained the same advantages, with valves inclined on either side of a cross-flow combustion chamber.

Triumph didn't take the Ford approach of flamboyant graphics and a basic interior. They made the Sprint a more luxurious car than the standard Dolomite, with wooden door cappings, velour seats and thick carpets. They also took it racing, finding notable success as British Touring Car Champions in 1974. It was keenly priced, too – only £300 more than an RS2000 or a Vauxhall Magnum 2300, £300 less than the Alfa Romeo Alfetta saloon and £850 less than the BMW 2002tii. Indeed, there was some danger of taking sales away from Triumph's own large model, the 2000 saloon, which cost £50 more than the Dolomite for a six-cylinder, 2-litre engine that gave considerably less power.

Today the Dolomite Sprint has a small but dedicated following. Once you appreciate its abilities, you wonder why Triumph wasn't allowed to develop a replacement when it departed in 1980. Well-equipped, comfortable, fun and fast, it anticipated the M-series BMW saloons of the 1980s and beyond.

**TOP:** The Dolly Sprint's interior was fairly basic by modern standards, but felt plush in 1975.

**MIDDLE:** In action on track at Dijon in 1976.

**BOTTOM:** A 1973 Dolomite Sprint at a retro rally event in 2012.

| 1975 Triumph Dolomite Sprint ||
|---|---|
| Length | 4,115 mm |
| Width | 1,567 mm |
| Weight | 1,005 kg |
| Wheelbase | 2,454 mm |
| Suspension | Independent via double wishbones, coil springs and telescopic dampers (front); live axle with trailing arms and telescopic spring and damper units (rear) |
| Brakes | Hydraulic discs (front); drums (rear) |
| Engine | 1,998 cc in-line four, OHC, 16v, two single-choke carburettors |
| Power | 127 bhp @ 5,700 rpm |
| Torque | 124 lb-ft @ 4,500 rpm |
| Transmission | Five-speed manual, rear-wheel drive |
| 0–60 mph | 8.7 sec. |
| Top speed | 117 mph |
| Cost new | £2,293 |
| Value today | £4,000–£15,000 |

# BMW

BMW builds around 2.5 million cars every year. It owns two iconic British brands – Mini and Rolls-Royce – and it makes more than 200,000 motorcycles each year too. Not bad for a company that started off building Austin Sevens under licence. In 1928 Bayerische Motoren Werke AG was already building engines for boats, lorries and motorcycles when it bought the Dixi factory in Eisenach, where the little Austins were constructed. The Dixi was soon replaced by larger, faster, better models, and a family of six-cylinder cars produced throughout the 1930s built the firm's reputation. The 328 was a particularly effective sports car and was one of the models imported to the UK by Frazer Nash up to 1939.

After the war, BMW struggled. The Eisenach factory was lost to nationalisation and ended up on the wrong side of the Iron Curtain with the formation of the German Democratic Republic (DDR) in 1949. Based solely in Munich, BMW launched large saloons and expensive sports roadsters, and it was eventually kept afloat by sales of the Isetta bubble car, licenced from Iso, the Italian creator and later sports-car builder. This strange, unbalanced range was rescued just in time by the model that saved the company – the 1500 cc 'Neue Klasse' saloon, introduced in 1962. Here, at last, was a medium-sized, mass-market car with an excellent engine, nice road manners and clean styling. It sold in large numbers, made BMW profitable again, and gave rise to both larger and smaller cars to fill various niches.

The company's transformation over the following ten or twelve years was astonishing. BMW went from building nothing but microcars and luxurious, loss-making V8s to a full range of small, medium and large saloons with coupé siblings. By 1973 they were winning races with the spectacular 3.0 CSL 'Batmobile' and revolutionising performance saloons with the 2002 Turbo. The success of these high-performance variants showed BMW how important such models would become to the brand's image, and the rise of the BMW M-division cars secured BMW a status it has never lost. Whatever Mercedes-Benz offered, BMW kept building the greatest performance saloons you could buy.

Success began with a car that wasn't a saloon at all: the M1 of 1979. This mid-engined supercar proved a dead end for BMW but gave its engine to the first M5 saloon and the M635CSi coupé. Then came the mighty M3, the first of an unstoppable line and a car with serious motorsport credentials. In the 1980s and 1990s BMW had an immensely strong image and an equally strong product range. The image was down to a perfect mix of consistent styling – those twin grilles harking back to the pre-war 328's frontal treatment – and the high praise heaped on each generation of BMW for its performance and handling.

The product range seemed ideal too, but in the twenty-first century it has evolved far beyond the old 3 Series, 5 Series and 7 Series staples, and that blue-and-white roundel badge remains just as sought-after. Today BMW could be the perfect example of success built on status. And that status came from a long line of superb performance cars.

# THROUGH THE YEARS

**CLOCKWISE FROM TOP LEFT:** A BMW 328; Isetta 300; 1500 Neue Klasse; E32 740; M1; 507.

# Lancia Stratos

Exciting-looking cars should be exciting to drive and there are very few that fulfil that requirement better than the Lancia Stratos. The aggressive, wedge-shaped side profile is reinforced by how short the wheelbase looks and how wide the car is for a diminutive two-seater. It flares out from a small, narrow roof to much wider doors and sills, so when you climb into the cabin – shoulder to shoulder with your passenger in a very narrow cockpit – you find the door bins really are large enough to carry a crash helmet. The engine, a crackling V6 from the Ferrari 246 Dino, seems to be right behind your head. Any cabin soundproofing is ineffectual as you wind it up through the gears, the engine snarling and then howling as it reaches peak revs. Then there's the handling, with steering as quick and nervous as a frightened cat. Suddenly that short wheelbase makes itself felt: enter a corner too fast, lift off the throttle and the car wants to swap ends in an instant. So you learn to use the powerful brakes before you turn for the apex and then power out, catching the back end with a flick of opposite lock. It must have taken great skill and bravery to throw these cars along loose-surfaced rally stages.

Yet that's where they found their greatest success, in the hands of rally legends like Sandro Munari, Björn Waldegård and Markku Alén. With these and other heroes at the wheel, Lancia won three manufacturer's prizes in the World Rally Championship, from 1974 to 1976. The car's outright performance on tarmac as well as loose surfaces saw it take five victories on the Tour de France Automobile (contested across different race tracks and closed stages), the last in 1980. Not bad for a car conceived as a styling exercise in 1970.

This was the Lancia Stratos Zero, a wild concept car low enough to drive under the barrier at the Lancia factory gates. It was coachbuilder and styling house Bertone's attempt to start a relationship with Lancia, and it worked. Bertone's Marcello Gandini, designer of the Lamborghini Miura, was put to work creating a shape for a new Lancia rally car. But it was Lancia's sporting director Cesare Fiorio who pushed the company to develop the Stratos and make it work. He was responsible for securing the supply of Dino V6 engines from Enzo Ferrari, which ensured the car would have the performance to be competitive.

Lancia needed to build 500 units of the Stratos to homologate it for Group 4 competition in rallying, and its these *Stradale* (street) versions that are now so valued as road cars. The competition versions, and indeed many replicas, still achieve great success in historic rallying. Enzo Ferrari saw the Stratos as potential competitor to the 246 Dino, and though it's much wilder and less civilised than the Ferrari, you can see why. For sheer adrenaline-pumping thrills, a drive in a Lancia Stratos takes a lot of beating.

TOP: Wide, short, squat and full of menace: one glance tells you the Stratos HF will be exciting.

BOTTOM: At speed in the San Remo Rally, 1975.

| 1974 Lancia Stratos | |
|---|---|
| Length | 3,710 mm |
| Width | 1,750 mm |
| Weight | 980 kg |
| Wheelbase | 2,180 mm |
| Suspension | Independent via double wishbones, coil springs and telescopic dampers (front); lower wishbones and Chapman struts (rear) |
| Brakes | Hydraulic discs (front and rear), servo-assisted |
| Engine | 2,419 cc V6, DOHC per bank, three twin-choke carburettors |
| Power | 187 bhp @ 7,000 rpm |
| Torque | 166 lb-ft @ 4,000 rpm |
| Transmission | Five-speed manual, rear-wheel drive |
| 0–60 mph | 6 sec. |
| Top speed | 143 mph |
| Cost new | n/a |
| Value today | £250,000–£500,000 |

# BMW 2002 Turbo

There have been books published on the history of classic cars that confidently identify the BMW 2002 Turbo as the first turbocharged production car. This ignores 9,607 1962 and 1963 Oldsmobile Jetfires with turbocharged V8s and the even more numerous 1962–66 Chevrolet Corvairs with turbocharged flat sixes. Which tells us two things – that British and European car enthusiasts sometimes don't pay enough attention to what's happening in America, and that the best way to get a turbocharged car noticed and remembered is to apply go-faster stripes and 'turbo' decals.

BMW dragged themselves back from the brink of bankruptcy with the excellent 'Neue Klasse' saloon in 1962. Rather than focusing on the unlikely and loss-making mix of microcars and immensely expensive sports roadsters and luxury cars, they aimed for the middle of the market with a high-quality compact executive saloon offered with a range of overhead camshaft four-cylinder engines. This platform was shortened in 1966 to give a slightly smaller, lighter derivative called the 02 series, while new, larger models took over from the Neue Klasse. The 02 was shorter and more nimble than its parent, with good performance from the strong M10 engines, especially the fuel-injected 2-litre version used in the 2002tii.

This formed the basis for the turbocharged engine. The idea of fitting exhaust-driven forced induction to the M10 formed part of a 1972 concept car that was too wild for production, but the engine gave BMW ideas. The tii engine already made an impressive 140 bhp at peak, but with a reduced compression ratio to avoid the problem of pre-ignition while under boost (known as 'knocking' and sometimes a cause of piston failure) and a large KK&K turbocharger, the 2-litre M10 was making 170 bhp – rather more than a 3-litre Ford V6 or a 3.5-litre Rover V8.

BMW prepared the 2002 by fitting bigger brakes and a limited-slip differential, but the impact the car made on launch in 1973 had much to do with the bolt-on wheel-arch extensions, spoilers and three-coloured stripes. Turbocharging was still a new discipline for road-car tuners, which meant the concept of turbo lag was understood but not yet cured. In an 02 Turbo, you can put your foot down hard at, say, 20 mph in second gear but for two or three seconds nothing much happens. This is because the engine has to produce more exhaust pressure to drive the turbo, to feed the engine with more mixture, and so on. Then, all of a sudden, boost builds up, the back tyres try to break traction and the car lunges for the horizon.

It's great fun, but it wasn't enough to save the 02 Turbo from slow sales when it was launched into the teeth of the oil crisis in 1973, and it lasted in production for just a year, so it was never made in right-hand drive. As with the later E30 M3, dedicated British BMW fans have to sit on the left. It's a landmark in Europe's car history and a perfect way to bring out the hooligan in any driver.

The 2002 Turbo script on the front spoiler was printed backwards so motorists knew what was filling their rear-view mirror!

**'Tremendous performance is available in a handy package.'**

*Autocar* magazine, 2 November 1974

| 1974 BMW 2002 Turbo | |
|---|---|
| Length | 4,221 mm |
| Width | 1,618 mm |
| Weight | 1,102 kg |
| Wheelbase | 2,502 mm |
| Suspension | Independent via MacPherson strut and lower link (front); independent via fixed differential, semi-trailing arms, coil springs and telescopic dampers (rear) |
| Brakes | Hydraulic discs (front); drum (rear), servo-assisted |
| Engine | 1,990 cc in-line four, OHC, Kugelfischer fuel injection and KK&K turbocharger |
| Power | 170 bhp @ 5,800 rpm |
| Torque | 117 lb-ft @ 4,000 rpm |
| Transmission | Five-speed manual, rear-wheel drive |
| 0–60 mph | 7.3 sec. |
| Top speed | 130 mph |
| Cost new | n/a |
| Value today | £30,000–£100,000 |

# Ferrari 365 GT4 Berlinetta Boxer

Enzo Ferrari took his time to launch a mid-engined 12-cylinder car. Although Maranello had had the V6 mid-engined Dino in production since 1967, *Il Commendatoré* felt no need to rush out a direct rival to the Lamborghini Miura. That would look weak, and besides, Ferrari had the new Daytona, which was already proving to be one of the most desirable cars in the world, regardless of where the engine sat.

When the 365 GT4 BB finally went on sale in 1973, two years after an exhibition prototype was displayed at the Turin show, everyone knew what was coming. The new car would have two sensational aspects – the engine's location and its format. Ferrari won the World Championship of Makes in sports-car racing for 1972 with the 312P and ran the 312B Formula One car that year, both with versions of the same flat-12 engine. Here was race-winning technology in a road car, just as many times before, with front-engined Ferraris using V12s that shared so much with successful competition machines.

The flat-12 layout should allow the engine to sit lower in the chassis and make the handling of this wide, low-slung car even more impressive. However, Ferrari chose to site the transaxle gearbox under the engine, so much of this advantage was lost. On the other hand, siting the gearbox under rather than behind the engine meant very little weight was left behind the rear axle line, which you can tell at a glance from the car's sawn-off tail. The longer nose housed the radiator plus the battery and spare wheel, in aid of better weight distribution, even though it left precious little luggage room.

Ferrari's innovation extended to the body, which used composite parts for the first time on a production Ferrari, here for the front and rear lower valance/bumper pieces, while the opening 'clamshell' sections over each end are aluminium. The rest of the structure is steel. This meant the 365 BB weighed just 1,235 kg, which, combined with the high-revving flat-12's 375 bhp, made it very fast indeed.

Perhaps it wasn't quite as fast as the initial hype would have it – there was no 200 mph top speed, not even 180 mph. It was, in fact, about equivalent in acceleration and top speed as its predecessor, the Daytona. If this seemed disappointing to some, road testers soon found out how much better it was to drive. The 365 BB brought finer, racier mid-engined handling, lighter steering, relatively soft springing, a light clutch pedal and excellent brakes. It was a less tiring way to cover the miles at the highest possible average speed. Yes, it was a supercar, but unlike the heavy-handling, hot Lamborghinis, or indeed the Daytona, it was a civilised one. It had more in common with the Maserati Bora, but with Ferrari's thrilling 12-cylinder soundtrack and performance to match. In 1976 it evolved into the BB 512, a lightly face-lifted version with a 5-litre engine, becoming the BBi in 1981 with the addition of fuel injection. It was phased out in 1984, and nowadays it's the first, lightest and purest of the line. The 365 GT4 BB: that's the one to have.

| 1974 Ferrari 365 GT4 BB | |
|---|---|
| Length | 4,360 mm |
| Width | 1,800 mm |
| Weight | 1,235 kg |
| Wheelbase | 2,500 mm |
| Suspension | Independent via double wishbones, coil-and-damper units (front and rear) |
| Brakes | Hydraulic discs (front and rear), servo-assisted |
| Engine | 4,390 cc flat-12, DOHC per bank, six twin-choke carburettors |
| Power | 375 bhp @ 7,200 rpm |
| Torque | 318 lb-ft @ 3,900 rpm |
| Transmission | Five-speed manual, rear-wheel drive |
| 0–60 mph | 6.5 sec. |
| Top speed | 175 mph |
| Cost new | £16,380 |
| Value today | £200,000–£350,000 |

## 'As an ultimate roadgoing performance machine, the Boxer has few equals'

*Road & Track* magazine, 1975

Long-nose, short-deck proportions and black composite trim gives the Boxer a menacing look.

# Lamborghini Countach

Just five years after the introduction of the Miura, Lamborghini stunned the world again. In March 1971 the covers came off the Countach LP500 prototype at the Geneva Motor Show, and it hardly seemed possible that they would bring such an outrageous show car into production. They wouldn't, would they?

After much testing, they did, and with far fewer modifications or compromises to the shape than anyone foresaw. The styling, a masterpiece of trapezoid forms and angled, almost-flat surfaces, was sure to cement Marcello Gandini's reputation as an original thinker among car stylists, if any confirmation were needed. The name of the car is an exclamation in Piedmontese dialect that literally means contagion or plague, but is used to express surprise, so translates better as 'Blimey!' or 'Good Lord!'. If anything, the alterations between show car and production car made the Countach even more dramatic, as they included a huge triangular air duct slashed into each side and scoops on the car's upper rear quarters, all in the hope of drawing in enough air for cooling the cabin, the engine and the brakes.

Gandini's design wasn't compromised by minor considerations like being able to see out, so there were originally no mirrors on the doors and so little rearward visibility that a small periscope mirror was installed in the roof of the first 150 cars to give you more chance of seeing what was behind. But when this was removed you were left trying to see out of the letterbox slot of the rear window. Then, of course, there were those doors.

Rising up like an unfolding blade from a penknife, they were there for two good reasons: to add another stunning design statement and to make it possible for occupants to get in and out if they parked in tight spaces. The Countach was so wide by the standards of the time, and the sills of the car so broad and high, that once it went on sale in 1974 Countach owners found that the safest way to reverse the car was to open the driver's door and drive it while sitting on the sill, looking over one shoulder.

Powering the Countach was Lamborghini's one and only engine – the quad-cam V12 in 4-litre form, later expanded to 4.8-litre and then 5.2-litre for the final four-valve per cylinder Countach QV. The true performance of the Countach in its steadily more outrageous forms gave schoolboys something to argue about for most of the 1970s and 1980s, because it certainly looked capable of 200 mph … even if the wings and spoilers that started appearing on the LP400S of 1978 added as much drag as drama. In truth, it's sometimes better not to know. Any Countach can make the driver sweat, with terribly heavy controls, not as much steering feel as you'd like from a 350 bhp supercar on extra-wide tyres, and terrible visibility. So is it worth putting up with the shortcomings to live with a legend? Of course it is.

| 1976 Lamborghini Countach ||
|---|---|
| Length | 4,140 mm |
| Width | 1,890 mm |
| Weight | 1,371 kg |
| Wheelbase | 2,451 mm |
| Suspension | Independent via double wishbones, coil-and-damper units (front and rear) |
| Brakes | Hydraulic discs (front and rear), servo-assisted |
| Engine | 3,929 cc V12, DOHC per bank, six twin-choke carburettors |
| Power | 375 bhp @ 8,000 rpm |
| Torque | 266 lb-ft @ 5,000 rpm |
| Transmission | Five-speed manual, rear-wheel drive |
| 0–60 mph | 6.8 sec. |
| Top speed | 178 mph |
| Cost new | £22,983 |
| Value today | £150,000–£400,000 (Periscopio: £1 million) |

TOP: A 1976 Countach Periscopio in Pebble Beach.

BOTTOM: A 1986 LP5000 showing the scissor-like door that helped make the Countach famous.

# Mercedes 450 SEL 6.9

The Mercedes S-class was already in with a good shout of stealing 'best car in the world' status from Rolls-Royce when the W116 went on sale in 1972. With most of the available engine options it was faster and (whisper it) better built than the Rolls-Royce Silver Shadow, with better road manners, superior safety features and very nearly the same spooky silence in the cabin. But the same year saw the launch of the Jaguar XJ12, which was also whisper-quiet, as smooth as silk, a delightfully competent handler and far less costly than either the Mercedes or the Rolls-Royce. And it was much faster than both.

Mercedes had produced a version of the previous 300 SEL with a supersized engine – the 6.3-litre model – so a successor was always likely. Nonetheless, Mercedes must have questioned the wisdom of introducing a vastly expensive range-topper with 12 mpg fuel consumption in the aftermath of the oil crisis, which was felt so acutely in Germany in late 1973 that driving on Sundays was banned. It's possible that the Jaguar's eye-catching performance figures helped persuade those in Stuttgart to press ahead with the 6.9-litre model.

It was mostly the same car as the 4.5-litre 450 SEL, but it differed in two very important ways: the enormous M100 V8 of 6,834 cc (derived from that created for the 600 limousine) and oleo-pneumatic suspension. Here, Mercedes had joined in with Rolls-Royce in imitating the Citroën system, but not to the extent of infringing the patent or buying a licence. In the Mercedes installation, three separate engine-driven hydraulic pumps supplied suspension, brake boost and power steering. The suspension pump pressurised a strut at each corner, each one connected to a sphere containing nitrogen gas at very high pressure. A butyl rubber diaphragm between the fluid and the gas allowed the soft, stable response of the suspension as a wheel deflected, while the system also self-levelled.

The results were enormously impressive. Here was a car weighing nearly two tons that could break traction on a dry road on kickdown, even with the 6.9 model's limited-slip differential. It fired itself to 60 mph from a standstill in 7.2 seconds: quicker than a Lotus Elite, a Lamborghini Urraco, a 'Sportomatic' Porsche 911, or indeed a Jaguar XJ12. Yet the ride was better than ever: controlled, soft as silk, capable in corners and dismissive of poor surfaces. There was only one shortcoming, and that was the interior. It was very nice, but then so were all the W116 S-class interiors, and the 6.9 was hardly any different. It had slightly more expensive-looking wood trim, a 170 mph speedometer and two extra warning lamps, but even at the immense asking price (40 per cent more than a standard 450 SEL), leather trim, heated seats and a sunroof were extra-cost options. For those addicted to the hand-finished charms of walnut and Connolly leather, the Mercedes couldn't hold a candle to Rolls-Royce. In every other way, the 450 SEL 6.9 was the best car money could buy.

**TOP:** Any Mercedes flagship should have an imposing look. Job done.

**BOTTOM:** The 6.9 badge, underlined for effect, leaves one in no doubt as to this car's power.

| 1976 Mercedes 450 SEL 6.9 ||
|---|---|
| Length | 5,060 mm |
| Width | 1,895 mm |
| Weight | 1,843 kg |
| Wheelbase | 2,595 mm |
| Suspension | Independent via double wishbones, hydraulic ram and damper units (front); independent via semi-trailing arms, hydraulic ram and damper units (rear) |
| Brakes | Hydraulic discs (front and rear), high-pressure assisted |
| Engine | 6,834 cc V8, OHC per bank, Bosch K-Jetronic fuel injection |
| Power | 286 bhp @ 4,250 rpm |
| Torque | 405 lb-ft @ 3,000 rpm |
| Transmission | Three-speed automatic, rear-wheel drive |
| 0–60 mph | 7.2 sec. |
| Top speed | 141 mph |
| Cost new | £21,995 |
| Value today | £15,000–£50,000 |

# Volkswagen Golf GTi

There can be few more influential cars than the first Volkswagen Golf GTi. Not only did it inspire the development of a whole new group of cars that survives to this day – hot hatchbacks – it also did much to kill off another group: those small two-seat sports cars that used to be the cheapest way to feel fast. Now, 50 years after it was announced, the GTi remains in production in its eighth generation. Not bad for a car Volkswagen thought of as a short-run special edition, hoping only to sell 5,000 units.

The reason for such pessimism was the 1973 oil crisis, which pops up repeatedly in the stories of cars in this chapter. It's hard to understand today, even in times of high fuel prices, climate change and global instability, but the 1970s saw a combination of widespread price inflation, difficult industrial disputes featuring frequent strikes and a crisis of confidence over the supply of petrol. Governments considered swingeing tax hikes to deter buyers from larger, more powerful cars, and manufacturers doubted they would break even on any new model other than economy-focused compacts. The fondness for sporting cars and driving for the sake of enjoyment was on the way out … or so many people thought. Yet it was the Golf GTi, as much as any car, that showed things didn't have to be this way.

The Golf had been launched in 1974 with the Herculean task of succeeding the VW Beetle. Wolfsburg's team had done their absolute best to judge what the market wanted, from the sharp, clean lines of Giugiaro's styling to exactly the right size and proportions, inside and out: two-door and four-door bodies, a hatchback (still a novelty at the time), and front-wheel drive with a new, transverse, water-cooled engine to save space and avoid the air-cooled VW's challenges of getting through tougher emissions standards. It was nice to drive, relatively affordable, came with a choice of a 1.1-litre or 1.5-litre engine and sold very well from the moment it was launched, passing 1 million units in less than three years. By then, of course, it had this exciting new variant.

The idea came from the head of VW's press office, Anton Konrad, and Alfons Löwenburg, a test engineer. They formed a small group to discuss a 'Sport Golf' and with expert input from other disciplines within Volkswagen had refined the idea enough to present it to senior colleagues early in 1975. Its appeal was obvious and new chairman Toni Schmücker gave it the go-ahead in May 1975. In September of the same year, the GTi was announced as a forthcoming model at the Frankfurt Motor Show. It would use a slightly larger engine of 1,588 cc and feature Bosch's K-Jetronic fuel injection system.

This proved to be a fantastic combination. K-Jetronic is a mechanical system that doesn't rely on a silicon chip to interpret information, and while it was more expensive to install than a pair of carburettors, it was almost immune to going out of tune or wearing significantly with age. This meant the GTi started promptly on frozen winter mornings and ran just as happily in mid-summer traffic jams. The engine's 9.5:1 compression ratio was high enough to give peppy performance without needing the costly five-star petrol that was already in danger of being phased out in the UK and elsewhere. With 110 bhp in a car weighing just 845 kg, acceleration felt even quicker than the ten-second 0–60 mph time would suggest.

The Golf GTi handled well too. Using slightly wider tyres than lesser Golf models, combined with the simple MacPherson strut suspension and front-wheel drive, struck a good balance between agility and safety. Put your foot down on a wet corner in a rear-drive sports car and you could spin. If you were rough with the accelerator in a Golf GTi, it just washed off the excess power in predictable understeer and tightened its line again as you eased off. It also looked good, with a black chin spoiler, side stripes and wheel-arch lips, plus a red outline to the grille and prominent GTi badging. Inside, you got a large rev counter, a golf-ball gear knob and the famous tartan cloth inserts in hip-hugging bucket seats.

Imports began to the UK in 1976, but in left-hand drive only, so it wasn't until 1979 when right-hand drive GTis appeared that sales took off here. By then, the GTi had moved up from a four-speed to a five-speed gearbox and came with distinctive BBS alloy wheels as standard. In 1982, the original 1.6-litre engine gave way to a 1.8-litre unit that still used the same injection system, distinguishable by its four-headlamp grille and (usually) a sunroof. It was only a little faster in top speed but delivered more torque for even more satisfaction when changing down to third gear and overtaking dawdling family saloons on country roads.

By this time, many other car-makers were imitating the Golf GTi and some of the best efforts appear in chapter 5. We were also witnessing the demise of the small sports car – the MG Midget, MGB, TR7 and Triumph Spitfire were pensioned off without replacements. Fiat's X1/9 kept selling, but you really had to want wind-in-the-hair motoring to choose a little two-seater, and Volkswagen soon had that covered too. The Golf GLi, a cabriolet version, joined the range when right-hand drive imports began in 1979. Arguably, the Golf GTi also stole some of the market for coupés like the Ford Capri. In 1980, for instance, it was the same price as a Capri 2000S and had it beaten in acceleration, top speed and economy. It was easier to get in and out of the Golf's back seats, visibility for the kids was better and it was easier to park too. GTi owners started to wonder if this was the only car they'd ever need.

Successive Golf generations always retained a GTi and it stayed true to its original aims, even if more extreme high-performance Golfs have sometimes been sold alongside it. For the original Mk 1 GTi, that prediction of 5,000 sales soon vanished. The final total between 1976 and 1983? An amazing 461,690. A star was born.

> 'The art of civilising the high-performance engine reaches new heights of excellence.'
>
> *Motor Sport* magazine, March 1977

TOP: A Mk 1 Golf GTi. Only two headlamps mean this example must have a 1.6-litre engine.

BOTTOM: Three letters that spell fun.

FOLLOWING PAGE: For the more outdoorsy type, the Mk1 also came in cabriolet form.

| Volkswagen Golf GTi (figures for 1977 model) | |
|---|---|
| Length | 3,721 mm |
| Width | 1,613 mm |
| Weight | 845 kg |
| Wheelbase | 2,400 mm |
| Suspension | Independent via MacPherson struts, lower arms (front); beam axle, trailing arms, coil-and-damper strut (rear) |
| Brakes | Hydraulic discs (front); drums (rear), servo-assisted |
| Engine | 1,598 cc in-line four, OHC, Bosch K-Jetronic fuel injection |
| Power | 110 bhp @ 6,100 rpm |
| Torque | 101 lb-ft @ 5,000 rpm |
| Transmission | Four-speed manual, front-wheel drive |
| 0–60 mph | 9.8 sec. |
| Top speed | 110 mph |
| Cost new | £3,986 |
| Value today | £8,000–£30,000 (Mk 1) |

# Lotus Esprit

In a modest, British kind of way, the Lotus Esprit was our homegrown Countach. Or rather, it was conceived and built in Norfolk but styled by an Italian, Giorgetto Giugiaro. Lotus founder Colin Chapman was at the Geneva Motor Show in 1971 when he was approached by Giugiaro. The stylist told Chapman he wanted to develop a show car to suggest a shape for the next Lotus generation, which fitted Chapman's plans very well. Chapman was keen to lift Lotus from making affordable sports cars and kits to rival Porsche and even Ferrari. He was planning three new models sharing just one or two engines. There would be a four-seat GT, a 2+2 fastback coupé and an out-and-out sports car, ideally mid-engined.

Lotus delivered a chassis from their mid-engined Europa model to Turin for Giugiaro to work on. Clothed in a new silver body, it appeared at the Turin Motor Show in November 1972. It looked sensational and wasn't far from the finished Esprit shape, yet between show car and production lay three years of hard work to refine the design and figure out a way to build it in glass-fibre, Chapman's preferred material. The Esprit would be powered by the Lotus 907 engine, a twin-cam four-cylinder unit slanted over to allow a space-efficient installation. The gearbox was a five-speed transaxle bought in from Citroën.

Lotus's Tony Rudd surprised Colin Chapman by picking him up from Heathrow Airport in the first running Esprit prototype early in 1975, only for a hub carrier to break on the way back to Hethel, the company's Norfolk base. Despite ongoing worries about chassis and suspension weaknesses, the Esprit went on sale later that year and magazine road testers got their hands on this long-awaited thrill. Its reception was generally good, with praise for the racing-car handling, exciting interior with bucket seats like tartan-panelled hammocks, and decent performance. But just 'decent'. Despite a respectable 160 bhp, the four-cylinder engine had neither the drama nor the output of a six- or eight-cylinder engine from Ferrari or Porsche.

Still, the car's dramatic shape grabbed a great deal of attention, none more important than that of Eon Productions, who cast the Esprit as James Bond's swimming supercar in *The Spy Who Loved Me* in 1977, leading to a second appearance in Turbo form in *For Your Eyes Only* in 1980. The Turbo Esprit was engineered in little more than a year by Martin Cliffe, who, with his boss Graham Atkin, reduced turbo lag to almost nothing. They gave the Esprit a 50 bhp boost and increased torque throughout the rev range. Finally, Lotus had supercar performance to go with the looks.

The original Esprit lasted until 1987 before replacement with a reworked shape, but it's the head-turning form of Giugiaro's pure angles that people love today. Drop into one of those banana-shaped seats and fire up the snarling engine just behind your headrest, and it's easy to think the Esprit is even more exciting from the inside than the outside.

| 1977 Lotus Esprit | |
|---|---|
| Length | 4,191 mm |
| Width | 1,854 mm |
| Weight | 1,032 kg |
| Wheelbase | 2,438 mm |
| Suspension | Independent via double wishbones with coil-and-damper units (front); independent via Chapman struts, semi-trailing arms and lower links (rear) |
| Brakes | Hydraulic discs (front and rear), servo-assisted |
| Engine | 1,973 cc in-line four, DOHC, two twin-choke carburettors |
| Power | 160 bhp @ 6,200 rpm |
| Torque | 140 lb-ft @ 4,900 rpm |
| Transmission | Five-speed manual, rear-wheel drive |
| 0–60 mph | 8.4 sec. |
| Top speed | 124 mph |
| Cost new | £8,219 |
| Value today | £20,000–£40,000 (S1) |

TOP: An original Esprit S1, the first and purest.

MIDDLE: A 1985 Turbo model.

BOTTOM: Underwater in *The Spy Who Loved Me* – the scene that made the Esprit a star.

# Porsche 928

Today, it's easy to dismiss the 928 as an oversized, overcomplicated car that failed its objective of replacing the 911. That would be a mistake because, in its day, it was the most sophisticated grand tourer on the market and a deserved winner of 1978's European Car of the Year – and it's still the only sports car to win that title.

The story begins with a period of some disruption at Porsche, when the Piëch and Porsche families had withdrawn from the company. So in 1971 Porsche had a new chairman, Ernst Fuhrmann, who favoured a radical rethink of the company's main product, because the 911 looked as though it would struggle to keep up with emissions regulations and crash safety standards, especially in the key American market. Instead, Fuhrmann envisaged a range of front-engined GT cars with transaxle gearboxes at the rear, which was nothing like any Porsche yet produced. In February 1972, work on an all-new model began at Weissach's development centre.

The engine would be an aluminium V8, water cooled and mounted in the front, but behind the front axle line. The rear axle would feature independent suspension but also a revolutionary passive rear-wheel-steering feature designed to avoid the very thing the 911 was always criticised for – lift-off oversteer. With the 928 you could lift off the throttle in mid-corner and the outside rear wheel would toe in, keeping its line through the corner, rather than toeing out and leading to a skid.

The 928's body was an unusual mix of steel, aluminium and polyurethane, the latter used for the front- and rear-impact bumpers and perfectly integrated into the shape. The body was styled by Anatole Lapine as a long-bonneted GT with a smooth, almost bulbous rear glasshouse with a hatchback tailgate, and Miura-like fold-up headlamps were a variation on the pop-up look. All this brilliance had to be put on hold in 1973 following the Arab–Israeli War and the resulting oil crisis. Eventually, with the American market too important to ignore, work restarted and the car launched at the Geneva Motor Show in March 1977.

The 928 was deeply impressive. Features included air conditioning that cooled the glove box; ergonomically adjustable pedals, foot rest and gear shift; and even a special cleaning fluid sprayed onto the windscreen from time to time to keep it streak-free. Above all, the 928 impressed with the way it drove – and it still does. It feels like a large, heavy car, but it's extremely well planted on the road, with such high cornering limits you never really find the edge of adhesion unless you're on a test track. Straight-line acceleration is relentless, like the take-off run in a private jet.

The 928 gained a little more power with S and S2 versions in 1979 and 1984, and much more with the 32-valve 5-litre 928 S4 in 1986. The last incarnations, the 1992–95 GTS models with 5.4-litre engines and 350 bhp, are true supercars, but all 928s are reminders of just how clever Porsche's engineers could be.

| 1978 Porsche 928 | |
|---|---|
| Length | 4,448 mm |
| Width | 1,836 mm |
| Weight | 1,519 kg |
| Wheelbase | 2,499 mm |
| Suspension | Independent via double wishbones with coil-and-damper units (front); independent via multiple links, inclined coil-and-damper units, anti-roll bar (rear) |
| Brakes | Hydraulic discs (front and rear), servo-assisted |
| Engine | 4,474 cc V8, OHC, fuel-injected |
| Power | 240 bhp @ 5,500 rpm |
| Torque | 257 lb-ft @ 3,600 rpm |
| Transmission | Three-speed automatic, rear-wheel drive |
| 0–60 mph | 7.5 sec. |
| Top speed | 138 mph |
| Cost new | £20,498 |
| Value today | £8,000–£40,000 (first series) |

TOP: The 928 S4 launched in 1986 with a more potent 32-valve V8.

BOTTOM: An original 928 with Porsche's distinctive Teledial alloy wheels.

# Saab 99 Turbo

At first glance, the differences between the Saab 99 Turbo and earlier turbocharged cars were subtle. BMW and Porsche, and before that Chevrolet and Oldsmobile, had used turbos to create thrilling high-performance models that could sit at the top of a model range. This was a fair description of the Saab 99 Turbo too, but the starting point was different. With a focus on efficiency over outright speed, Saab's goal was to create a car with the performance of a class above with the economy and weight almost unchanged.

This was a crucial difference, because it showed the world it was worthwhile turbocharging almost any model at any price level. Through the 1990s and beyond, it became normal for sensible family cars to feature engines fed by turbochargers, because they could deliver just what Saab had realised in the mid-1970s. For diesel-engined cars, the advantages were even more dramatic, and it's been a long time since any diesel car was built without a turbo.

Early Saab models had been produced one at a time, with an odd combination of advanced streamlined bodywork and two-stroke engines driving the front wheels, but that changed with the launch of the Saab 99. Here was a much less esoteric machine, still front-wheel drive, but with a conventional four-stroke, four-cylinder engine in a larger and more spacious bodyshell.

The programme to turbocharge the 99 was initiated by Saab's head of engine development, Per Gillbrand, around 1974. Early experiments used a Holset turbocharger from a truck engine but the results were unpromising. Then he met Geoff Kershaw, a young British engineer working as a technical sales representative for the American turbocharger specialist Garrett. Kershaw brought over Garrett's new T3 turbo in November 1975, the first one ever made to suit a car engine and produce boost at lower revs. After two years of refinement, the 99 Turbo was launched at the Frankfurt Motor Show. Deliveries began in 1978 and the waves made by this exciting new car spread worldwide.

What impressed everyone was the car's docility. It drove like a normal, civilised 2-litre saloon on light throttle openings but then built power quite steadily as boost came on, eventually delivering a shove that no other car in its class could manage. This contrasted with the Porsche 930 and the BMW 2002, which were felt to have 'top-end only' boost, to quote *Motor Sport* – lacking urgency at lower revs, then with extra power delivered in a sudden rush that was hard to control. Exciting, yes, but undesirable for a five-seat family car.

The 99 Turbo feels remarkably modern to drive. Letting it build boost and accelerate faster and faster, well beyond the legal limit and all in top gear, is a remarkable feeling that seems alien in a saloon car designed nearly 60 years ago. Saab introduced the 900 for 1978 and it soon gained a turbo as well. This was finally phased out in 1993, but by then Saab had been offering the larger 9000 model for seven years and there was a new Vauxhall-based 900 coming, both of which were offered as turbo versions. For Saab, the turbocharger was the gift that kept on giving, and it gave the rest of the industry a vital boost too.

| 1978 Saab 99 Turbo | |
|---|---|
| Length | 4,529 mm |
| Width | 1,689 mm |
| Weight | 1,233 kg |
| Wheelbase | 2,477 mm |
| Suspension | Independent via double wishbones (front); beam axle, trailing arms and Panhard rod (rear) |
| Brakes | Hydraulic discs (front and rear), servo-assisted |
| Engine | 1,995 cc in-line four, OHC, fuel-injected and turbocharged |
| Power | 145 bhp @ 5,000 rpm |
| Torque | 174 lb-ft @ 3,000 rpm |
| Transmission | Four-speed manual, front-wheel drive |
| 0–60 mph | 8.9 sec. |
| Top speed | 123 mph |
| Cost new | £7,950 |
| Value today | £8,000–£25,000 |

TOP: A three-door 99 Turbo with the special wheels, badge and spoilers setting it apart from other Saabs.

MIDDLE: This car can pull. A five-door example with boat trailer in tow.

BOTTOM: The 99 Turbo was quickly joined by the slightly longer, better-equipped 900 Turbo, which was offered in convertible form from 1986.

# Mazda RX-7

If you've read the entry on the NSU Ro80 in chapter 3 (p. 128), you might think the clever German saloon would have been the end of production cars with Wankel engines. Would anyone ever conquer those twin challenges of rotor-tip sealing and high fuel consumption? Yes and no.

Mazda was the other great pioneer of rotary engines, introducing its Cosmo 110S sports car after the NSU Wankel Spider but before the Ro80, and it was the first car to feature a twin-rotor engine. From there, Mazda produced a couple of saloon-based coupés with rotary engines – the R130, the RX-2 and the RX-4 – until the much sleeker, more purposeful RX-7 was launched in 1978. Designed by a team led by Matasaburo Maeda, it was a return to the purer, more sporting approach of the Cosmo. The RX-7 looked like a direct rival to the Datsun 260Z and 280Z and similar small GTs and sports coupés. In the UK, that meant the Ford Capri, Opel Manta and MGB, but Mazda chose a surprising route.

The list price was set at £8,549 – more than double what the car cost in America, and 40 per cent more than even a 3-litre Capri, which made it seem very expensive indeed. Other cars in Mazda's range were competitive with home-market rivals, so it may have been a deliberate decision to pitch this exciting new coupé as something exclusive … or they may simply have looked at the price of the surprisingly costly Datsun 280Z (£8,641) and decided to match that. Both were still £500 cheaper than the Porsche 924, with similar performance. Would anyone choose the Mazda over a famous marque like Porsche?

Enough people did to keep Mazda importing them and over the years the model built a following. In America it was doing very well indeed, thanks to the much more competitive price and the new open-minded attitude to Japanese sports cars started by the Datsun 240Z. The durability problems of early rotary engines had become less acute with years of patient development, so the reputation for trouble began to fade, though the reputation for excessive thirst wasn't going anywhere. An average of 18.2 mpg versus 27.8 mpg for the 924 wasn't great for a car producing just 105 bhp at peak.

It was, though, a very tuneable engine. In the UK, TWR offered a potent turbo conversion and by late 1983 Mazda had developed its own. Increasing power was a strong theme from then on, with the redesigned second generation in 1985 and especially for the third generation RX-7 in 1991, which boasted engines making up to 276 bhp and became hugely popular in the Japanese tuning scene. Mazda persisted with the Wankel engine for the RX-7's eventual replacement, the RX-8 of 2003–12, showing that the design's main advantages – smoothness, small size, light weight and prodigious power – could outweigh economy and durability concerns in the sports-car market. The RX-7 was the classic that proved the concept, which makes the rare UK-market survivors something special in today's scene.

| 1979 Mazda RX-7 | |
|---|---|
| Length | 4,285 mm |
| Width | 1,674 mm |
| Weight | 1,025 kg |
| Wheelbase | 2,421 mm |
| Suspension | Independent via MacPherson struts (front); live axle, trailing arms, coil springs (rear) |
| Brakes | Hydraulic discs (front); drums (rear), servo-assisted |
| Engine | 1,146 cc twin-rotor Wankel, two carburettors |
| Power | 105 bhp @ 6,000 rpm |
| Torque | 106 lb-ft @ 4,000 rpm |
| Transmission | Five-speed manual, rear-wheel drive |
| 0–60 mph | 10.1 sec. |
| Top speed | 115 mph |
| Cost new | £8,549 |
| Value today | £3,000–£15,000 |

TOP: A 1981 coupé participating in a classic car rally in Greece.

BOTTOM: A 1990 RX-7 convertible.

# Porsche

Ferdinand Porsche was one of the most remarkable and versatile design engineers in motoring history. Any one of his creations would guarantee fame: a series of four-wheel-drive electric and petrol-electric hybrid carriages called Lohner-Porsches from 1900; huge Austro-Daimler racing cars of 1912 with overhead camshafts and five valves per cylinder; the supercharged 7.1-litre Mercedes models of the 1920s; the astonishing rear-engined Auto-Union racing cars of the 1930s; and of course the KdF-Wagen, which became the Volkswagen Beetle.

The firm he created in 1931 was a consultancy rather than a car-maker and it wasn't until 1948 that the first Porsche-branded car appeared. Porsche himself was imprisoned for his wartime activities until the same year, so it was his son, Ferry Porsche, who organised the first prototypes of the 356. The number 356 refers to the job number – the 356th project since Ferdinand Porsche's first design for an electric vehicle in 1898. Ferdinand Porsche died in 1951, but by then the business was established enough to survive. Right from the beginning, racing versions of their road cars, and indeed purpose-built racers, were a key part of the firm's activity, almost all using the air-cooled flat-four engine Porsche had developed from the VW unit.

The six-cylinder engine for the apparently immortal 911 was a major step forward and the result of a third generation of the Porsche family contributing to design – the 911 was Butzi's baby, Butzi being the nickname for Ferry's son, Ferdinand Alexander Porsche. Through the 1960s, Porsche moved up through the capacity classes in sports-car racing. It was the eight-cylinder and then twelve-cylinder Le Mans cars that dazzled racegoers later in the decade, and the stunning 240 mph Porsche 917K gave the marque its first overall victory at Le Mans in 1970. Porsche would go on to become the most successful constructor of all at the famous 24-hour race, with 19 overall victories as of 2024. The 917 was created under Ferdinand Piëch, grandson of Ferdinand Porsche and a later hugely influential figure in VW, Porsche and Audi history.

Turbocharging defined Porsche's new generations in the 1970s, both on track and off, when the 911/930 Turbo showed what the technology could offer to sports cars. Smaller models had always been part of Porsche's range too, with the 912 and then 914 offering a more affordable entry to Porsche ownership, as the 924, 944, 968 and eventually the Boxster would do.

Like many sports-car makers, Porsche struggled to stay profitable in the 1990s but engineered an amazing turnaround fuelled by diverse new models – including the Boxster and the very popular SUVs, the Cayenne and Macan – allowing the holding company Porsche AG to gradually take a controlling stake in Volkswagen during the 2000s. Corporate restructuring created a new company identity, Porsche SE, in control of a business comprising not just VW but also Audi, Bentley, Lamborghini, Porsche, SEAT, Skoda, Scania and MAN trucks, Ducati motorcycles, and many others. Its operating income is around €5.4 billion a year – not bad for a small family business that started off making sports versions of the Beetle.

# THROUGH THE YEARS

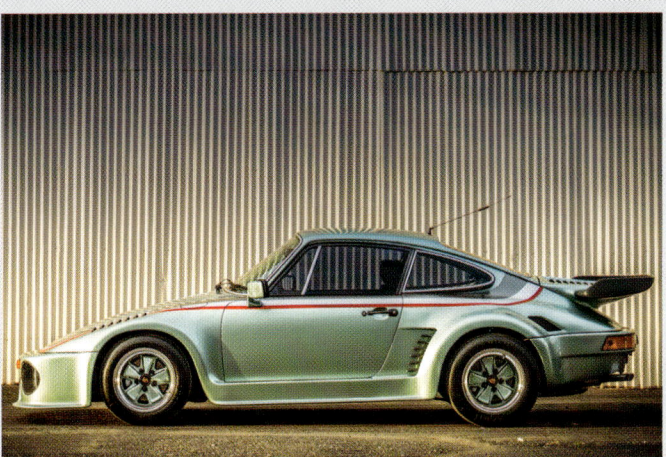

**CLOCKWISE FROM TOP LEFT:** A 550 Spyder 1500 RS; 930 'flatnose'; 914; Cayenne; 944; 917K.

# Vauxhall Chevette HS/HSR

Ford's fast road cars got most of the attention in the 1960s and 1970s, as they still do today, but Vauxhall ensured they didn't have things all their own way. There were the twin-carb Brabham Viva and the faster 2-litre Viva GT in the 1960s, while the Firenza 'Droop Snoot' and Magnum Sports Hatch challenged the Escort Mk 2 RS2000 in terms of wedge-shaped nose jobs, with performance to match. But it was the Vauxhall Chevette HS that came with real motorsport credibility.

Dealer Team Vauxhall had been racing these muscled-up Chevettes since 1976. The road-going homologation special took two years to appear, launching in 1978 with a 2.3-litre slant-four like the Firenza and Magnum, but with a new 16-valve cylinder head. Vauxhall went further than simply dropping in a big engine and adding go-faster stripes: they gave the car new suspension with a double-wishbone arrangement at the front, adapted from the Opel Kadett GT/E, and they located the live rear axle with twin trailing arms and a Panhard rod. The feeling of a competition car for the road was kicked up a notch by the use of a Getrag five-speed manual gearbox, with first gear in a dog-leg down to the left, leaving second and third in the same plane and fourth and fifth in the same plane, just like some much larger, faster and more exotic machinery.

Inside, the trim left you in no doubt you were in something special. Tartan may have been visual shorthand for 'sports-car cockpit', what with the Golf GTi and Lotus Esprit choosing the same route, and Vauxhall went all out with red-and-black check on the door cards and seat panels. There was no choice: you got silver paint and a black-and-red interior. It made for a distinctive road car that could also boast of being slightly quicker in acceleration and faster in top speed than the Escort RS 2000, but because of the extra work Vauxhall put into the suspension, engine and running gear, it was a lot more expensive: £5,577 versus £4,057 in 1979. This made for slow sales and only 400 were built.

However, it did great things for Vauxhall's image on the rally stages, winning major events in the hands of British drivers Tony Pond and Jimmy McRae and Finnish driver Pentti Airikkala, who used one to win the British Open Rally Championship in 1979, breaking the Escort's eight years of dominance. In 1981 Vauxhall won the manufacturer's prize at the same championship. To stay competitive, they developed the Chevette HSR, with bulging glass-fibre wings, bonnet and boot lid to save weight. Revised rear suspension improved the handling still further, but very few were built. Group 4 regulations required only 50 to be constructed as an evolution of the previous model, which Vauxhall achieved by modifying unsold Chevette HSs and rebuilding customers' cars. Today, these exciting, loud and unmistakable machines are rarer than the much-fancied Fords but a little less expensive, which makes them a tempting nostalgia trip for fans of 1970s rallying.

| 1978 Vauxhall Chevette 2300 HS | |
|---|---|
| Length | 3,993 mm |
| Width | 1,580 mm |
| Weight | 1,014 kg |
| Wheelbase | 2,388 mm |
| Suspension | Independent via double wishbones, coil springs and telescopic dampers (front); live axle, twin trailing arms, Panhard rod and coil springs (rear) |
| Brakes | Discs (front); drums (rear), servo-assisted |
| Engine | 2,279 cc in-line four, DOHC |
| Power | 135 bhp @ 5,500 rpm |
| Torque | 134 lb-ft @ 4,500 rpm |
| Transmission | Five-speed manual, rear-wheel drive |
| 0–60 mph | 8.5 sec. |
| Top speed | 117 mph |
| Cost new | £5,577 |
| Value today | £10,000–£30,000 |

TOP: A 1978 Chevette HS.

BOTTOM: Showing it's still got what it takes at a retro rally event in 2020.

# Talbot Sunbeam Lotus

Here was the fastest of all the British rally-inspired specials around in the 1970s, and it came from the least likely source – an American-owned conglomerate of old British names in the process of being sold to the French.

The parent company, Rootes Group, revived the pre-war Talbot Ten in 1945 by adding in the name of another noble old British marque and calling it the Sunbeam-Talbot Ten. The Talbot part of the name dropped away after 1954 and the Rootes Group was slowly sold off in various chunks to the Chrysler Corporation's European arm in the mid-1960s. In 1977, Chrysler launched a small rear-wheel-drive hatchback, the Chrysler Sunbeam, turning the old Sunbeam company name into a model name. This was confused further in 1979 when Chrysler Europe was sold off by the American parent company to PSA/Peugeot-Citroën. They changed all the Chrysler-badged cars to Talbots and so created the Talbot Sunbeam … meaning that both Sunbeam-Talbots and Talbot Sunbeams existed, 30 years apart.

While the little hatchback Sunbeam was still a Chrysler, the company's competition manager Des O'Dell approached Lotus about fitting it with a slant-four Lotus engine, as found in the Elite, Esprit and Eclat. The idea was a repeat of the theory behind creating the Ford Cortina Lotus and Escort Twin-Cam: take a humble, rear-wheel-drive car and give it Lotus power. Colin Chapman and Mike Kimberley led a newly formed consultancy, Lotus Engineering, and took on the project. The first cars were promising but Chrysler wanted more torque, so Kimberley and Chapman encouraged them to fund a new version of the engine with an increased capacity of 2.2-litres.

O'Dell agreed to this and it made the Sunbeam very fast indeed. It also benefited Lotus enormously, as they used the larger version of the engine in their road cars, much to Chrysler's displeasure, as they felt they'd paid for Lotus's own engine development. Nonetheless, with 150 bhp in road-going form and an untouchable 250 bhp in full rally tune, the 960-kg Sunbeam was born to win. It took first place in the Lombard RAC Rally in 1980 and the following year Chrysler won the manufacturer's prize in the World Rally Championship.

The road-going version was unveiled in Geneva in the spring of 1979 as the Sunbeam Lotus, but as the Chrysler takeover was completed the first production cars were delivered as the Talbot Sunbeam Lotus: all either black and silver or blue and silver. The performance was dazzling: 0–60 mph times were a full second quicker than obvious rivals like the Escort RS 2000 and Chevette 2300 HS, with a top speed in excess of 120 mph. It was priced at £7,205, thousands more than the Ford and the Vauxhall, yet Chrysler sold an impressive 2,308 of them from 1979–81, before the Sunbeam model was discontinued. Today they're revered, but survivors are scarce. Some led hard lives on rally stages and terrible rust problems scrapped many others. Find a good one and it remains one of the most exciting British cars of the decade.

| 1979 Talbot Sunbeam Lotus | |
|---|---|
| Length | 3,830 mm |
| Width | 1,603 mm |
| Weight | 960 kg |
| Wheelbase | 2,413 mm |
| Suspension | Independent via MacPherson strut, lower link and anti-roll bar (front); live axle, twin trailing arms, coil springs and telescopic dampers (rear) |
| Brakes | Hydraulic discs (front and rear), servo-assisted |
| Engine | 2,172 cc in-line four, DOHC, two carburettors |
| Power | 150 bhp @ 5,750 rpm |
| Torque | 150 lb-ft @ 4,500 rpm |
| Transmission | Five-speed manual, rear-wheel drive |
| 0–60 mph | 7.4 sec. |
| Top speed | 121 mph |
| Cost new | £7,205 |
| Value today | £10,000–£50,000 |

TOP: Power-sliding around a corner in the RAC Rally in 1980.

BOTTOM: In road-going form: a 1982 Sunbeam Lotus.

# THE BOOM IS BACK
## 1980 TO 1989

# AUDI QUATTRO

| Audi Quattro (figures for 1981 model) ||
|---|---|
| Length | 4,404 mm |
| Width | 1,725 mm |
| Weight | 1,414 kg |
| Wheelbase | 2,525 mm |
| Suspension | Independent via MacPherson struts, lower wishbones (front and rear) |
| Brakes | Hydraulic discs, servo-assisted (front and rear) |
| Engine | 2,144 cc in-line five, OHC, turbo-charged, fuel-injected |
| Power | 200 bhp @ 5,500 rpm |
| Torque | 210 lb-ft @ 3,500 rpm |
| Transmission | Five-speed manual, four-wheel drive |
| 0–60 mph | 7.3 sec. |
| Top speed | 137 mph |
| Cost new | £14,500 |
| Value today | £15,000–£50,000 |

The Audi Quattro was another game-changer from the VW-Audi group, and one which took shape remarkably quickly considering the technological revolution it brought. In just three years the project went from an idea to a debut at the Geneva Motor Show in March 1980. In fact, the creation of an all-new model was really the development of an existing four-wheel-drive system with a floorplan from the Audi 80. Nonetheless, it was an impressive achievement because the choice to package the car as a high-performance, turbocharged model meant it had to be good enough to show the purpose of using all-wheel drive. In this, it succeeded brilliantly.

The idea of four-wheel drive for road cars was not new by 1977. Jensen had shown what was possible with the FF (p. 120) but had also built in some problems the model could never overcome, namely weight, thirst, a high price and the lack of a left-hand-drive option. Land Rovers and Jeeps had been around for decades, and American buyers were used to a four-wheel-drive option on some pickup trucks. All of these were perfectly happy on-road, if a little slower and less comfortable than conventional cars. The Range Rover addressed that, but it was still costly, heavy, thirsty and unavailable in the US.

The real pioneer in applying all-wheel drive systems to smaller, more affordable cars was Subaru. They launched their Symmetrical All-Wheel Drive (SAWD) system as an option on the Leone estate in 1972. It launched in Australia in 1973, the United States in 1974 and the UK in 1977, by which time the system had shown it made these small, light cars with punchy flat-four engines almost unstoppable in mud, snow or sand. Saloon and pickup versions could also be optioned with Subaru's SAWD, long before Subaru became a force on the world rally scene; the emphasis was on utility rather than performance. The little Leone seemed aimed at those couldn't afford a large 4x4, not at typical car buyers who might benefit from four-wheel drive in poor road conditions. In 1985 Subaru launched the XT coupé, a sleek, turbocharged sports machine with four-wheel drive. If they'd done so six years earlier, the Audi Quattro might not have received the credit heaped on it ever since.

As it was, early in 1977, Audi's chief chassis engineer Jörg Bensinger was testing a lightweight off-roader, the Volkswagen Iltis, in the snow and he began to wonder whether the little vehicle's four-wheel-drive system could work in a road car. He approached his boss, Ferdinand Piëch, the technical engineering manager at Audi at that time. It was Piëch who suggested making it a high-performance model, which was a crucial difference from the Subaru and ensured that Audi would be launching a car with no direct rival. The price would be high, but not too high — less than a base-model Porsche 911, more than a Lotus Eclat and about on a par with a BMW 628CSi coupé — but with two features none of them could boast: a turbocharger and the all-important four-wheel drive.

The Quattro avoided the problems of bulk and weight that the Jensen FF suffered with an ingenious design that removed the need for a transfer case. Most off-road vehicles sent the power to all four wheels using a conventional manual or automatic gearbox and then a separate box that distributed drive to the front and rear axles. Audi used a conventional layout: the engine arranged north–south, not transverse, with a clutch and gearbox behind it. The gearbox was the revolutionary part. First, it did away with the need for a transfer case by using a hollow shaft within the gearbox casing, just alongside the gear cluster, that sent drive forwards. There, to the side of the clutch, was a front differential and the output for two front driveshafts.

Second, there was a small centre differential the size of a grapefruit at the back of the gearbox. This fed motion to both the transfer shaft going forwards and the conventional propshaft that drove the rear axle. That centre differential could be locked with a control in the cabin, ensuring the front and rear axles received equal amounts of torque for optimal traction in really slippery conditions, but in normal road use it could be left open to allow for the smoothest driving experience.

Rather like the VW Golf GTi, the initial sales forecast of only 400 now looks extremely pessimistic, but it just happened to be enough to homologate the Quattro for motorsport. This was in Piëch's mind from early in the project and Audi made a modest re-entry to international rallying with the front-wheel-drive 80 in 1978. The Quattro's first appearance in the World Rally Championship was in 1981, and the car's potential was clear when Hannu Mikkola won in Sweden and at the Lombard RAC Rally, while Michèle Mouton won the San Remo Rally in Italy. The following season was better still and Audi won the manufacturer's championship. They won the driver's championship in 1983 and 1984, with Mikkola and Stig Blomqvist respectively, and took the manufacturer's prize again in 1984. That year, Audi developed the fearsome Sport Quattro S1 for Group B rally regulations, with a 20-valve cylinder head on the five-cylinder engine and even more turbo boost, resulting in almost 450 bhp in competition trim.

The Quattro changed rallying; four-wheel traction proved unbeatable and after 1982 no two-wheel drive car would win the World Rally Championship again. It also changed the way we thought of four-wheel drive in road cars, because the Quattro was both faster and safer than any rival on wet roads, and still huge fun in the dry. Audi fitted the Quattro four-wheel-drive system to its saloons and estates, and has continued using and developing the system across its range to this day. Most major manufacturers followed suit and in almost every sector, from superminis to supercars, four-wheel drive is now a common option. We should be grateful that the Audi Quattro showed how big the advantages can be.

PREVIOUS PAGE: An original WR-series Quattro.

TOP: The Sport Quattro, with a shorter wheelbase, bulging bodywork and up to 450 bhp.

BOTTOM: In action at the San Remo Rally in 1981.

# Renault 5 Turbo and Turbo 2

You don't need psychic powers to guess how this muscular little car came into being. Renault had been building the familiar R5 hatchback since 1972, but it would never have threatened the podium places on a World Championship rally, even in the souped-up Gordini and Gordini Turbo forms. No, it would take something a bit more radical to make Renault's runabout competitive with the glut of rally specials on the stages in the late 1970s and early 1980s. Yes, a turbocharger would be important, but Renault's vice-president of production, Jean Terramorsi, had a more fundamental change in mind: move the engine behind the front seats.

Out with the rear seats and the simple old rear suspension: in with a 1,297 cc pushrod four-cylinder engine, heavily turbocharged and fed fresh air through huge wing vents on either side of the much-revised widebody styling. The new model's look was designed by Marc Deschamps at Bertone, while his boss Marcello Gandini went to town on the interior. This would only appear in the road-going version, of course, but it was a major selling point for the first R5 Turbo – a concept-car statement of bold colours and angles, a celebration of bright plastics on the dash, and bucket seats that were more about style than comfort.

With 158 bhp in the standard road-going form, the Turbo's engine was pushing out well over 100 bhp per litre, but to provoke that kind of output you had to floor the throttle and wait till the rev counter showed at least 4,000 rpm, at which point the boost from the Garrett T3 turbocharger would pile in like a rugby forward and heave the 970-kg Renault down the road in a lunge. To drive the rear wheels, Renault's engineers used the five-speed gearbox from the Renault 30, a large front-wheel-drive saloon with a V6 engine; they just had room to squeeze it in behind the small, mid-mounted four-cylinder engine. The rear suspension was adapted from that of the Alpine A310, a mid-engined sports coupé built by Renault's sporting subsidiary, Alpine, in Dieppe, where the R5 Turbo would also be put together.

The Turbo was homologated for Group 3 and Group 4 rallying as soon as 400 were constructed, and soon found its home on tarmac rallies above all else. Jean Ragnotti won the Rallye Monte Carlo at the first attempt in 1981 and would go on to win other tarmac-based events, including two first places at the Tour de Corse. On loose surfaces it couldn't compete with the new generation of four-wheel-drive Group B cars, even when the Maxi version was boosted to 345 bhp. As a road car, it continued as the Turbo 2 after the homologation number was reached, with a much less costly interior from an R5 Alpine and steel panels where the original Turbo used aluminium. Nowadays, both are sought after for their cartoonish looks and terrific performance. Never a run-of-the-mill hot hatch, the R5 Turbo remains as brash as it was brilliant.

**TOP:** All flared wheel arches and oversized air intakes, the Renault 5 Turbo is hard to miss.

**BOTTOM:** The interior is just as outrageous.

| 1981 Renault 5 Turbo ||
|---|---|
| Length | 3,724 mm |
| Width | 1,778 mm |
| Weight | 970 kg |
| Wheelbase | 2,431 mm |
| Suspension | Independent via double wishbones, torsion bars, telescopic dampers (front); independent via double wishbones, coil-and-damper struts (rear) |
| Brakes | Hydraulic discs, servo-assisted (front and rear) |
| Engine | 1,397 cc in-line four, overhead valve, turbocharged, fuel-injected |
| Power | 158 bhp @ 6,000 rpm |
| Torque | 155 lb-ft @ 3,250 rpm |
| Transmission | Five-speed manual, rear-wheel drive |
| 0–60 mph | 7.7 sec. |
| Top speed | 122 mph |
| Cost new | n/a |
| Value today | £25,000–£70,000 |

# DeLorean DMC-12

A great car? Perhaps not. A great success? Quite the opposite. A classic? Well, yes – the DeLorean seems guaranteed everlasting fame by its own tragic story and its starring role in the *Back to the Future* films. And such fame brings with it a considerable following.

It could have been a winner. Almost everything else John DeLorean touched turned to gold during a shining career in the American car industry – see the Pontiac GTO (p. 108). He was the youngest division chief in General Motors history when he was promoted to run Chevrolet in 1969, but he left in 1973 and founded the DeLorean Motor Company in 1975. He commissioned Giorgetto Giugiaro to style the new DeLorean Safety Vehicle, an angular coupé that would lead to the design for the DMC-12.

Lotus was brought in to engineer the car and based it on a backbone chassis derived from their own mid-engined Esprit. However, the DeLorean would be rear-engined, and with a heavy iron V6 engine instead of an alloy four-cylinder, handling seemed likely to be compromised even before the first car was built. To build them, DeLorean searched the globe for somewhere with an enticing package that would provide financial aid to start a car factory in an area of high unemployment. The British government put up $120 million (*c.*£65 million in 1978) to help create the DeLorean plant in Dunmurry on the edge of Belfast, Northern Ireland. When production eventually got underway, 18 months late, they were building an exciting car: stainless steel cover panels on a glass-fibre body and gullwing doors – nothing else looked like a DeLorean. Exports to the crucial American market began in spring 1981, but the delays had more than doubled the car's target launch price of $12,000.

Dunmurry had no history of car-making and poor quality control led to dreadful build standards, while road testers found the car sluggish and heavy to handle. Warranty claims flooded into DeLorean dealers in America and negative word-of-mouth did the new car no good. DeLorean needed to sell at least 10,000 to break even in the first year and might have done so had it not been for these early production problems … and the weather. A fierce, icy winter paralysed much of the USA for several weeks from December 1981 and everything froze – including car sales. DeLorean's business had no cash flow.

The house of cards came down with around 6,000 cars built: the UK government refused to cough up any more, debts were called in, and the DeLorean Motor Company collapsed with the loss of 2,600 jobs and hundreds of millions of dollars of investors' money – most of it the British public's. Then, in 1985, this ultimate symbol of hubris was reborn as a time machine in *Back to the Future*. It would be decades later before it was appreciated enough to rise in value, but today it's almost a legend. Sure, it's no sports car, but it's a charismatic machine absolutely everyone recognises. And no, nothing happens when you hit 88 mph!

| 1981 DeLorean DMC-12 ||
|---|---|
| Length | 4,267 mm |
| Width | 1,989 mm |
| Weight | 1,289 kg |
| Wheelbase | 2,431 mm |
| Suspension | Independent via double wishbones, coil springs, telescopic dampers (front); independent via Chapman struts and trailing arms (rear) |
| Brakes | Hydraulic discs, servo-assisted (front and rear) |
| Engine | 2,849 cc V6, overhead valve, fuel-injected |
| Power | 130 bhp @ 5,500 rpm |
| Torque | 162 lb-ft @ 2,750 rpm |
| Transmission | Five-speed manual, rear-wheel drive |
| 0–60 mph | 10.5 sec. |
| Top speed | 109 mph |
| Cost new | $25,000 (c.£14,300) |
| Value today | £25,000–£70,000 |

TOP: Cruising serenely, with difference in front and rear wheel sizes evident.

BOTTOM: Gullwing doors and brushed stainless steel body panels made the DeLorean a styling success, at least.

# Alfa Romeo

This noble old Milanese marque had been making cars since 1910, but it wasn't until the six-cylinder overhead-valve RL series appeared in 1921 that there were hints of greatness. From there, Alfa Romeo's rise was nothing short of meteoric, thanks mainly to a supercharged straight-eight engine designed by Vittorio Jano, recently poached from Fiat. This engine allowed the Alfa Romeo P2 to win the first grand prix the company ever entered – the French Grand Prix at Lyons in 1924. The following year Alfa Romeo took the World Championship and in 1926 Jano's designs filtered down to road cars.

His six- and eight-cylinder overhead camshaft engines were close to state of the art for motorsport, and though detuned for road use they made Alfa Romeo serious rivals for Bugatti. A full account of the racing glories of Alfa Romeo through the remainder of the pre-war years would fill this book (it has filled several others already), but it's the road cars that kept the money coming in, and which are now so sought-after as classics. The 6C 1750, especially in Super Sport or Gran Sport form with a supercharger and 95 mph performance, is exceeded only in desirability by the 8C 2300 and the glorious 8C 2900. The latter was the ultimate pre-war Alfa – a 220 bhp race engine with twin superchargers in a road-going body.

When car production resumed after the Second World War, Alfa Romeo continued with its pre-war approach: very fast, beautiful and expensive road cars like the 6C 2500 selling off the back of heroic grand prix success. Then everything changed in 1950 when the 1900, a smaller four-cylinder model, was launched. Out went the old separate chassis and coachbuilt bodies, in came a more affordable, accessible Alfa. They downsized again in 1954 with the Giulietta model, a 1,290 cc coupé that was soon joined by a small saloon version. With the Giulietta came a new twin-cam engine, like the 1900's in principle, but with an aluminium engine block rather than iron and many design differences. It would go on to power a golden generation of classic Alfa Romeos.

The next-generation Giulia of 1963 raised Alfa's popularity still further, with saloon, coupé, convertible and, eventually, Duetto Spider versions available, all with the free-revving, energetic twin-cam. The Giulia Sprint GTA was a light-alloy homologation special and a wonderful driver's car, which indeed was the reputation so many Alfa Romeos had gained. In the 1970s and 1980s the model range diversified with the front-wheel-drive Alfasud and its successor, the 33, while the Alfetta family of saloons and coupés brought in a rear transaxle and, in 1979, a V6 engine. This became just as well-loved as the twin-cam, thanks to the wonderful sound it made.

In the 1990s Alfa Romeo launched a new front-wheel-drive Spider and hard-top GTV sibling, while the range evolved with nippy hatchback models and both large and small saloons. After the glorious 8C of 2007 and the agile mid-engined 4C that launched in 2013, Alfa Romeo currently makes three SUVs and one saloon – but no sports car. Surely a situation that won't last long.

# THROUGH THE YEARS

**CLOCKWISE FROM TOP LEFT:** An RL Targa Florio; 8C 2900B Touring Spider; Giulia Sprint GTA; 8C Competizione; Alfetta; Giulietta 750 Sprint.

# Rover SD1 Vitesse

The new Rover 3500 of 1976 had none of the innovation and sophistication of the previous P6 model, with its clever suspension, novel structure and overhead-cam engine. Here was a larger, cruder car with a pushrod engine already more than 15 years old and basic live-axle rear suspension, which would make it tricky for the new car ever to match the old car's ride quality. But that apparently outdated engine would become the big Rover's key point of difference to its rivals.

The ageing Buick-sourced aluminium V8 actually had plenty of life left in it, and it was the obvious choice on which to base a new model. Stylist David Bache had effectively finished his striking Ferrari Daytona-inspired design way back in November 1971. This being British Leyland, it was five more years before the SD1 was launched, but it was warmly received – at least until terrible quality-control problems damaged its image and sales figures. The V8's blend of performance, high-geared economy and price – 20 per cent less than a BMW or Jaguar of similar abilities – won a lot of friends.

In 1980, work began to create a faster version, inspired by some disappointing results for 3500s racing in the British Saloon Car Championship and the launch of the BMW M535i. The power target would be 200 bhp, the suspension would be firmer and the brakes would be from the successful police versions of the 3500. Inside, the car would feature model-specific trim, while front and rear spoilers and alloy wheels distinguished the exterior. Quite late in development, a change from a thirsty multi-carburettor set-up to Bosch L-Jetronic fuel injection, plus a raised compression ratio, gave 190 bhp and excellent manners.

The new model was christened Vitesse. Launched at the NEC Motor Show in October 1982, it was heaped with praise when journalists got their hands on it, with *Motor* magazine calling it a 'poor man's Aston Martin'. In fact, it felt like a well-dressed muscle car and offered a thrilling V8 bellow under hard acceleration that none of its straight-six-engined rivals could produce. At its best bullying lesser rivals down the fast lane of the motorway, the Vitesse belongs to an era before speed cameras, when senior executives could set new personal bests between one city and another: 'Leader by nature, Paris by lunchtime, car by Rover', as one famous advert put it.

It became faster still from November 1985, thanks to an improved induction arrangement developed by Lotus, and the 'Twin-Plenum' Vitesse was homologated for the 1986 European Touring Car Championship. On the road it felt exhilarating, but it was a last hurrah for this great British bruiser. Production ended in July 1986 and the front-wheel drive 800 series came along to replace the SD1. In Vitesse form especially, many mourned its passing – some police forces snapped up unsold V8s in 1986 and kept them in service until 1989. Now the most valuable of the SD1 range, the Vitesse was not necessarily the car our dads and grandads had … but it was definitely the car they wanted.

| 1982 Rover Vitesse | |
|---|---|
| Length | 4,699 mm |
| Width | 1,768 mm |
| Weight | 1,423 kg |
| Wheelbase | 2,814 mm |
| Suspension | Independent via MacPherson struts and lower wishbones (front); live axle with trailing arms, Watts linkage, coil springs, telescopic dampers (rear) |
| Brakes | Hydraulic discs (front) and drums (rear), servo-assisted |
| Engine | 3,528 cc V8, overhead valve, fuel-injected |
| Power | 190 bhp @ 5,280 rpm |
| Torque | 220 lb-ft @ 4,000 rpm |
| Transmission | Five-speed manual, rear-wheel drive |
| 0–60 mph | 7.6 sec. |
| Top speed | 133 mph |
| Cost new | £14,950 |
| Value today | £8,000–£30,000 |

TOP: The Vitesse's large air dam and purposeful stance are obvious.

BOTTOM: Conceived to win on track as well as on the motorway commute, the Vitesse did just that.

# Peugeot 205 GTi

If the Golf GTi was the first proper hot hatch, perhaps the 205 GTi was the best. Peugeot had the ideal starting point with the 205. This was a neat, cute, up-to-date car with lots of youth appeal and, from a dynamic point of view, it had a 'wheel at each corner' look that suggested agility. The suspension – MacPherson struts at the front and torsion bars in a transverse beam at the back – took up little space and was relatively cheap to build. The spare wheel moved from the under-bonnet location common to various French cars at the time to beneath the boot floor, which had the dual advantages of lowering the bonnet line for better aerodynamics and improving weight distribution. Not that buyers of the 45 bhp, 954 cc base model felt much benefit from either, but there was soon a much quicker 205 on the horizon. The well-proportioned three-door model arrived in 1984, a year after the 205's launch in five-door form. And with the three-door came the first GTi.

All Peugeot had to do was fit their new XU 1.6-litre overhead-cam engine, add fuel injection, a red pinstripe and a body kit. The first 205 GTi could only boast 105 bhp, but this was enough to make it quicker than the Ford Escort XR3i. It lagged slightly behind the VW Golf GTi with its 1.8-litre engine but was a good deal cheaper, while it actually beat its ageing French rival, the Renault 5 Gordini Turbo, in acceleration and top speed. Talk to owners, though, and they don't bang on about the performance – they want to tell you about the handling.

It was so quick to change direction that it was easy to get carried away. Turn into a corner too fast, back off the throttle and find the 205 GTi's built-in flaw: lift-off oversteer. The weight would transfer to the front of the car and, despite that spare wheel in the back, the rear of the car would go light, lose traction and spin. However, once you knew this you drove around the problem. Keeping the nimble 205 balanced on tiptoe, you revelled in the car's high adhesion limits when you kept your foot down and in the joyfully talkative steering. Rarely has any car egged the driver on to go fast quite as effectively as a 205 GTi.

It went faster still in 1986 when the 1.6-litre version was given bigger valves for an extra 10 bhp, but the big news was the 1.9-litre GTi with nearly 130 bhp and the kind of performance usually reserved for executive expresses or high-priced rally specials. It would clear 120 mph and hit 60 mph from rest in 7.8 seconds, more than half a second quicker than even the 16-valve version of the Golf GTi. Sadly, the hot hatch scene became synonymous with car crime and joyriding, and rising insurance premiums deterred buyers. The GTi 1.6 departed in 1992 and the 1.9 a couple of years later; both were soon regarded as nailed-on classics of their breed.

**TOP:** Much like its Renault competitor, the GTi's interior left no doubt that this was the 'hot hatch' version of the 205.

**BOTTOM:** A 1991 205 GTi in classic Sorrento Green.

| 1987 Peugeot 205 GTi 1.9 ||
|---|---|
| Length | 3,705 mm |
| Width | 1,572 mm |
| Weight | 910 kg |
| Wheelbase | 2,420 mm |
| Suspension | Independent via MacPherson struts and lower wishbones (front); trailing arms with transverse torsion bars, telescopic dampers (rear) |
| Brakes | Hydraulic discs (front and rear), servo-assisted |
| Engine | 1,905 cc in-line 4, OHC, fuel-injected |
| Power | 130 bhp @ 6,000 rpm |
| Torque | 118 lb-ft @ 4,750 rpm |
| Transmission | Five-speed manual, front-wheel drive |
| 0–60 mph | 7.8 sec. |
| Top speed | 123 mph |
| Cost new | £9,295 |
| Value today | £6,000–£25,000 |

# Mercedes-Benz 190E 2.3-16

Here is another homologation special, but the story for this road-going racer began with a twist. Mercedes had a serious eye on rallying in the late 1970s and early 1980s and decided its new 190 saloon could be competitive – with the right engine. After all, it had more sophisticated suspension than any of the rear-wheel-drive rivals and it was sure to be nimbler than the big V8-powered 450 SLC that Mercedes had been using. Mercedes approached the British tuning firm Cosworth and asked them to develop a racing version of the four-cylinder M102 engine.

This was a good starting point. It was an 'oversquare' design, meaning the bore was larger than the stroke, and would be more willing to rev than a long-stroke engine. The tough iron-block design seemed capable of taking much more power, which is exactly what Cosworth provided. They created a new 16-valve twin-cam cylinder head and, in competition tune, found the engine's peak output exceeded 300 bhp. Then Audi began rallying the new Quattro and by the autumn of 1982, when the 190 saloon was launched, it was obvious there was no point developing a new rally car without four-wheel drive.

Rather than scrap the project, Mercedes went racing instead. The rules of the German Touring Car Championship (*Deutsche Tourenwagen Meisterschaft* or DTM) meant the Cosworth-headed engine had to go into a production car. In 1983, a year after the 190's launch, Mercedes introduced the 190E 2.3-16, a 2.3-litre engine with 16 valves. It made 183 bhp in road-going trim and was geared rather high for an impressive top speed of 143 mph, but it still managed to dash from rest to 60 mph in a fraction under eight seconds. This being Mercedes-Benz, the body kit it wore was not merely decorative – it reduced both lift and drag.

Inside, it was at the luxury end of the performance saloon market. Many buyers chose an automatic gearbox, revealing that these cars were often bought by those who liked a racy image and a surge of power to overtake, but spent most of their time behind the wheel commuting in city traffic. In manual form, though, it was a highly satisfying driver's car, with neutral handling, a flexible, willing engine and excellent brakes. There was impressive technology to help it work this well: a hydraulic pump powered both self-levelling rear suspension and an optional automatic locking rear differential that kicked in if one rear wheel began to spin.

On-track, it began a classic era of head-to-head contests with the BMW M3; to keep pace the engine size rose to 2.5-litres before successive Evo 1 and Evo 2 versions brought power increases up to 235 bhp and more outrageous body kits. With the exception of the rather extreme Evo 2, all versions remain surprisingly civilised, quiet and smooth-riding executive saloons … until you put your foot down. The 190E Cosworths are more practical and affordable than the E30 M3 and, in their own understated way, they are just as impressive to drive.

| 1985 Mercedes-Benz 190E 2.3-16 ||
|---|---|
| Length | 4,430 mm |
| Width | 1,707 mm |
| Weight | 1,341 kg |
| Wheelbase | 2,664 mm |
| Suspension | Independent via struts and lower wishbones with separate coil springs (front); multiple links, coil springs and self-levelling ram (rear) |
| Brakes | Hydraulic discs (front and rear), servo-assisted |
| Engine | 2,299 cc in-line 4, DOHC, fuel-injected |
| Power | 185 bhp @ 6,200 rpm |
| Torque | 173 lb-ft @ 4,500 rpm |
| Transmission | Five-speed manual, rear-wheel drive |
| 0–60 mph | 7.8 sec. |
| Top speed | 143 mph |
| Cost new | £21,045 |
| Value today | £10,000–£30,000 (Evo much more) |

TOP: A 190E 2.3-16 in Smoke Silver, photographed at the Nürburgring when new.

BOTTOM: Klaus Ludwig drives a 190E Cosworth in a DTM race at the Nürburgring in 1993.

# Ford Sierra RS Cosworth

The Sierra Cosworth has become a symbol of the turbo era: that huge rear wing, the immense performance, the tuning potential that pushed power higher and higher. Even by the standards of the day, when many manufacturers built high-speed specials with body kits and souped-up engines, it looked extreme. This, it said, is how far Ford is prepared to go to win. So that word 'homologation' appears yet again: 5,000 had to be built before Ford could take it racing, plus a further 500 of any evolved version. At least Ford, with its immense production capabilities, wouldn't have a problem coping with that. But what, exactly, were they going to build?

The Sierra Cosworth's origin story centres on Stuart Turner. Ford's director of motorsport may well have had a plan before he took Ford's chairman, Walter Hayes, and their American bosses to the British Grand Prix in 1983. The main support race was a round of the British Touring Car Championship, in which the Rover Vitesse took all three podium places, and the best-placed Ford was a 3-litre Capri in ninth. BMW, Toyota and General Motors all finished in front of Ford, and Stuart Turner faced some uncomfortable questions, to which he could only say that there wasn't a Ford road car that was fast enough to beat the V8 Rover, the 635 CSi, Supra or Opel Monza.

Shortly afterwards, Turner took the same group to visit Cosworth Engineering in Northampton, where he knew he could show them an exciting twin-cam version of the Ford Pinto engine. On to a pub lunch, and out came the suggestion of turbocharging that engine, fitting it to a Sierra and winning some touring car races. It got the nod, and after exploring various alternatives a prototype was created in time for the Geneva Motor Show in March 1985. That body kit, and particularly the whale-tail wing at the back, were products of wind-tunnel testing and really did provide downforce for stability at three-figure speeds – new territory for a road car.

The Cosworth YB engine made an impressive 204 bhp from 1,993 cc but used a turbo much larger than was ideal for street use, so the race teams could extract up to 350 bhp. This made for considerable turbo lag (and major thrills!) on the road. The Sierra was given a better suspension set-up by Speciality Vehicle Engineering, the spiritual successor to Ford's old AVO factory, and the plushest interior of any Sierra, with special Recaro sport seats.

Once the Cosworth was homologated in August 1987, on-track success was instant. The World Touring Car Championship came first, then European, Australian and German titles. In 1990 the evolved RS500 version (even bigger turbo, more power and a stronger cylinder block) won the British Touring Car Championship. On the street, nothing else looked like it or went like it – as the car thieves and joyriders soon discovered. Those examples that avoided being stolen, thrashed and crashed have now become very valuable.

| 1986 Ford Sierra RS Cosworth | |
|---|---|
| Length | 4,493 mm |
| Width | 1,697 mm |
| Weight | 1,217 kg |
| Wheelbase | 2,446 mm |
| Suspension | Independent via MacPherson struts with anti-roll bar (front); independent via semi-trailing arms, coil springs, telescopic dampers, anti-roll bar (rear) |
| Brakes | Hydraulic discs (front and rear), servo-assisted |
| Engine | 1993 cc in-line 4, DOHC, fuel-injected and turbocharged |
| Power | 204 bhp @ 6,000 rpm |
| Torque | 203 lb-ft @ 4,500 rpm |
| Transmission | Five-speed manual, rear-wheel drive |
| 0–60 mph | 6.2 sec. |
| Top speed | 145 mph |
| Cost new | £15,950 |
| Value today | £25,000–£80,000 (RS500 more) |

TOP: The all-important badge.

BOTTOM: Extra air intakes, large rear spoiler – this car means business.

205

# Bentley Turbo R

As a marque, Bentley came close to dying out in the 1970s. Rolls-Royce had owned Bentley since 1931 and after 1946 had built Bentleys that shared a great deal with Rolls-Royce models. By the mid-1960s this had become what was disparagingly known as 'badge engineering'; in other words, you engineered a new Bentley by changing the badge on a Rolls-Royce. Fewer and fewer customers saw the point. Bentley's appeal had been as a more sporting alternative to the all-out luxury of Rolls-Royce, so when the performance and handling were identical and the only difference was the shape of the radiator grille, why bother? By the early 1980s, just one in twenty of the cars Rolls-Royce built at Crewe was a Bentley.

Back in 1973, chief executive David Plastow saw the folly in maintaining two brand names where only one was wanted, but rather than delete the Bentley name he wanted 'something in the locker'. In other words, he wanted a project that might one day revitalise the marque. He chose turbocharging, and tuning company Broadspeed was given the job of fitting a turbo to an old Silver Shadow. The results were dramatic – crude but brutally quick – and the installation was developed further in Crewe's engineering department. They refined it until the boost arrived much lower in the rev range and the under-bonnet area maintained a tolerable temperature in all conditions. Then it was put on the back burner until a new model arrived.

This was the SZ generation of 1980: the Rolls-Royce Silver Spirit and Bentley Mulsanne. The intention had always been to launch the turbocharged version as a Bentley, which was timed for 1982 and caused a huge sensation. There was one large Garrett turbocharger driven by the exhaust of one bank of the V8 engine, feeding a Solex carburettor sealed in a cast-aluminium chamber. It gave nearly 300 bhp, 135 mph and an unlikely 0–60 mph lunge in seven seconds flat. Find a corner, though, and trouble started.

The Mulsanne Turbo's suspension was still limousine soft, so Rolls-Royce quickly introduced an optional handling pack but cured the problem properly with the Turbo R ('R' for roadholding) in 1985. It had almost twice as much roll stiffness, better damping, better location for the rear subframe and wide, low-profile Pirelli P7s. It was a smash hit by Crewe standards and in the five years from 1981 to 1986, Bentleys had risen from 5 per cent of the factory's output to 40 per cent.

The Turbo R developed steadily, with fuel injection providing better power delivery and much improved hot starting and reliability. Adaptive suspension gave limo-like comfort when cruising and a much-stiffened response in fast bends. Longer wheelbase models (Turbo RL) gave an even more opulent option as power climbed through the 1990s, but all Turbo Rs share the same unique feel: huge power and torque from low revs, a sense of disbelief than anything so large can shift so quickly, and a wish for the journey to last longer. The finest British bruiser ever made.

| 1987 Bentley Turbo R | |
|---|---|
| Length | 5,268 mm |
| Width | 1,887 mm |
| Weight | 2,252 kg |
| Wheelbase | 3,061 mm |
| Suspension | Independent via double wishbones, coil springs, telescopic dampers, anti-roll bar (front); independent via semi-trailing arms, coil springs, telescopic dampers, self-levelling rams, anti-roll bar (rear) |
| Brakes | Hydraulic discs (front and rear), high-pressure pump-assisted |
| Engine | 6,750 cc V8, overhead valve, one Solex carburettor, turbocharged |
| Power | 328 bhp @ 4,500 rpm |
| Torque | 203 lb-ft @ 4,500 rpm |
| Transmission | Three-speed manual, rear-wheel drive |
| 0–60 mph | 7.0 sec. |
| Top speed | 146 mph |
| Cost new | £58,613 |
| Value today | £7,000–£70,000 |

TOP: Very little chrome – the body-colour grille surround tells you this is a Turbo R.

BOTTOM: By 1995, the Turbo R's massive V8 engine was concealed beneath tasteful covers.

# Lancia

At the time of writing, Lancia has almost disappeared – but not quite. From 2015, only one model was offered, and that was a hatchback based on the Fiat 500 and available only in Italy. In 2021 the parent company, Fiat Chrysler Automobiles, was merged with the French PSA group (Peugeot and Citroën) and it looked as though the old Lancia name would be allowed to die off. Instead, the new parent company, Stellantis, made Lancia part of a group with Alfa Romeo and DS automobiles, the upscale Citroën brand. Why bother saving an old marque that made nothing but one home-market runabout?

The answer is in Lancia's heritage. It's an ancient firm, founded in 1906, with an extraordinary history of innovation, and after Fiat's takeover in 1969 Lancia had come to dominate world rallying. It's just too important to be allowed to fade away.

Vincenzo Lancia was a racing driver for Fiat right at the birth of motorsport, manhandling ever larger and faster machines on famous races like the Gordon Bennett Cup and the Targa Florio, until in 1908 he concentrated on building his own cars. He was an early adopter of various technologies, offering a car with a rear transaxle – a gearbox mounted at the back – in 1911, electric lighting in 1913 and the first standardised full electric system on a European car the following year. But it was in the 1920s that Lancia gained a worldwide reputation, with the revolutionary Lambda of 1922. Not only did it do away with a conventional chassis by using a punt-type floorpan, it offered independent front suspension on sliding, coil-sprung pillars with an internal damper. The engine was a V4, but with the v-angle so narrow that both banks were covered by the same cylinder head and operated by the same overhead camshaft.

Lancia used that front suspension until 1963, alongside numerous other innovations: a five-speed gearbox on the little Ardea saloon in 1948; the first production V6 engine for the Aurelia in 1950, which also re-introduced the front engine/rear transaxle idea, later taken up by Alfa Romeo and others; and a water-cooled flat-four engine mounted in front of the gearbox driving the front wheels appeared on the Flavia of 1961. When the same format appeared on the Alfa Romeo Alfasud a decade later, you didn't need to look far for the inspiration.

But innovation costs money, costs put prices up, and higher prices harmed sales to the point where Fiat bought out Lancia. Positioned as an upmarket alternative to Fiat, Lancia's image was given a huge boost by the rally success of the Fulvia, the Stratos, the 037, the Delta S4 and especially the Delta Integrale, making it the most successful marque in World Rally Championship history. In the UK, though, one unhappy scandal involving Lancia Betas with rusty subframes damaged the marque's reputation and it never recovered, eventually being withdrawn from all right-hand-drive markets in 1994. It has faded still further since then, so it's reassuring to know the Lancia story isn't over yet.

# THROUGH THE YEARS

**CLOCKWISE FROM TOP LEFT:** A Lambda 221 Spider Casaro; Ardea; Aurelia B24; Beta Montecarlo; Fuliva Coupé.

# BMW M3

If the Peugeot 205 is reckoned to be the best-handling hot hatch of the first generation, the BMW M3 of 1986 has the same reputation amongst the rear-wheel-drive super saloons of the era. The rivalry between the M3 and the Mercedes 190E 2.3-16 was the reason interest in the German Touring Car Championship (the *Deutsche Tourenwagen Meisterschaft* or DTM) peaked in the late 1980s and early 1990s. But it's the M3's legend as a road car that has grown ever since.

To distinguish it from the many later M3 models, it's often referred to as the E30 M3, with E30 referring to the shape of 3-series BMWs made between 1982 and 1994. The fact that so many more M3s came later is down to the success, both on-track and off, of this first one. The recipe of bulging wheel arches, spoilers and a hotter engine looked simple enough, but every panel was new bar the roof and bonnet, while changes to suspension and steering perfected the set-up.

The S14 four-cylinder unit was the car's fiery heart. It had no turbocharger but used a twin-cam 16-valve cylinder head for higher revs – the redline was 7,250 rpm. At launch it made 197 bhp, which increased when new Evo and Sport Evo versions arrived to keep the M3 competitive. There were special editions named after the successful racing drivers who helped make the car famous – Johnny Cecotto and Roberto Ravaglia. Indeed, it was the most successful car in the history of the DTM, with many victories in Group A Touring Car competitions elsewhere too.

Surprisingly, for such a motorsport-focused model, the M3 was also available as a convertible. It was clear that demand for the M3 was high, so offering an open-air version was good business. Though homologation required only 5,000 M3s to be built, BMW sold almost 18,000 by the time production ceased in 1992. None of those left the factory in right-hand drive and perhaps this has added to the E30 M3's mystique in the UK. It was certainly a purist's choice when compared with slightly more practical rivals from Ford or Mercedes-Benz.

This car found its place a clear step above the hot hatches, with status and performance no hatchback GTi could achieve. The M3 was for a more affluent, more informed buyer, who might choose one over a Porsche. Sometimes the car's awesome reputation can tint reality – that dog-leg manual gearbox is the same one used in the 190E 2.3-16, where it's sometimes criticised for its shift quality: not a complaint you hear about the M3. Yet the BMW still has a rare ability to enthral the driver. Find any magazine poll on 'greatest drivers' cars' and the E30 M3 is near the top.

Strapping into that highly bolstered bucket seat behind the businesslike dash doesn't give much of a clue to the delight that awaits. But warm it up, work the engine hard, then revel in the perfect chassis balance and quick steering to make any twisty road a joy. Not supercar fast, no, but rapid and tremendously satisfying.

| 1986 BMW M3 | |
|---|---|
| Length | 4,345 mm |
| Width | 1,680 mm |
| Weight | 1,255 kg |
| Wheelbase | 2,562 mm |
| Suspension | Independent via MacPherson struts (front); semi-trailing arms (rear) |
| Brakes | Power-assisted discs (front and rear) |
| Engine | 2,302 cc DOHC in-line four, fuel-injected |
| Power | 197 bhp @ 6,750 rpm |
| Torque | 170 lb-ft @ 4,750 rpm |
| Transmission | Five-speed manual |
| 0–60 mph | 6.3 sec. |
| Top speed | 144 mph |
| Cost new | £22,750 |
| Value today | £45,000–£75,000 (Sport Evo twice that) |

**TOP:** Bulging aerodynamic bodywork meant only the roof and bonnet were shared with the standard E30 model.

**BOTTOM:** The M3 Cabriolet was a small bonus for BMW, adding 783 sales to the E30 M3's total.

# Ferrari F40

There have been so many great sports cars, GTs and supercars from Maranello that it's tricky to pick between them. In the case of the F40, the classic Ferrari market has probably done that all by itself, as values have gone up since the early 2010s from less than £500,000 to £2 million and more. Yet these are not particularly rare cars. They look strikingly aggressive with that ground-hugging shape and huge rear wing, but there were 1,311 F40s built between 1987 and 1992. More, in fact, than the production run of the Daytona, which is now worth about a fifth of the price of an F40. So the surge in popularity of this unmistakable Ferrari must be attributed to something else.

It is, of course, down to the intoxicating blend of features the F40 offers. It's 'only' a V8 rather than the V12 you find in most other truly great Ferraris, but two turbochargers give it a staggering rush of performance. The spartan cockpit and racing-car-like suspension and steering were arranged for one purpose only – to give the finest, most focused experience to a keen driver on a fast road or, better yet, on a track day. Then there's its looks. It was shaped by Piero Camardella at Pininfarina but engineered by Ferrari's Nicola Materazzi, who was a key figure in the creation of the car that led directly to the F40: the Ferrari 288 GTO.

This was the second car to use those famous three initials, and the 'O' – *Omologato* – referred to Group B: not the fearsome high-powered rally class but the racetrack equivalent. The options were a 4-litre naturally aspirated engine or a 2.8-litre turbo. Ferrari opted for the latter and used the 308 GTB as a base, before modifying it radically. The 288 ended up almost all-new, with the V8 engine rotated from a transverse to an in-line arrangement. Group B was cancelled in 1986 while Ferrari was developing an *Evoluzione* version of the 288 with boxed-out front arches and a low, flat nose, clearly a precursor to the F40.

Even then, Materazzi was only allowed to continue the development and launch of the F40 in 1987 because 89-year-old Enzo Ferrari knew it could be his last car and wanted to leave behind something special. In this he succeeded: the F40 was rumoured to lap Ferrari's test track faster than their own Formula One car of nine years before. Its stated power output of 472 bhp was really more like 500-plus, and its complete lack of modern driver aids meant wheelspin could be induced even when you were already doing 120 mph. Speculators jumped at the chance to buy them, forcing their value up to many multiples of the list price before the bubble burst in 1989. Ever since then, with periodical road tests on TV and in magazines to reinforce the legend, it's been building fame and fortune like its own twin-turbo boost.

| 1988 Ferrari F40 ||
|---|---|
| Length | 4,430 mm |
| Width | 1,981 mm |
| Weight | 1,101 kg |
| Wheelbase | 2,649 mm |
| Suspension | Independent via double wishbones, coil springs and telescopic dampers (front and rear) |
| Brakes | Discs, front and rear |
| Engine | 2,936 cc V8, DOHC per bank, two IHI turbochargers, fuel injection |
| Power | 478 bhp @ 7,000 rpm (as listed) |
| Torque | 425 lb-ft @ 4,000 rpm |
| Transmission | Five-speed manual |
| 0–60 mph | 4.5 sec. |
| Top speed | 199 mph |
| Cost new | £163,000 |
| Value today | £1.5 million–£2.5 million |

TOP: No leather, no radio, not even a carpet – a pure driving machine.

BOTTOM: The F40's combination of swooping lines and sharp angles on display.

# Porsche 959

What started as an attempt to extend the life of the old Porsche 911 turned into a technical tour-de-force that redefined what supercars could be. Before the 959, going fast was just about more and more power, but Porsche added serious engineering innovation. It wasn't just the quickest car you could buy in 1986, it was the cleverest, by a mile.

The project had its roots in the early 1980s when Porsche, like everyone else who'd seen the Audi Quattro's launch, began considering four-wheel drive for their own models. They had a 4WD 911 Turbo Cabriolet at the 1981 Frankfurt Motor Show, but it wasn't intended for production. Instead, they chose a motorsport route to develop their all-wheel drive approach. The remarkably permissive rules of Group B were exciting interest from lots of manufacturers and depending on which source you trust, Porsche set the 959 program in motion to tackle Group B rally events or Group B race events – perhaps both.

Porsche's boss at the time, Peter Schutz, put his backing into the project. His belief was key to the creation of the 959, as he didn't want to create just another homologation special with a big turbo and a body kit – he wanted the ultimate expression of what the 911 could be, using the new car as a test-bed for all kinds of sophisticated systems. This is exactly what it became, leaving the 911 basis so far behind that only the door and window apertures remained the same. The body was panelled in a bulging, flowing form made of aluminium and Aramid, a Kevlar derivative. It was aerodynamically tested to produce zero lift and a drag factor of just 0.31. The floorpan was new, in order to fit the computer-controlled four-wheel drive system, new suspension and an engine that had also taken a leap on from anything fitted to a 911.

It was still a rear-mounted flat six, but this one had water-cooled cylinder heads (though still air-cooled cylinders) and twin turbochargers working in sequence. The first turbo starts operating at 1,200rpm, then the second kicks in under hard driving at 4,000rpm, providing additional boost right up to the 8000rpm redline. The engine was based on those used in the 956 and 962 endurance racers and produced 450bhp from just 2.8-litres.

Drivers of modern performance cars are used to having different modes to choose from, and all that started here. The 959 gave you three ride-height settings and four transmission modes, though these varied between the 'Sport' and 'Confort' models, with the former able to give a greater torque split to the rear wheels. The factory's 959 team finished first, second and sixth on the 1986 Paris-Dakar Rally, while a racing 959 took a class win at Le Mans the same year. The premature end of Group B meant the 959 retired young, but it made its greatest impact as a road car. For once, those crazy performance figures claimed by supercar makers were being backed up in road tests. Here was a new high-water mark, both in ambition and accomplishment, that left the rest struggling to catch up.

| 1986 Porsche 959 | |
|---|---|
| Length | 4,260 mm |
| Width | 1,840 mm |
| Weight | 1,450 kg |
| Wheelbase | 2,272 mm |
| Suspension | Independent via double wishbones, coil springs and electronic damper units (front and rear) |
| Brakes | Discs, front and rear, servo-assisted ABS |
| Engine | 2,849 cc flat six, DOHC, twin-turbocharged, intercooled and fuel injected |
| Power | 450 bhp @ 6,500 rpm |
| Torque | 369 lb-ft @ 5,500 rpm |
| Transmission | Six-speed manual |
| 0–60 mph | 3.7 sec. |
| Top speed | 197 mph |
| Cost new | £129,000 |
| Value today | £800,000–£1.2m |

TOP: Comfortable, safe, easy to drive – and the fastest road car in the world, when new.

BOTTOM: The huge wrap-around rear spoiler is the 959's signature styling feature.

# Lancia Delta Integrale

Lancia had already won the World Rally Championship four times before the creation of the Delta Integrale, but in between those victories several other marques put their names on the trophy too. Once the four-wheel-drive turbocharged Delta was ready, nobody else got a look in. Lancia won the World Rally Championship manufacturer's title *six* years in a row, from 1987 to 1992, and in four of those years they also won the driver's title. This was better than anything achieved by the Audi Quattro, the later Subaru Impreza, the Mitsubishi Lancer Evo, or indeed any other single model.

That extraordinary record on its own would be enough to guarantee classic status, but the road-going version of this most dominant competition car was a great sporting machine in its own right. It was a mix of several tempting ingredients: four-wheel drive for unshakeable roadholding in any conditions; a highly turbocharged engine to take advantage of all that traction; and a thrilling beefed-up look. Even the cabin seemed exciting, with lurid yellow numbers on black dials and hip-grabbing sports seats. It felt a long way from its planned niche as the Fiat empire's upmarket shopping car.

Fiat had absorbed Lancia in 1969, which to purists was the end of the engineering-led era of classic Lancia models. But Fiat brought investment, so first there was the Beta range of mid-sized saloons, coupés and other models, and then the Delta arrived in 1979 as an overdue replacement for the smaller Fulvia saloon. It used MacPherson strut suspension from the Beta and small overhead-cam engines from the Fiat Strada hatchback, all wrapped in a neat five-door body created by Italdesign Giugiaro and understandably similar to the Mk 1 Golf styled by the same firm.

A nippy hot-hatch version, the Delta HF, came in 1983, then an HF Turbo. In 1986, a new range-topping Delta was unveiled at the Turin Motor Show: the Delta HF four-wheel drive. The all-wheel-drive system was a clever variation on earlier approaches by Audi and others, in that it used three differentials (one central and one in each of the front and rear axles) but featured a novel way of splitting the drive between the front and rear using an epicyclic gear at the back of the gearbox. The engine was a 2-litre twin-cam with balance shafts and a Garrett turbo, fed by an intercooler to make the air-fuel mixture denser, hence increasing power.

This car became the Integrale with a few changes to the suspension, final drive ratio (lower, for even better acceleration) and the bodywork in particular, which flared out to allow wider wheels and tyres. To keep the rally versions on top, Lancia kept improving the breed, launching a 16v version in 1989, an *Evoluzione* version in 1991, and in June 1993 the Evo II in various special editions in extrovert colours. They share the Integrale trademarks: exhilarating acceleration, claw-like grip and a firm ride with instant steering response that can feel like a skateboard compared to the more civilised Audi Quattro. It brings Italian flair to four-wheel-drive performance, and it's an addictive mix.

| 1989 Lancia Delta HF Integrale ||
|---|---|
| Length | 3,900 mm |
| Width | 1,700 mm |
| Weight | 1,267 kg |
| Wheelbase | 2,480 mm |
| Suspension | Independent via MacPherson/Chapman struts, lower links and anti-roll bars (front and rear) |
| Brakes | Discs, front and rear, servo-assisted |
| Engine | 1,995 cc in-line four, DOHC, turbo-charged, intercooled, fuel-injected |
| Power | 185 bhp @ 5,300 rpm |
| Torque | 223 lb-ft @ 3,500 rpm |
| Transmission | Five-speed manual |
| 0–60 mph | 6.4 sec. |
| Top speed | 130 mph |
| Cost new | £15,455 |
| Value today | £25,000–£50,000 (Evo II can exceed £100,000) |

TOP: At the RAC Rally in 1988.

BOTTOM: An Evo I Delta Integrale.

# Nissan Skyline R32

It probably never occurred to the people buying 1980s European performance cars such as the BMW M3, Audi Quattro, Ford Sierra Cosworth, Mercedes 190E 2.3-16 and the Lancia Delta Integrale that a Japanese firm was about to build something that would make them look old fashioned ... and rather slow. Still less that it was Nissan: the same firm that had built those rusty little Datsuns of the 1970s and 1980s.

There had been clues. The hugely successful 240Z and its successors showed that Nissan could build great sporting cars, but in Europe you had to be a serious student of the Japanese motor industry to know about the Skyline family, and especially the GT-R sports variant. The first of these arrived in 1969 as a saloon but soon launched as a coupé, using an impressive 2-litre straight-six engine with 160 bhp, and two overhead camshafts like a Jaguar, Lotus or Alfa Romeo. The GT-R badge dropped away for a couple of generations as the Skyline changed shape every few years, though Skylines found success in Australian touring car racing after the introduction of a turbocharged engine in 1983.

It was the boxy-looking R31 Skyline of 1985 that showed the way things were going. Here was the new RB engine, another twin-cam straight-six but with four valves per cylinder and sophisticated fuel injection, engine management and intake controls. That wasn't all – four-wheel steering was introduced to increase agility and cornering stability. The hottest GTS-R version offered 207 bhp from a turbocharged 2-litre RB engine. Then, in 1989, out came Godzilla.

Godzilla was the nickname given to the new Skyline GT-R by an Australian motoring magazine. The car was created to defeat all-comers in Group A touring car competitions, which had some specific rules: in the class that their turbocharged car would find itself, a tyre could be no more than 250 mm wide. In that case, thought Nissan's engineers, let's make it four-wheel drive. They achieved this by adapting their existing ATTESA system (Advanced Total Traction Engineering System for All-Terrain), with its central viscous limited-slip differential and transfer case, and developing a computer-controlled torque splitting mechanism that allowed anything from 100 per cent of the engine's output to reach the rear wheels, to a perfect 50:50 split from front to rear. To most drivers, it would feel as 'chuckable' as a rear-wheel-drive car until the extra traction was required.

Meanwhile, a larger version of the RB engine was designed to allow a 2.6-litre capacity with potential for extensive further tuning and the road-going car was launched with 276 bhp. This wasn't an earth-shaking figure in a car weighing nearly a ton and a half, but no car had ever been so good at putting the power to the road. In 1989, a Skyline GT-R lapped the Nürburgring Nordschleife in 8 minutes and 22.38 seconds, a record for any production car ... and in damp conditions too. Since then, they've only got faster with each successive generation and through the efforts of a tuning scene that worships the Skyline GT-R like a mechanical deity. Figures of 300, 400, 500 and even 600 bhp have been extracted from the R32, so the legend about Godzilla breathing fire must be true!

| 1990 Nissan Skyline GT-R (R32) | |
|---|---|
| Length | 4,547 mm |
| Width | 1,755 mm |
| Weight | 1,430 kg |
| Wheelbase | 2,616 mm |
| Suspension | Independent via struts, multiple links and anti-roll bars (front and rear) |
| Brakes | Discs, front and rear, servo-assisted |
| Engine | 2,568 cc in-line six, DOHC, turbocharged, intercooled, fuel-injected |
| Power | 276 bhp @ 6,800 rpm |
| Torque | 260 lb-ft @ 4,400 rpm |
| Transmission | Five-speed manual |
| 0–60 mph | 5.6 sec. |
| Top speed | 156 mph |
| Cost new | n/a |
| Value today | £20,000–£60,000 |

## 'You don't have to like it. You just have to stay the hell out of its way.'

*Automobile* magazine, 1990

In its original form the Skyline gives little away – but underneath the unassuming bodywork is a speed machine.

# Alfa Romeo SZ

The SZ, or Sport Zagato, is surely the boldest piece of car styling to reach production in the 1980s. It's as though a piece of brutalist architecture has been uprooted, turned on its side and given wheels. No wonder the Italians nicknamed it *Il Mostro* – the monster. It's the kind of thing that would have been laughed off as an indulgent novelty if it were just a show car, but it wasn't. Alfa Romeo put it into production in 1989 and eventually sold 1,036, and then another 278 of the even more monolithic RZ convertible version.

Zagato, the famous Italian styling house and coachbuilder, created some of the most curvaceous and beautiful cars of the post-war years, like the Aston Martin DB4 GT Zagato and Alfa Romeo's racing TZ and TZ2, before the design language performed a handbrake turn. Suddenly, Zagato's products were all about straight lines and angles, flat surfaces and challenging proportions. This geometric phase, as Zagato called it, resulted in the excitingly angular Alfa Romeo Junior Z and the slab-like Bristol 412. All of which seem in retrospect to point to its ultimate style statement – the SZ – but although Zagato built the SZ, it was not responsible for the design.

The man given credit for originating the shape was French stylist Robert Opron, which seems remarkable when you know that he was responsible for the slippery-smooth Citroën SM. By the mid-1980s Opron was working for Fiat, which had absorbed Alfa Romeo in 1986. The SZ project came from a wish to revive some of Alfa's sporting prestige, so Fiat invited design proposals from its own Centro Stile, Alfa Romeo's styling team and Zagato. With some irony – bearing in mind the car would be an Alfa Romeo, built and badged by Zagato – it was the proposal from Fiat that succeeded. Antonio Castellana developed Opron's initial sketches and created the car's final look.

The chosen basis was the Alfa Romeo 75, which used a transaxle gearbox between the rear wheels, stabilised by a de Dion rear axle and driven by a V6 engine up front. The SZ was equipped with a tuned version of the 3.0-litre 'Busso' V6, with a power boost of around 25 bhp over the 75. Alfa fans, or *Alfisti*, will tell you it's one of the best-sounding engines ever made, and it certainly adds to the drama in a car that already overdelivers on that score.

The SZ would have remained a historical quirk if it hadn't been so good to drive. Despite the composite panels over a steel frame, the SZ was marginally heavier than the 75 saloon, but it was also impressively stiff and benefited from the suspension set-up of the Alfa 75 Group A racing car. The delightful handling balance combined with the histrionic howls from the V6 made it seem faster and more satisfying than it should have been on paper. As for the opposition, well … if you had the self-confidence to own an SZ, everything short of a Lamborghini seemed dull. Now revered as an unrepeatable moment of excess, the SZ's values have climbed alongside its reputation as a driver's car.

TOP: An SZ coupé, challenging everything we thought we knew about Italian car design.

BOTTOM: An RZ convertible.

| 1989 Alfa Romeo SZ | |
|---|---|
| Length | 4,059 mm |
| Width | 1,730 mm |
| Weight | 1,256 kg |
| Wheelbase | 2,510 mm |
| Suspension | Independent via upper and lower wishbones and anti-roll bar (front); De Dion axle, Watt's linkage, coil springs and telescopic dampers (rear) |
| Brakes | Discs, front and rear, servo-assisted |
| Engine | 2,959 cc V6, OHC, fuel-injected |
| Power | 207 bhp @ 6,200 rpm |
| Torque | 245 lb-ft @ 4,500 rpm |
| Transmission | Five-speed manual |
| 0–60 mph | 7.0 sec. |
| Top speed | 152 mph |
| Cost new | £40,000 |
| Value today | £40,000–£80,000 |

# TO A NEW CENTURY
## THE 1990s AND BEYOND

# Vauxhall-Lotus Carlton

Not many cars can claim to have caused headlines in the newspapers, but such was the reaction to the Lotus Carlton's performance figures in 1990. *Autocar* ran an uncharacteristically up-in-arms piece on the car's huge top speed of 176 mph and this was picked up by the rest of the press. The *Daily Mail* campaigned to have the car banned and the Association of Chief Police Officers branded it 'an outrageous invitation to speed'.

Never mind that quite a few Italian and German supercars already surpassed this figure – this was a four-door saloon with a Vauxhall badge, which seemed to be enough to cause an uproar. Lotus, led by Mike Kimberley, could only wait for the fuss to die down. Which it did, as some of the same magazines that had been frowning at the car's outrageous numbers took advantage of the press fleet to record road tests of their own. Of course they loved it, and a new hero car was born.

Kimberley suggested the car in 1986 after General Motors took control of Lotus, to give Lotus Engineering an exciting new project and Opel and Vauxhall something to shout about. In other words, a traditional halo model to shed some glory over its less costly siblings. It was partly a GM/Vauxhall 'bitsa': it borrowed the differential from a Holden Commodore; the self-levelling pump and bellows rear dampers from a top-line German Omega saloon; the six-speed manual gearbox from a Corvette ZR1; the power steering from the Senator; and sundry other parts, as suited. There was also a great deal of Lotus-Carlton-specific engineering too, particularly in the engine and suspension.

Lotus expanded the capacity to 3.6-litres, insisting not just on a larger bore or longer stroke, but on a whole new engine-block casting, capable of producing the extra power without flexing. The crankshaft had to be milled from a piece of steel billet, while Mahle made new pistons to Lotus's specifications, suitable for use with the twin-turbocharged and intercooled induction set-up. This, together with carefully programmed fuel injection and ignition management, produced a peak power figure that surpassed the BMW M5 by more than 60 bhp and even out-did most of the supercars on the market.

Production was less than slick. Completed Opel Omegas (left-hand drive) and Vauxhall Carlton GSis (right-hand drive) were shipped from the factory at Russelsheim in Germany and then stripped: their wheel arches chopped out with a plasma cutter and wider ones welded in; the new engine and rear suspension fitted; and the seats re-covered, before every car received its coat of Imperial Green. The required 130 work hours added on to already completed cars contributed to a list price of £48,000. Combined with the notoriety create by the press, this asking price was no help as the recession of the early 1990s bit. The sales target of 1,100 was narrowly missed – 950 were built in all, mostly Lotus Omegas, including 286 right-hand-drive Lotus Carltons for the UK. An invitation to speed? Well, perhaps. It would be hard to resist if you saw a Ferrari 348 in front of you, trying its best to get away … and failing.

| 1990 Vauxhall-Lotus Carlton ||
|---|---|
| Length | 4,768 mm |
| Width | 1,933 mm |
| Weight | 1,663 kg |
| Wheelbase | 2,371 mm |
| Suspension | Independent via MacPherson struts, lower wishbone, anti-roll bar (front); independent via five-link design, coil springs, telescopic dampers (front and rear) |
| Brakes | Hydraulic discs, servo-assisted (front and rear) |
| Engine | 3,615 cc in-line six, DOHC, twin-turbocharged, intercooled, fuel-injected |
| Power | 377 bhp @ 5,200 rpm |
| Torque | 419 lb-ft @ 4,200 rpm |
| Transmission | Six-speed manual, rear-wheel drive |
| 0–60 mph | 5.2 sec. |
| Top speed | 176 mph |
| Cost new | £48,000 |
| Value today | £35,000–£80,000 |

**TOP:** A 1990 brochure shot of the Carlton.

**BOTTOM:** The engine bay with proud Lotus badging.

# Lamborghini Diablo

The Countach was a hard act to follow. But even the greats are not immortal and by the mid-1980s the need for a successor was clear. How do you approach such a task? Lamborghini bosses brought back the Countach's stylist, Marcello Gandini, to see if he could work his old magic. However, after his initial drawings were completed Lamborghini was taken over by Chrysler, who decided they didn't like what they saw. Chrysler's own stylists were given the task of shaping the new Lamborghini and Gandini, disgusted at this development, sold his design to fledgling supercar-maker Cizeta-Moroder. They produced a remarkably brave but unsuccessful car with a V16 engine. In retrospect it looks like a more outrageous Diablo, because Gandini was eventually invited back to finish the Lamborghini, after Chrysler didn't like their own stylists' ideas either. So *disegno Marcello Gandini* badges appeared on the new car.

The Diablo was essentially an improved Countach. Ferrari's Testarossa had shown that 180 mph, 12-cylinder, mid-engined supercars could also be pleasant to drive over long distances, so Lamborghini made successful efforts to enlarge the cabin and allow the driver to see out of the car properly. While the Countach was stunning to look at, the shape wasn't created with aerodynamics in mind. The Diablo was – with a drag coefficient of just 0.31, a startling top speed would be easier to reach. There was also one important technical innovation: the plan for the drivetrain.

Four-wheel drive was spreading throughout the car industry in the wake of the Audi Quattro's success and it reached the supercar market with the amazing Porsche 959 in 1986. What if the team at Sant'Agata could make a car that was as civilised as a Testarossa, as fast and capable in all conditions as the 959, and as dramatic as only a Lamborghini can be? They came up with a brilliantly packaged solution: turn the V12 round so the gearbox is pointing forward, sending the propshaft to the front axle. From the clutch housing, take a separate drive to a shaft that runs backwards, right alongside the sump to a differential for the rear axle, in a unit at the back of the engine. Boost the capacity to 5.7-litres, add computer-controlled fuel injection for easy starting and 485 bhp, and you had a genuine 200 mph road car.

But it was not four-wheel drive, or not at first. Development wasn't quite finished in time to replace the Countach in certain markets where it was no longer meeting standards, so for the first three years the Diablo was rear-wheel drive. The four-wheel-drive Diablo VT arrived in 1993, adding electronically adjustable dampers. The two-wheel-drive version survived in supertuned form as the Diablo SV, while roadster options arrived for both models. The last Diablos used a 6-litre engine and made 575 bhp. All of them are wild – despite the new-found traction and user-friendly cabin, a Diablo is a beast. Let it off the leash if you dare … and try not to get bitten.

**TOP:** This SV model proudly advertises its status.

**MIDDLE:** The VT model, with larger rear wing.

**BOTTOM:** Picking up where the Countach left off, the Diablo maintained Lamborghini's reputation for poster-worthy cars.

| 1990 Lamborghini Diablo | |
|---|---|
| Length | 4,460 mm |
| Width | 2,040 mm |
| Weight | 1,652 kg |
| Wheelbase | 2,649 mm |
| Suspension | Independent via double wishbones, anti-roll bar, coil springs and telescopic dampers (front); independent via double wishbones, upper anti-roll bar, twinned coil springs and telescopic dampers (rear) |
| Brakes | Hydraulic vented discs, servo-assisted (front and rear) |
| Engine | 5,707 cc V12, DOHC per bank, fuel-injected |
| Power | 485 bhp @ 7,000 rpm |
| Torque | 428 lb-ft @ 5,200 rpm |
| Transmission | Five-speed manual, rear-wheel drive |
| 0–60 mph | 4.5 sec. |
| Top speed | 202 mph |
| Cost new | £152,614 |
| Value today | £70,000–£175,000 |

# Honda NSX

After the Nissan Skyline GT-R, here was the second Japanese supercar. Rather than evolving over generations to homologate a dominant racing machine, the NSX came into being precisely because Honda did not have a road car that showed the public what they were achieving on track. They had found considerable success in Formula One as an engine builder for Williams and McLaren, yet the road car offerings were all front-wheel-drive hatchbacks and saloons. What to do?

Rather than try to detune a Formula One engine and build a record-setting hypercar, Honda took aim at Ferrari, Lotus and Porsche. The NSX would be as light as possible (no more than 5 kg per horsepower) but practical too. A spacious cabin and a decent boot, capable of taking a set of golf clubs, were thought to be key to sales in the USA.

Honda achieved this with extensive use of aluminium, not just for the panels but for the car's monocoque structure and suspension arms, and even for the scissor jack. Honda dodged some of the normal mid-engined packaging issues by opting for a 3-litre V6 (aluminium, of course) set across the car, not along it. The engine itself was a masterpiece – Honda's ingenious VTEC cylinder-head design allowed for valve timing to vary as revs rose, producing an almost turbo-like lunge as the rev counter passed 4,500 rpm on its way to an 8,000 rpm rev limit. It was engineered, like the rest of the car, to a standard all Honda owners would be familiar with. No highly strung behaviour here, or design flaws indulged as 'character' – it just worked.

That's not to say it wasn't exciting. Honda judged the handling balance very carefully, using Ayrton Senna (then a McLaren-Honda driver) for a few test sessions and fellow Formula One driver Satoru Nakajima for many more, eventually stiffening the chassis by more than 50 per cent on the original design. While road tests of the new model often mentioned how easy it was to drive, with a familiar Honda dashboard and controls, its delicately judged suspension was meant to provide a rewarding challenge to a skilled driver. Aiming for a neutral cornering poise meant that clumsy handling or a sudden lift in mid-bend could cause a rapid spin … but only at speeds that would be insane on a public road.

The praise flooded in soon after the first cars went on sale in 1990, at least for the manual version. The automatic, again thought a necessity for the American market, lost 20 bhp, lacked the limited-slip differential and used less-tactile power steering, while costing £3,000 more. With the manual version, and especially the lighter NSX-R of 1992, Ferrari, Porsche and Lotus all had something to worry about. It was only badge snobbery that kept annual sales modest, and the length of time that the NSX stayed in production is testament to its success: a match for the Ferrari 348 when new (and £16,000 cheaper), it was still in production 15 years later. In its day it was a great car and now it's an interesting modern classic.

TOP: The contrast in colour to the always-black roof and cabin was meant to suggest a fighter jet's cockpit.

BOTTOM: Black dashboard plastics were neat but less exciting than rival supercars.

| 1990 Honda NSX | |
|---|---|
| Length | 4,404 mm |
| Width | 1,811 mm |
| Weight | 1,340 kg |
| Wheelbase | 2,530 mm |
| Suspension | Independent via wishbones and upper links, coil-and-damper struts, anti-roll bar (front and rear) |
| Brakes | Hydraulic vented discs, servo-assisted (front and rear) |
| Engine | 2,977 cc V6, DOHC per bank, variable valve lift and timing, fuel-injected |
| Power | 270 bhp @ 7,100 rpm |
| Torque | 210 lb-ft @ 3,500 rpm |
| Transmission | Five-speed manual, rear-wheel drive |
| 0–60 mph | 5.8 sec. |
| Top speed | 162 mph |
| Cost new | £52,000 |
| Value today | £40,000–£80,000 (NSX-R and special editions much more) |

# Mitsubishi Lancer Evo

When Lancia's grip on the World Rally Championship finally slackened, three Japanese manufacturers were waiting to tear it away from them. Toyota was the first to succeed in the constructor's championship with the Celica Turbo four-wheel drive in 1993 and 1994, but it was the developing battle between Subaru and Mitsubishi that would capture fans' imaginations in the mid-1990s. Subaru did the double in 1995 and took the constructor's title the next two years, but Mitsubishi nabbed the driver's championship from 1996–99, bagging the constructor's prize in 1998 too.

It had taken Mitsubishi a while to find their feet. They phased in the new Lancer Evo in the 1993 season but only took two podium places. They were hardly any better the next season, with three podiums in ten rallies and still no wins, but the car was developing all the time. Each year brought a new Evo: Evo II in January 1994, Evo III in February 1995 and Evo IV in August 1996, each time a little better. The Evo III made the breakthrough on the rally stages, thanks in part to the masterful efforts of Tommi Mäkinen, who won five rallies and took the driver's title in 1996. Yet on the road, these cars were still largely unknown in Europe and the USA.

Mitsubishi could build and sell enough of them in Japan to satisfy the rules for participation in the World Rally Championship, but eventually unofficial 'grey imports' spread the word about the almost unbelievable performance and tenacity of these road-going rally cars. Mitsubishi began marketing them through its Ralliart dealers in the UK and Europe, beginning in 1998 with the Lancer Evo V. It soon developed a fanatical following and the Evo VI followed in 1999. Mitsubishi saw a fine marketing opportunity, launching a special Tommi Mäkinen edition – now the most sought-after of all.

Every generation of the Evo shared a basic plan: a transverse in-line four-cylinder engine, turbocharged and driving all four wheels via limited-slip differentials. From there, much evolution took place. The engine and transaxle of the Evo IV were rotated 180 degrees to improve balance and remove torque steer, aided by active yaw control, then the Evo V and VI brought improvements to engine durability and cooling, while the Evo VII had an active centre differential. Curiously, the official power rating never seemed to climb above 276 bhp, which reflected a gentleman's agreement between Japanese manufacturers, though this didn't apply in the UK. Special edition Evo VII and VIII models started appearing with 305, 320, 340 and eventually 405 bhp for the 2004 FQ-400 version. Blasting from 0–60 mph in 3.8 seconds, it was a supercar beater – at least up to 120 mph. But then a Ferrari wouldn't dare follow it though a forest rally stage …

Discontinued in 2015 with the end of the Evo X, all Evo models are already rising in value from the performance bargains they once were to investable classics. Which is a pity, as they're much more fun on a greasy British B-road than locked away in a collection.

| 1998 Mitsubishi Lancer Evo IV GSR ||
|---|---|
| Length | 4,330 mm |
| Width | 1,690 mm |
| Weight | 1,350 kg |
| Wheelbase | 2,510 mm |
| Suspension | Independent via lower wishbones and MacPherson struts, anti-roll bar (front); and via multiple links with coil-and-damper strut (rear) |
| Brakes | Hydraulic vented discs, servo-assisted (front and rear) |
| Engine | 1,997 cc in-line four, DOHC, turbocharged, fuel-injected |
| Power | 276 bhp @ 6,500 rpm |
| Torque | 260 lb-ft @ 3,000 rpm |
| Transmission | Five-speed manual, four-wheel drive |
| 0–60 mph | 5.1 sec. |
| Top speed | 147 mph |
| Cost new | c.£20,000 |
| Value today | £10,000–£40,000 (standard editions) |

**TOP:** The Evo IV edition of the Lancer.

**BOTTOM:** Tommi Mäkinen in rally action in 1998 – here without one of his wheels.

# Subaru Impreza WRX STi

It's rare for one car to be so closely associated with another, because genuinely competitive pairings are rare in motorsport, never mind in the kind of motorsport that has direct equivalents on the road. Yet that was the case in the second half of the 1990s, when Subaru and Mitsubishi duked it out, as detailed with the Lancer Evo on p. 230. It was a rivalry felt keenly in the UK because two of the star drivers were British – Colin McRae of Scotland and Richard Burns of England. Burns drove for both teams: Mitsubishi from 1996 to 1998, then Subaru from 1999 to 2001, winning the World Rally Championship in the final year. McRae had been with Subaru from 1993 to 1998 and in 1995 he was the first Briton to win the World Rally Championship, in his Impreza.

Subaru had a longer history of all-wheel-drive cars than Mitsubishi, longer than almost any manufacturer. They had established a layout in the 1970s that would stay with the Impreza throughout its production life. The engine was a flat-four, mounted in front of the gearbox, which in the front-wheel-drive 'shopping' versions of the Impreza sent drive straight out to the front wheels. In all the four-wheel-drive variants, up to the WRX and STi models, there was a propshaft to the rear axle as well. This driveline kept the centre of gravity low and helped give this modest, mid-market saloon or short-decked station wagon a limpet-like grip.

The WRX designation stood for World Rally eXperimental and implied four-wheel drive and a turbocharger. Subaru Technical International is equivalent to Mitsubishi's Ralliart, developing cars for competition use, so the STi versions were the cars Subaru homologated for rallying, featuring larger turbochargers and different transmissions and suspension. Trying to keep track of all the different WRX and STi Subarus can be dizzying; there were six versions of the first generation, roughly one a year between 1993 and 2000. The second generation started as the 'Bugeye' model before having a facelift to become the 'Blobeye' and 'Hawkeye' styles, while the WRX STi cars were augmented with at least five different special editions boasting 315 bhp engines. In 2007, Impreza fans were dismayed by the third-generation model and its hatchback styling, particularly as it seemed a little softer and less involving to drive.

The first two generations of the WRX STi are remarkable cars to experience on a twisty road. They possess so much mechanical grip, traction and power that niceties like handling balance and steering feel become secondary. You lunge from one bend to the next, the low, off-beat engine sounding more like a V8 than a four-cylinder, throw the car at the apex, plant your right foot again, and gape as it claws its way round, almost regardless of conditions. The pick of the bunch? Hardcore 'Scooby' fans would insist on the rare two-door P1 version created by Prodrive in Britain. In fact, they're all breathtaking.

| 2001 Subaru Impreza WRX STi ||
|---|---|
| Length | 4,405 mm |
| Width | 1,730 mm |
| Weight | 1,430 kg |
| Wheelbase | 2,525 mm |
| Suspension | Independent via lower wishbones and MacPherson struts, anti-roll bar (front); independent via multiple links with coil-and-damper strut (rear) |
| Brakes | Hydraulic vented discs, servo-assisted (front and rear) |
| Engine | 1,994 cc flat four, DOHC, turbocharged, fuel-injected |
| Power | 276 bhp @ 6,400 rpm |
| Torque | 275 lb-ft @ 4,000 rpm |
| Transmission | Six-speed manual, four-wheel drive |
| 0–60 mph | 5.0 sec. |
| Top speed | 156 mph |
| Cost new | c.£21,000 |
| Value today | £12,000–£40,000 (special editions more) |

TOP: A 1995 Impreza in Subaru's classic colour scheme of blue with gold wheels.

BOTTOM: McRae in rally action in 1994.

# MCLAREN F1

| McLaren F1 (figures for 1992 model) ||
|---|---|
| Length | 4,288 mm |
| Width | 1,820 mm |
| Weight | 1,137 kg |
| Wheelbase | 2,718 mm |
| Suspension | Independent via double wishbones, coil springs and anti-roll bars (front and rear) |
| Brakes | Hydraulic vented discs (front and rear) |
| Engine | 6,064 cc V12, DOHC, variable valve timing, fuel-injected |
| Power | 627 bhp @ 7,500 rpm |
| Torque | 455 lb-ft @ 4,000 rpm |
| Transmission | Six-speed manual, rear-wheel drive |
| 0–60 mph | 3.2 sec. |
| Top speed | 240 mph |
| Cost new | £540,000 |
| Value today | £15 million–£22 million |

In the early 1990s it was difficult to see why anyone would bother creating a new supercar. A recession in the UK was reflected in other economies, and the Jaguar XJ 220 had just been caught in the middle of the panic. This five-metre-long, 500-bhp projectile was unveiled in 1988, promising (but never reliably achieving) a 220 mph top speed. Around 1,500 deposits were taken from interested buyers, or perhaps speculators. It went on sale in 1992 as the recession bit hard, at a price of £470,000. Five of every six potential buyers asked for their deposit back. In Italy, Lamborghini and Ferrari were stable enough thanks to the protection of Chrysler and Fiat ownership respectively, and both companies claimed a 200 mph top speed for their flagship models: the new Diablo and the F40. Porsche could also touch the 200 mph mark with its own halo model, the 959. The idea that a small British firm with no experience of building road cars was about to redefine our idea of a supercar, and to consign the opposition to the slow lane, was ludicrous.

Yet that's what happened in 1992 when McLaren launched the F1. Yes, McLaren is a Formula One constructor, but the F1 shared nothing with the racing cars, other than some of the materials used to create the body tub. It was thought anything faster than a Porsche 959 would need NASA-like technological advancement to make it driveable, but the McLaren jumped the other way: no turbochargers, no four-wheel drive, no anti-lock brakes – not even any power steering.

This was entirely the choice of the car's creator, Gordon Murray. He was already a successful designer of Formula One cars for Brabham and McLaren when he persuaded McLaren's bosses to back a road car project. The new car would be the culmination of everything he'd learned to that point, and of everything he wanted. Simply building the fastest car in the world wasn't enough.

The most obvious difference between the F1 and any other contemporary was the central driving position. Two passenger seats, one either side of the driver, meant the car offered accommodation for three in a package 20 cm shorter and 15 cm narrower than a two-seat Ferrari Testarossa. It was also capable of carrying a useful amount of luggage, with fitted suitcases and soft bags fitting in capacious side lockers. Murray gave a lot of consideration to ride quality after he was enchanted by Honda's then-new NSX on a visit to Japan. If that underrated everyday supercar struggles for recognition against the Italian exotics, the fact that Murray made the NSX's ride and handling a target for the F1's development should be all the credibility it needs.

That just left the performance to sort out. Murray tried hard to persuade Honda, then the engine supplier to McLaren's Formula One team, to build a new 4.5-litre V10 or V12 engine to power the F1 road car, but they declined. This left Murray looking for alternative power and as he set strict conditions his options were llimited: no turbo power nor superchargers – he didn't want the extra complexity, weight, heat or throttle lag that these could introduce. He wanted a 550 bhp engine no more than 600 mm long and weighing no more than 250 kg. Murray approached BMW, and engineer Paul Rosche of 'M' division created a specially modified version of the S70 V12 engine used in the BMW 850CSi. The key to its performance was variable valve timing, using a system BMW calls VANOS.

This impressive engine was 15 kg heavier than Murray wanted, but it delivered 77 bhp more – an incredible 627 bhp at 7,400 rpm. It even fitted the 600 mm limit for block length. Famously, Murray lined the engine bay with gold film to resist heat transfer. Cost, both to McLaren for the build and to the consumer when the final price tag was worked out, was of no regard. In short, the F1 was going to combine perfect handling balance, ride comfort, a dash of practicality and utterly dazzling performance in a way no road car had achieved before, and few had ever attempted. So how would all this come together?

A carbon-fibre monocoque was styled by Peter Stevens, who is perhaps best known for reworking the Lotus Esprit and creating the M100 Elan (which donated its super-slim front sidelight and indicator cluster). Gordon Murray shared some of Lotus founder Colin Chapman's philosophy on the importance of lightness – weight is the enemy in handling dynamics, ride control, performance and just about everything else a car designer is striving for. Aluminium and magnesium fixing points set into the carbon-fibre reinforced polymer body tub attached the car's driveline and suspension. Then there are the dihedral doors, which take in part of the roof on each side and allow the driver to step into the central seat. Well, almost. It's better than crawling across from a normal door aperture.

The F1 was an instant, scene-changing phenomenon. Nothing else cost £540,000 and nothing else could do 230 mph ... or 240 mph, as it turned out when Andy Wallace drove the ageing prototype on the 8.7 km straight at VW's Ehra-Lessien test track in March 1998. Only 64 road-going versions were built, each one taking three-and-a-half months. More than 30 years after launch, it is still the fastest naturally aspirated production car ever made.

As if all this isn't enough, there is the car's racing career. It was conceived, designed and built as a road car, and yet with a few modifications to aerodynamics, suspension and engine management (a mandatory air restrictor cut power to 591 bhp) it won the 24 Hours of Le Mans at its first attempt – and came third, fourth and fifth in the same race too. Nowadays, the McLaren F1 is the only car made in numbers greater than one or two that looks capable of challenging the Ferrari 250 GTO's values. It's not there yet, but with prices rising from perhaps £5 million in 2010 to £10 million in 2015 and around £20 million now, it's claiming its place at the very top of the tree. A living legend.

**TOP:** A GTR Longtail in competition livery.   **BOTTOM:** Is it really a supercar if the doors don't open upwards?   **PREVIOUS PAGE:** The sweeping profile of a 1995 McLaren F1.

# Aston Martin DB7

Today, we might think of the DB7 as just another ageing Aston: something of a bargain if you buy one carefully but a liability if anything goes wrong. It doesn't have the kudos of the old DB models of the 1960s, nor did it manage to get itself into a James Bond film, but if you look at the effect it had on the company's fortunes it's the most important Aston Martin since the 1950s.

By 1990, handbuilding cars in the traditional Aston Martin manner was becoming unaffordable. The cheapest Aston cost more than the dearest Ferrari because each Aston Martin took 1,500 hours to construct. Sales, as you might expect, were low. The company remained in profit – just – but without any resources to develop more mechanised production. The solution presented itself via a partial buyout by Ford, which took a 75 per cent stake in the company in 1987. Ideas circulated for a lower-priced Aston, but it was only when Ford bought Jaguar in 1990 that the stars aligned.

The DB7's genesis was a blend of two stillborn projects: a sleek successor for the Jaguar E-type, known as the F-type, and a high-performance Jaguar XJ-S derivative developed by Tom Walkinshaw Racing (TWR). Ian Callum, a Ford stylist who had moved to TWR, knew about the F-type and suggested placing that body design on an XJ-S platform. Jaguar didn't go for it, preferring to invest in a different revision of the XJ-S, code-named the X100, which would become the XK8 (see p. 244). Ian Callum's idea was dead … until Aston Martin's new chairman, ex-Ford boss Walter Hayes, pounced on it. What would have been too expensive for Jaguar to build made much more sense at the Aston Martin price point.

Ian Callum worked up a new shape that took the F-type as a loose starting point, creating a superbly elegant fastback coupé with faired-in headlamps and muscular haunches. Walter Hayes wanted a straight-six to continue the six-cylinder heritage of the old DB6. This would be Jaguar's 3.2-litre AJ6 engine, modified in various ways and supercharged to give 335 bhp. Launched in 1994, it fulfilled the brief perfectly – fast and exciting, elegant and luxurious, and much more affordable than the V8 Virage. In 1996 a convertible version joined the range and broadened the appeal, and then in 1999 the straight-six made way for a 5.9-litre V12. The old Vantage name was revived, and with a few hikes in power and special editions the DB7 stayed relevant until a successor was ready in 2004.

In the flesh, the DB7's beauty is mixed with a charismatic presence and it is impressive to drive thanks to a serious turn of speed. The V12 Vantage kicks the performance up to Ferrari-rivalling levels. Only the too-familiar Ford switchgear in the cabin takes the gloss off the experience, but it's worth remembering that they're affordable now because there are so many about: 7,000 sales made the DB7 the best-selling Aston Martin yet. From that springboard, the company has gone from strength to strength.

**TOP:** The sleek looks suggest Aston Martin DNA, despite its Jaguar origins.

**BOTTOM:** The Vantage Volante DB7.

| 1994 Aston Martin DB7 ||
|---|---|
| Length | 4,631 mm |
| Width | 1,820 mm |
| Weight | 1,650 kg |
| Wheelbase | 2,591 mm |
| Suspension | Independent via double wishbones, coil springs (front only); anti-roll bar (front and rear) |
| Brakes | Hydraulic vented discs, front and rear, power assisted |
| Engine | 3,239 cc in-line six, DOHC, supercharged, fuel-injected |
| Power | 335 bhp @ 5,500 rpm |
| Torque | 360 lb-ft @ 3,000 rpm |
| Transmission | Five-speed manual, rear-wheel drive |
| 0–60 mph | 5.8 sec. |
| Top speed | 157 mph |
| Cost new | £78,000 |
| Value today | £10,000–£30,000 |

# Lotus Elise

There is a common theme in the history of sports car-makers in the 1990s: increasingly expensive cars lead the marque away from its roots, low sales make it hard to invest in new production, and the business is at risk. Lotus had needed saving twice already by the time the Elise was launched, first in 1983 when a consortium of British investors bought the firm. By 1985 they realised they couldn't fund development of new models and sought a buyer, which led to a complete takeover by General Motors by the end of 1986. What should have been a sporting jewel in their crown wasn't looking attractive, and in 1993 they sold Lotus to Romano Artioli, the Italian businessman who also owned Bugatti.

Soon after, work began on a new model. Lotus's only product at this point was the Esprit, still with just four cylinders and a turbo. Sales were dipping sharply as it struggled to compete with Ferrari and Porsche rivals. Designer Julian Thompson and chief engineer Richard Rackham took the original Lotus formula of a small, light, two-seat sports car with a fizzing twin-cam engine and updated it thoroughly. The new car was mid-engined and didn't use a steel backbone chassis but a tub of extruded aluminium, bonded rather than welded together. On top of this, a glass-fibre composite bodyshell offered a targa-top arrangement.

The car's kerb weight was an eye-catching 723 kg, which was the key to its remarkable cornering ability and performance. From a 1.8-litre Rover K-series engine making just 118 bhp (the same as the contemporary eight-valve VW Golf GTi) it managed the 0–60 mph sprint in just 5.6 seconds. But it's the way an Elise handles that magnifies this performance to something greater. The Series 1 car, launched in September 1995 before Lotus was sold yet again to Malaysian car-maker Proton, has a cockpit like a racing car. You sit low within a very small, low-slung body, and the only soft furnishings are the seats themselves and pads on the sills where your leg touches. No carpet on the floor, no gaiters on the gearstick or handbrake. Even the window winder (no electric windows, of course) is drilled for lightness.

The engine is right behind you and you can feel as well as hear the revs rise, as the car's structure tingles with the noise. The steering is so quick you have to readjust from almost any other car, or you turn into corners too early and risk kissing the kerb. The little Lotus changes direction like a housefly, finding any series of switchback bends or hairpins laughably easy to dismiss without slowing down. When you have to brake, the tiny weight allows impressive stopping power. Sales, of course, were many times more than the Esprit and guaranteed Lotus's future. The Elise's ability was developed extensively with more powerful special editions and a hardcore, hard-roof version called the Exige. A Series 2 Elise took over from 2001 to 2011, with the Series 3 ending Elise production in 2022. The best small sports car of the 1990s, and beyond.

'By the time I'd parked it that night, I was convinced that I'd driven the future.'

*Autocar* magazine, 1996

| 1996 Lotus Elise | |
|---|---|
| Length | 3,726 mm |
| Width | 1,820 mm |
| Weight | 723 kg |
| Wheelbase | 2,300 mm |
| Suspension | Independent via double wishbones, coil springs, telescopic dampers (front and rear) and front anti-roll bar |
| Brakes | Hydraulic vented discs, front and rear |
| Engine | 1,796 cc in-line four, DOHC, 16-valve, fuel-injected |
| Power | 118 bhp @ 5,500 rpm |
| Torque | 122 lb-ft @ 3,000 rpm |
| Transmission | Five-speed manual, rear-wheel drive |
| 0–60 mph | 5.6 sec. |
| Top speed | 124 mph |
| Cost new | £18,950 |
| Value today | £10,000–£30,000 (some special editions more) |

An S1 Elise. The extreme fore and aft positions of the wheels contribute to its nimble handling.

# MG

MG is surely Britain's best-loved and most-recognised classic car marque. In its long lifespan, it has produced affordable sports cars based closely on components from humble family cars. So as many MG models have aged, the same things that made them popular when new make them appealing to own now. Parts supply is easy, they're fun to drive, inexpensive to buy and run, and they're supported by some of the biggest and best owners' clubs in the country.

The origin of the company as Morris Garages was one of those happy accidents that change the course of history. An Oxford Morris dealer's efforts to make a sports car out of the Bullnose model led to one of the foundations on which British Motor Corporation (BMC), then British Leyland and eventually the Rover Group were built. The lineage of British history ended in 2005 and today the brand survives in Chinese ownership. By 2005 the range of cars MG had created was beyond anything Cecil Kimber of Morris Garages could have imagined in 1924.

MG became a separate company in 1927, with its own factory in Cowley. It was the smallest MGs that found most fame, starting with the M-type Midget. Low, narrow and on a wheelbase just two metres long, it felt nippy to drive, and when a supercharged version arrived in 1932, just £250 bought you a car that could hit 80 mph. Even more exciting was the K3 Magnette, with a small six-cylinder OHC engine of just 1,087 cc and a supercharger, making an amazing 120 bhp. This gave MG serious competition credibility – Tazio Nuvolari won the 1933 Ulster Tourist Trophy race in a K3, among many other successes.

MG built an impressive range of larger Wolseley-based saloons and drophead coupés with elegant flowing wings, but the likes of the SA, VA and WA did not reappear after the war. Instead, MG set off to conquer America, as the TC, TD and TF Midget models popularised the idea of the small British roadster in that hugely important market. An MG saloon returned in 1953, when the handsome ZA Magnette introduced the new B-series engine. At the end of the 1950s, the Magnette Mk III introduced MG to badge engineering, in which the MG octagon was used on sporty versions of the small Austin/Morris 1100 and 1300 saloons.

While the MGA and MGB carried the flag, the reappearance of the Midget name helped sales when the Mk 2 Austin-Healey Sprite gained an MG badge. Following the transformation of British Leyland into Austin Rover and then the Rover Group, badge engineering returned as the traditional sports cars disappeared, creating the MG Montego, Maestro and Metro, and later the MG ZR, ZS and ZT, all of which now have their own following. Two sports cars did emerge – the RV8 of 1994, a reworked MGB shell with a Rover V8, and the MGF of 1995, a properly new mid-engined two-seater. The spirit of MG isn't dead – a new battery electric roadster, the MG Cyberster, went on sale in the UK in 2024, 100 years after MG's creation.

# THROUGH THE YEARS

**CLOCKWISE FROM TOP LEFT:** An M-Type; Magnette; Maestro; MGF; RV8; Midget.

# Jaguar XK8

It's tempting to see this car as the long-lost twin of the Aston Martin DB7, as their development stories intertwine, but in fact they don't share a great deal. While both were inspired by 1980's concepts to update the long-gone E-type, the XK8 was the more advanced and expensive car to develop. In 1991, Jaguar had launched an update of the XJ-S that changed its name very slightly by removing the hyphen, so the XJS with the rounded tail and smoothed-off edges held the fort for a few years while a new sports car was developed. In 1992, this had barely got off the ground. Four different clay models were under consideration; two came from Jaguar's own studio, one from Ford at Dearborn in America and one from Ghia in Turin, also owned by Ford.

One of Jaguar's own designs was eventually chosen, then refined with a shorter boot. It discarded the old XJ-S suspension, itself developed from the E-type, and used that from the forthcoming X300 XJ saloon. Equally important was the new powerplant. For Jaguar to be allowed its own V8 engine while Ford USA built V8s by the million was key – something perceived to be borrowed from a pickup truck or even a Mustang was not the right image for Jaguar, so the AJ26 V8 engine went ahead in 1992. This is all the more surprising when you know that Jaguar was losing more than $1 million a day at this point. Plunging sales, the UK recession and the terrible dollar-sterling exchange rate meant Jaguar's very existence was uncertain. The new sports model, code-name X100, simply had to succeed.

For a while in 1993, it looked as though it would never happen. Funding ran out and work ceased, but eventually some investment from Ford and the UK government pushed it ahead. The X300 saloon, the latest update of the long-established Jaguar XJ, took up much of the company's attention before launch in 1994, so it was March 1996 before the XK8 was introduced at the Geneva Motor Show. It looked every inch a Jaguar: Fergus Pollock and Geoff Lawson perfected a slightly hunched, aggressive stance with large wheels, and the headlamps and grille aperture suggesting a snarl.

The coupé and convertible both used the new 32-valve V8, which made a smooth and tuneful 290 bhp, teamed with a five-speed automatic transmission and no manual option. This was to be a relaxed, high-speed grand tourer to take on the big coupés from Mercedes and BMW rather than Ferrari or Porsche, though these more sporting marques were challenged in 1997 by the XKR version, offering 370 bhp and a 0–60 mph sprint in 5.4 seconds. From 2002, the engine size increased from 4 litres to 4.2 litres and the five-speed transmission (borrowed from Mercedes) was replaced by a six-speed ZF automatic. Today they make tempting modern classics, as impressive production figures – a profitable 90,000 sold in nine years, helping Jaguar survive – mean there is plenty of choice.

TOP: The XK8's interior was luxurious, stylish and bang up to date in 1996.

MIDDLE: The XK8's sleek shape was given an aggressive stance by the use of large wheels.

BOTTOM: Like the E-type, the XK8's convertible shape was as graceful as the coupé.

| 1996 Jaguar XK8 ||
|---|---|
| Length | 4,760 mm |
| Width | 1,829 mm |
| Weight | 1,653 kg |
| Wheelbase | 2,588 mm |
| Suspension | Independent via double wishbones, coil springs, telescopic dampers and anti-roll bar (front); independent via lower wishbones, telescopic dampers, coil springs (rear) |
| Brakes | Hydraulic vented discs (front and rear) |
| Engine | 3,996 cc V8, DOHC, 32-valve, fuel-injected |
| Power | 290 bhp @ 6,100 rpm |
| Torque | 290 lb-ft @ 4,250 rpm |
| Transmission | Five-speed automatic, rear-wheel drive |
| 0–60 mph | 6.4 sec. |
| Top speed | 156 mph |
| Cost new | £44,200 |
| Value today | £3,000–£25,000 |

# Porsche Boxster

By late 1991 Porsche was in trouble. Annual sales had dropped from 40,000 to 15,000 as the company struggled to shift an increasingly expensive range. There were painful redundancies and changes at board level too. Nonetheless, an idea was taking shape for a small roadster that could share components with the next generation of the 911. As research and development director Horst Marchart sought board approval for this plan, a young American-born designer called Grant Larson was suggesting something very similar elsewhere in the company.

Approval from the board to do a pre-study on what became the Boxster brought some optimism, and the design team decided to build a show car to explore the look the little roadster might have – and to tease the public a little. Larson loved two small competition models from Porsche's past: the 718 RSK and the 550 Spyder. But Porsche were so keen on the project that he found himself working on the show car and the production car at the same time, using the show car to demonstrate what they really wanted and prevent the production car getting too far from the mark.

Packaging the new roadster was going to be a challenge, because this was Porsche's first mid-engined road car, yet it had to share many components with the new generation of water-cooled 911, the 996. Today, with Porsche's immense success, it seems hard to imagine, but cost savings in the early and mid-1990s were about saving the company. So if the Boxster had to share the headlamps, wheels, radiators and countless other items with the 911, Larson's design had to cope with that. And it did, very nicely, putting down a marker in a relatively cautious market. The car's obvious rivals, the BMW Z3 and the Mercedes SLK, were launched a few months before the Boxster with conventional front-engined layouts and a driving experience that felt more about looking good than sports-car motoring.

An early Boxster feels light and nimble, and the six-cylinder engine gives it a punch well beyond its four-cylinder rivals, even in the first 2.5-litre form. It's less intimidating to drive than a contemporary 911, though you're aware it would be wise to slow down in the wet – the relatively short wheelbase and mid-engined balance would make it challenging to catch a spin on a greasy corner. On dry roads the limits are extremely high and it's as quick along a British B-road as its rear-engined big brother. In 3.2-litre Boxster S form, its 0–60 mph time dipped below six seconds and the top speed rose above 160 mph, which bridged the gap between 'affordable roadster' and 'serious performance car'.

The first generation 986 Boxster lasted until 2004, by which time it was an irreplaceable part of the Porsche line-up so simply had to continue as the next-generation 987 Boxster. Two further generations followed and the Boxster remains with us today. It was one of the foundations on which the Porsche empire rebuilt itself and it remains a joyous car to experience down a twisty road on a sunny day.

**TOP:** The Boxster came in fun colours to match its fun price tag.

**BOTTOM:** Despite our unpredictable weather, Porsche's little convertible was always a strong seller in the UK.

| 1996 Porsche Boxster | |
|---|---|
| Length | 4,315 mm |
| Width | 1,778 mm |
| Weight | 1,252 kg |
| Wheelbase | 2,415 mm |
| Suspension | Independent via lower wishbones, coil-and-damper struts and anti-roll bar (front); independent via semi-trailing arms, lower and transverse links, coil springs and telescopic dampers (rear) |
| Brakes | Hydraulic vented discs (front and rear), servo-assisted, ABS |
| Engine | 2,480 cc flat-six, DOHC, 24-valve, fuel-injected |
| Power | 201 bhp @ 6,000 rpm |
| Torque | 177 lb-ft @ 5,000 rpm |
| Transmission | Five-speed manual, rear-wheel drive |
| 0–60 mph | 6.9 sec. |
| Top speed | 152 mph |
| Cost new | £44,200 |
| Value today | £3,000–£25,000 |

# TVR Cerbera

The British sports-car-maker TVR is a rare survivor from the post-war boom of independent 'special' builders and kit-car companies. Like Lotus, it made a successful leap to the production of fast, desirable two-seaters and GTs and, like Lotus, sailed close to the rocks of financial ruin more than once. After plunging sales and cash-flow worries, in 1981 TVR's then-chairman Martin Lilley sold out to Peter Wheeler, a successful chemical engineer in the oil industry. In Wheeler's time TVR increased its proportion of convertible models and turned to Rover V8 engines, yet the most exciting road car built in Wheeler's ownership had neither a folding roof nor a Rover-derived engine.

This was the Cerbera, a long, low coupé with 2+2 seating that went on sale late in 1995. Under the bonnet was TVR's first homegrown engine, the 4.2-litre Speed Eight. Until this point, all TVRs had been powered by bought-in engines from a variety of sources, most recently Rover and Ford; but they created an in-house replacement for a new generation of high-performance roadsters and coupés. It was designed by engineering consultant Al Melling and developed by Melling, John Ravenscroft and Peter Wheeler, with their first initials creating the AJP8 nickname.

It was a bold design that had much in common with racing engines. The AJP8 used a flat-plane crankshaft, a feature common to racing V8s and all of Ferrari's road-going V8s, rather than the conventional cross-plane crankshaft of American pushrod designs like the Rover. This allowed for a lighter crankshaft, while an angle of 75 degrees between cylinder banks, rather than 90 degrees, made for a more compact unit. The AJP8 used one overhead camshaft per bank with just two valves per cylinder rather than four, as Melling believed he could achieve excellent gas flow without the extra weight and complexity of multi-valve designs. It was made in aluminium and tipped the scales at only 121 kg, around 50 kg lighter than the Rover. What the engine was most notable for, though, was its outrageous power.

Two versions were offered: 360 bhp from 4.2-litres and 420 bhp from 4.5-litres, though that was later raised to 450 bhp with a factory tweak called the Red Rose upgrade. Jaguar's all-aluminium, 4.2-litre, double overhead cam V8 needed a supercharger to reach 360 bhp, but the TVR was naturally aspirated. Development delays prevented its use in the Griffith and Chimaera models, but it found a home in the Cerbera, which rapidly acquired a reputation as one of the fastest production cars you could buy, if not the very fastest. *Top Gear* famously ran a standing mile drag-race in 1996, involving a Dodge Viper, a Porsche 911/993 Turbo, an Aston Martin Vantage, a Lotus Esprit V8 turbo, a Caterham Seven JPE and the Cerbera: not even the 4.5-litre version, just the 4.2-litre. Despite being the second-cheapest car bar the hot-rod Caterham, the Cerbera won.

TVR built 1,490 Cerberas between 1996 and 2006, but compared with contemporary Ferraris and Porsches they remain something of a secret. It's the wildest of a pretty wild bunch.

| 1996 TVR Cerbera | |
|---|---|
| Length | 4,280 mm |
| Width | 1,865 mm |
| Weight | 1,160 kg |
| Wheelbase | 2,566 mm |
| Suspension | Independent via double wishbones, coil springs, telescopic dampers and anti-roll bars (front and rear) |
| Brakes | Hydraulic vented discs (front and rear), servo-assisted |
| Engine | 4,185 cc V8, OHC per bank, fuel-injected |
| Power | 360 bhp @ 6,500 rpm |
| Torque | 320 lb-ft @ 4,500 rpm |
| Transmission | Five-speed manual, rear-wheel drive |
| 0–60 mph | 4.2 sec. |
| Top speed | 180 mph |
| Cost new | £40,000 |
| Value today | £7,000–£25,000 |

TOP: The futuristic interior.

MIDDLE: The V8 sits well back in the engine bay.

BOTTOM: The Cerbera's length was well disguised, but it allowed reasonable rear seats.

# Pagani Zonda

Predicting the death of the supercar has been popular since the 1990s, and certainly since the McLaren F1 appeared to put a lid on every previous effort. By 1999, the Toyota Prius had been on sale for two years in Japan and the Honda Insight had just arrived. Hybrid cars were a reality and fully electric vehicles were on the horizon. Lamborghini had been bought by Audi in 1998, so it seemed likely that the old craziness would be toned down for the Diablo's replacement. The Ferrari F50 had left production and Porsche hadn't listed a range-topping hypercar since a few street versions of the 911 GT1 Le Mans car were built in 1997. Where was the next hero – the next supercar worthy of a poster on a bedroom wall?

The unlikely answer came in the form of a totally new player. Horacio Pagani had overseen Lamborghini's composites department before founding his own design and engineering consultancy. Alongside this, he developed his own idea of what a supercar should be, and by the mid-1990s had secured a deal with Mercedes to supply V12 engines. It took until 1999 for the project to reach fruition, when Pagani launched the Zonda C12 at the Geneva Motor Show.

The Zonda startled the world. Here was a car that looked wilder and more imaginative than any Ferrari or Lamborghini, that claimed performance beyond anything the big-name rivals were offering (0–100 mph in 9.2 seconds), and which cost more than all of them at £300,000. The interior looked like the bridge of a starfighter, with shiny alloys in curving organic shapes and glossy carbon-fibre wrapping around sills and doors. The spacecraft theme seemed to continue outside, thanks to a pod-like cabin that was mostly glass, sitting in the centre of a wide body with huge side scoops, twin rear wings and four exhausts gathered together like rocket thrusters. It was all incredibly bold, but then motoring history is littered with bold ideas for low-production supercars that have died with only a few examples ever completed. What was different about Pagani?

First, Pagani's experience with composites meant he could create a very light, very stiff carbon composite structure that kept weight to just 1,250 kg, despite the 6-litre, quad-cam Mercedes AMG V12 behind the cabin. This allowed eye-popping performance and handling like a supersized Lotus Elise. Second, the build quality matched the imagination of the design, so buyers didn't have to forgive the foibles typical of hand-built sports cars. Third, there wasn't anything else quite so exciting.

The Zonda rose in price, evolved in power and established Pagani as a permanent player at the top table of performance-car constructors. But it did more than that, showing other manufacturers that there was indeed a market for the wildest and most expensive cars that pushed the boundaries of speed and acceleration. Without the Zonda, would we have seen the Bugatti Veyron, or the success of Koenigsegg? The year 2000 wasn't the end of the supercar: it was the beginning of the new generation.

**TOP:** The Zonda S introduced a 7-litre version of the V12 engine with 542 bhp.

**MIDDLE:** The rear of a Zonda 760 MD, with the 'rocket pod' exhaust on display.

**BOTTOM:** Pagani made sure the Zonda was as wild inside as it was outside.

| 1999 Pagani Zonda C12 ||
|---|---|
| Length | 4,345 mm |
| Width | 2,055 mm |
| Weight | 1,250 kg |
| Wheelbase | 2,730 mm |
| Suspension | Independent via double wishbones, coil springs, telescopic dampers and anti-roll bars (front and rear) |
| Brakes | Hydraulic vented discs (front and rear), servo-assisted |
| Engine | 5,987 cc V12, DOHC per bank, fuel-injected |
| Power | 394 bhp @ 5,200 rpm |
| Torque | 420 lb-ft @ 3,800 rpm |
| Transmission | Six-speed manual, rear-wheel drive |
| 0–60 mph | 4.0 sec. |
| Top speed | 186 mph |
| Cost new | £300,000 |
| Value today | £2.5 million-plus |

# Tesla Roadster

The Tesla Roadster has shown itself to be the first electric vehicle (EV) capable of rising in value like a traditionally investable classic. The early Japanese hybrids of the late 1990s were important landmarks, technologically speaking, but they've struggled to stir the emotions of owners, as has the first mass-produced EV, the Nissan Leaf. But they were small family cars, which always have to wait a long time to develop a following. Sports cars have a head start and here the Tesla Roadster is out on its own.

Tesla's first model was based on a Lotus Elise chassis platform and equipped with a 53 kWh lithium-ion battery. With electric motors of either 248 bhp or 288 bhp, and an instant 295 lb-ft of torque available from zero revs, it could accelerate like a supercar: 0–60 mph in 3.7 seconds. Around 2,500 were built from 2008 to 2012 and initially the Roadster was greeted with wonder – here was a battery-powered car you could really use, with a range of 150–200 miles in the real world plus staggering acceleration and fine handling. But then a few problems began to appear.

The technology for getting the sudden torque delivery of electric motors to the wheels was underdeveloped, with transmission failures occurring after a few thousand miles. Production started very slowly; only 27 cars were built in the first six months, despite a considerable waiting list. Reviews of the Roadster mentioned build quality and materials choice that didn't fit with a $100,000 car, and customers who thought their deposits were locked in to a purchase price found thousands of dollars being added for options that had originally been standard. Then there was the phenomenon of 'bricking'.

If you let your Tesla go uncharged for a couple of months, it could drain the battery to the point where it refused to take a charge at all. The car would effectively be locked in gear and have to be craned away for reactivation or repair. But all of these worries have faded away in a surprisingly short time, helped in part by a more powerful updated battery pack released in 2015, four years after the car left production. Tesla went from strength to strength and the EV market grew exponentially, so the first model started looking like a desirable piece of history.

Today there is a premium for collectable first-year Roadsters. It's an American-led market, where values have jumped. Figures around $40,000 (£30,200) were standard in 2019, but by 2023 and 2024 prices of $70,000–$80,000 (£53,000–£60,000) were the new normal, with first-year cars on tiny mileages breaking $100,000 (£76,000). There is a sharp step down for cars at the end of their battery life, which adds an interesting wrinkle to the second-hand value of any EV, because fitting a replacement battery can cost £20,000. What's impressive about the rise in appreciation for the Tesla Roadster is that there's enough value in a re-equipped car to make it worth doing. Cars may be changing fundamentally, but what makes a classic – good looks, the thrill of driving and a keen following – remains.

TOP: Elon Musk's personal car in space.

BOTTOM: A rare sight, but the Roadster is set to become the first classic EV.

| 2012 Tesla Roadster | |
|---|---|
| Length | 3,940 mm |
| Width | 1,722 mm |
| Weight | 1,235 kg |
| Wheelbase | 2,443 mm |
| Suspension | Independent via double wishbones, coil springs and telescopic dampers (front and rear) with front anti-roll bars |
| Brakes | Hydraulic vented discs (front and rear), servo-assisted |
| Engine | Three-phase, four-pole electric induction motor |
| Power | 288 bhp @ 5,000–6,000 rpm |
| Torque | 273 lb-ft @ 0–5,400 rpm |
| Transmission | Twin or single-speed, rear-wheel drive |
| 0–60 mph | 3.9 sec. |
| Top speed | 125 mph |
| Cost new | £86,000 |
| Value today | £40,000–£90,000 |

# Index

24 Hours of Le Mans race 26, 44, 52, 54, 88, 112, 134, 180, 237
AC Cars 4, 92
   AC/Shelby Cobra 92–3
Alfa Romeo 4, 34, 44, 98, 114, 154, 196–7, 208, 218
   6C 1750 196
   8C 2900B Touring Spider 197
   8C Competizione 197
   75 220
   Alfasud 146–7, 196, 208
   Alfetta 197
   'Duetto' Spider 124–5
   Giulia 196, 197
   Giulietta 196, 197
   Junior Z 220
   RL Targa Florio 197
   SZ 220–1
   TZ 220
Allard 92
   J2 44
Alvis 30, 62
   4.3-litre Vanden Plas Tourer 34–5
   TB21 44
Aston Martin 98, 104, 106, 112–13
   Bulldog concept car 113
   DB1 44, 112, 113
   DB4 90, 112, 113, 220
   DB5 94–5
   DB6 238
   DB7 238–9, 244
   Ulster 113
   V8 Vantage 112, 113, 248
Audi 39, 106, 120, 180, 216, 250
   Quattro 188–91, 202, 214, 216, 218, 226
Austin 62
   A40 62
   Seven ('Baby Austin') 16–17, 22, 156
   Seven Swallow 54
Austin-Healey 242
   100 62–3
   3000 136
Austin/Morris Mini 80–3
Austro-Daimler 180
Auto-Union 52, 180
Autokraft 92

Bache, David 110, 198
Bamford & Martin 112
Bashford, Gordon 42, 142
Bentley, Walter Owen 24, 26, 112
Bentley 18, 22, 28, 34, 39, 180
   4½-litre 'Blower' 26–7
   Arnage 28
   Continental 48
   Mk VI 28, 68

R-type 28, 68
R-type Continental 60–1, 68
S-series 68, 90
Turbo R 206–7
Benz, Bertha 8, 18
Benz, Carl 8, 9, 18
Benz Patent Motorwagen 8–9
Berkeley 82, 84
Bertone 122, 158, 192
Blackburne 22
BMC 72, 82, 100
BMW 4, 18, 28, 48, 83, 136, 138, 152, 154, 156–7, 176, 190, 198, 204, 236, 244, 246
   328 156, 157
   507 156, 157
   1500 cc 'Neue Klasse' 156, 157, 160
   2002 Turbo 160–1, 176
   E32 740 156, 157
   M1 156, 157
   M3 156, 160, 202, 210–11, 218
   M5 156, 198, 224
   see also Mini; Rolls-Royce
Bond, James 82, 94, 112, 172, 238
Bosch 168, 198
Brabham 236
Bristol
   400 44
   401 48–9
   411 152
British Leyland 54, 100, 154, 198, 242
British Motor Corporation (BMC) 54, 242
British Saloon Car Championship 106, 198
British Touring Car Championship 154, 204
BSA 84
Bugatti, Ettore 20, 24
Bugatti 24, 34, 39, 44, 104, 196, 240, 250
   Type 35 20–1
Buick 110, 126, 142, 198

Cadillac 44, 92, 126
   Coupe de Ville 1959 78–9
   V16 24
Carrozzeria Ghia 144
Carrozzeria Touring 74, 94, 120
Caterham Cars 72, 248
Centro Stile 220
Chapman, Colin 72, 102, 106, 172, 184, 236
Chevrolet 176, 194
   Bel Air 76–7, 78
   Corvair 118, 160
   Corvette 92, 108, 144, 224
   Corvette Sting Ray 104–5

Chrysler 32, 48, 62, 84, 108, 120, 184, 226, 236
Citroën, André 30
Citroën 42, 58, 148, 166, 172, 208
   2CV 46–7, 58, 66
   CX 126
   DS 4, 30, 58, 66–7, 110, 128
   H-van 56
   SM 220
   Traction Avant 30–1, 32, 34, 46, 66, 110
Cizeta-Moroder 226
Cord 24, 126
Cosworth 72, 106, 150, 202, 204
Coventry Climax 72, 102, 154

Daimler, Gottlieb 18
Daimler SP250 'Dart' 84–5, 130
Daimler-Benz 18
Datsun 178, 218
   240Z 138–9
David Brown Ltd 112
de Dion 58, 110, 220
De Tomaso Pantera 144–5
DeLorean, John 108, 194
DeLorean DMC-12 194–5
DS automobiles 208
Dunlop 82, 120
Dusenberg
   Model A 24
   Model J 24–5

Earl, Harley 78, 104
electric vehicles (EVs) 180, 252–3
European Touring Car Championship 106, 198

Ferrari, Enzo 54, 74, 75, 98, 148, 158, 162, 212
Ferrari 18, 74–5, 90, 94, 104, 108, 116, 144, 148, 172, 228, 236, 238, 240, 244, 248
   125 S 75
   166 MM 75
   238 224, 228
   246 Dino 75, 158, 162
   250 GTO 96–9, 122
   250 Lusso 75
   288 GTO 212, 237
   308 GTB 75, 212
   365 GT4 Berlinetta Boxer 162–3
   365 GTB/4 'Daytona' 134–5
   Daytona 74, 94, 134–5, 162, 198, 212
   F40 4, 212–13, 236
   F50 250
   Testarossa 74, 98, 226, 236
Fiat 58, 74, 146, 169, 196, 208, 216, 220, 236

Fiat Chrysler 208
Ford, Henry 14
Ford 34, 54, 70, 72, 92, 110, 126, 130, 144, 160, 182, 210, 238, 244, 248
   Capri 132–3, 169, 178, 204
   Cortina 72
   Cortina Lotus 106–7, 184
   Escort 106, 200
   Escort RS1600 150
   Escort RS2000 150–1, 154, 182, 184
   Escort Twin-Cam 184
   Falcon 118
   Model T 4, 14–15, 16
   Mustang 118–19, 132
   Popular 103E 64
   Sierra RS Cosworth 106, 204–5, 218
   Thunderbird 126
Formula One 58, 112, 228, 236
Frankfurt Motor Show 168, 176, 214
Frazer Nash 48, 156

Gandini, Marcello 122, 144, 158, 164, 192, 226
Geiger, Friedrich 64, 114
General Motors (GM) 78, 104, 108, 126, 194, 204, 224, 240
Geneva Motor Show 88, 164, 172, 174, 190, 204, 244, 250
German Touring Car Championship 202, 210
Ghia 58, 74, 244
Giugiaro, Giorgetto 148, 172, 194
Grand Prix 22, 24, 82, 196, 204

Hayes, Walter 106, 238
Hitachi 138
Hitler, Adolf 32, 38
Holden Commodore 224
Holset 176
Honda 250
   NSX 228–9, 236

Isetta bubble car 156, 157
Issigonis, Alec 50, 82
Italdesign Giugiaro 216

J. A. P. 22
Jaguar 4, 54–5, 84, 104, 112, 130, 198, 218, 238, 248
   C-type 55
   E-type 4, 88–91, 94, 98, 100, 107, 114, 136, 138, 152, 238, 244
   Mk 2 Saloon 55, 84, 106
   Mk IX 55
   SS Jaguar 100 55
   XJ 244

XJ6 152
XJ12 152–3, 166
XJ220 236
XJS (XJ-S) 55, 90, 238, 244
XK8 238, 244–5
XK120 44–5, 60, 62, 88
XK150 84
Jeep 190
   Wagoneer 142
Jensen 62
   FF 120–1, 190

Kaiser Jeep 142
Karmann 136
Kimber, Cecil 100, 242
Kimberley, Mike 184, 224
King, Spencer 142, 154
Koenigsegg 250

Lagonda 34, 112
Lamborghini, Ferruccio 122
Lamborghini 39, 116, 144, 162, 166, 180, 220, 236, 250
   Countach 144, 148, 164–5, 172, 226
   Diablo 226–7, 236, 250
   Miura 122–3, 148, 158, 162, 164
Lancia, Vincenzo 208
Lancia 208–9
   221 Spider Casaro 209
   Ardea 208, 209
   Aurelia 208, 209
   Aurelia B20 58–9, 208
   Beta 208, 209, 216
   Delta Integrale 216–17, 218
   Flavia 146, 208
   Fulvia 208, 209
   Stratos 158–9, 208
Land Rover 42–3, 83, 142, 190
Lea-Francis 62
Lefebvre, André 30, 66
Leyland 54, 83
Lincoln Continental 126
Lincoln-Mercury 144
Lockheed 78
Lohner-Porsche 180
Lombard RAC Rally 184, 190
London Motor Show 50, 62
Lord, Sir Leonard 62, 82
Lotus 84, 166, 184, 198, 218, 224–5, 228, 248
   Eclat 184, 190
   Elan 20, 102–3, 106, 236
   Elise 240–1, 250, 252
   Elite 184
   Esprit 172–3, 182, 184, 194, 236, 240, 248
   Exige 240
   Seven 72–3, 92
Lyons, Sir William 44, 54, 84, 88

McLaren 228
   F1 234–7, 250
MacPherson 216
McRae, Colin 232, 233
Mahle 224
MAN 39, 180
Maserati 66, 94, 98, 144
   Bora 148–9, 162

Ghibli 148
Khamsin 148
MC12 148
Mistral 148
Mazda
   RX-7 178–9
Mercedes-Benz 18–19, 34, 78, 98, 106, 112, 128, 136, 152, 156, 180, 210, 244, 246, 250
   190E 2.3-16 202–3, 210, 218
   260D 18
   290 saloon 19
   300SL 'Gullwing' 18, 19, 64–5, 66, 114
   450 SEL 6.9 152, 166–7
   770-series 'Grosser' Mercedes 18
   Mercedes-AMG 18, 250
   S-class saloon W116 18, 19
   'Silver Arrows' 18
   SL 'Pagoda' 114–15
   SLS 18
   SSK 18, 19, 52
   Vision EQXX 18
MG 22, 62, 84, 100, 169, 242–3
   M-Type 243
   Maestro 242, 243
   Magnette 242, 243
   MGA 242
   MGB 100–1, 138, 169, 178, 242
   MGC 136
   MGF 243
   Midget 169, 242, 243
   RV8 242, 243
Michelin 30, 58
Mille Miglia 52, 58, 90
Mini 4, 42, 50, 122, 156
   see also Austin/Morris Mini
Mitsubishi 232
   Lancer Evo 216, 230–1
Morgan
   Aero / Super Sports 'three-wheeler' 22–3
   Plus 136
Morris
   Minor 50–1
   see also Austin/Morris Mini
Moss, Stirling 90, 98, 114
Mundy, Harry 106, 154
Murphy 24

Nardi 58
Nissan 138, 228, 252
   Skyline R32 218–19
NSU Ro80 128–9, 178
Nürburgring 52, 203, 218

Ogle Design 84, 130
oil crisis 1973 82, 144, 160, 166, 168, 174
Oldsmobile 108, 160, 176
   Toronado 126–7
Opel 178, 182, 204
   Omega 224

Pagani 106
   Zonda 250–1
Paris–Dakar Rally 214
Peugeot 116, 208

205 GTi 200–1, 210
Quadrilette 16
Piëch, Ferdinand 180, 190
Pininfarina 58, 74, 124, 134, 212
Pontiac GTO 108–9, 194
Porsche, Ferdinand 32, 38, 52, 116, 180
Porsche, Ferdinand Alexander (Butzi) 116, 180
Porsche, Ferry 52, 180
Porsche 18, 39, 106, 172, 176, 178, 180–1, 210, 214, 228, 236, 240, 244, 248
   356 52–3, 114
   550 Spyder 1500 RS 181
   911 116–17, 166, 174, 180, 190, 214, 246, 248, 250
   912 180
   914 180, 181
   917 180, 181
   928 174–5
   930 176, 181
   959 214–5, 226, 236
   Boxster 180, 246–7
   Cayenne 180, 181
Pressed Steel 54
PSA group 184, 208

RAC Rally 83, 184, 185, 217
Rambler Rebel V8 108
Range Rover 142–3, 190
Reliant 82
   Scimitar 84, 130–1
Renault 5 Turbo and Turbo 2 192–3, 200
Reutter 52
Riley 62
Rochdale 84
Rolls, Hon. Charles 28, 206
Rolls-Royce 18, 26, 28–9, 60, 78, 152, 156, 166
   40/50 hp 'Silver Ghost' 10–13, 14, 28
   armoured car 12
   Phantom 12, 13, 28, 29, 60, 68
   Silver Cloud 29, 68–9
   Silver Dawn 68
   Silver Seraph 28
   Silver Shadow 29, 152, 166, 206
   Silver Spirit 28, 206
   Silver Spur 29
   Silver Wraith 64, 68
   Turbo R 28
Rootes Group 184
Rover 42, 48, 100, 128, 134, 142, 154, 160, 204, 240, 242, 248
   2000/2200/3500 110–11
   SD1 Vitesse 198–9, 204
Royce, Henry 12, 24, 28

Saab 99 Turbo 176–7
San Remo Rally 158, 190, 191
Sayer, Malcolm 54, 88
Scania 39, 180
SEAT 39, 180
Senna, Ayrton 228
Singer 22
Skoda 39, 180

Speciality Vehicle Engineering 204
SS Cars Ltd 54
Standard 54
Stellantis 208
Stromlinien Karosserie Gesellschaft 32
Subaru 190, 230
   Impreza WRX STi 216, 232–3
   Symmetrical All-Wheel Drive (SAWD) 190
Swallow Sidecars 54

Talbot Sunbeam Lotus 184–5
Targa Florio 20, 52, 98, 208
Tata 54
Tatra 77 and 87 32–3, 38
Tesla Roadster 252–3
Tom Walkinshaw Racing (TWR) 238
Tour de France Automobile 98, 158
Touring of Milan 112
Toyota 42, 138, 204, 230, 250
Triumph 110, 169
   1800 roadster 62
   Dolomite Sprint 154–5
   Renown 64
   Roadster 62
   Spitfire 169
   Toledo 154
   TR 100
   TR3 84
   TR6 136–7, 138
   TR7 136, 169
Turin Motor Show 122, 146, 162, 172, 216
TVR
   AJP8 248
   Cerbera 248–9

Vauxhall 34, 70, 110, 154, 176, 184
   Chevette HS/HSR 182–3, 184
   Firenza 182
Vauxhall-Lotus Carlton 224–5
Vignale 74, 120
Viotti 58
Volkswagen 28, 32, 46, 52, 56, 116, 180, 236
   Beetle (KdF-Wagen) 4, 14, 38–41, 42, 46, 50, 52, 56, 116, 168, 180
   Golf GLi 169
   Golf GTi 116, 146, 168–71, 182, 190, 200, 240
   Type 2 56–7
   VW-Audi 128, 190
Volvo
   121 'Amazon' 70–1
   PV 444 70

Weber 94
Williams 228
Willys Jeep 42
World Rally Championship 158, 184, 190–2, 208, 216, 230, 232

Zagato 112, 114, 220

# Acknowledgements

Thanks are due to my understanding family for their patience – my wife Karagh and especially my sons William and John, who put up with me debating the final choice of cars. At Harper Collins I'd like to thank Samuel Fitzgerald for his guidance throughout, designer Kevin Robbins, copy-editor Denise Cowle, commissioning editor Gerry Breslin, Craig Balfour and also Keith Moore, for thinking of me in the first place.

## Image Credits

*Unless otherwise specified, all images are courtesy of Shutterstock*

front cover (top) Goddard Automotive/Alamy Stock Photo; (bottom) Erik Fuller Photography/Alamy Stock Photo
back cover (left) Retro AdArchives/Alamy Stock Photo; (middle and right) adsR/Alamy Stock Photo
p. 5 Nigel Boothman
p. 9 (top) Bettmann/Getty Images
p. 13 Motoring Picture Library/Alamy Stock Photo
p. 15 (bottom) Shawshots/Alamy Stock Photo
p. 19 (top left) Jimlop Collection/Alamy Stock Photo
p. 23 (bottom) Carnundrum/Alamy Stock Photo
p. 27 (bottom) Dave Donaldson/Alamy Stock Photo
p. 33 (top) Ian Bottle/Alamy Stock Photo
p. 35 (top) Autocar/Stringer/Getty Images
p. 35 (bottom) Malcolm Haines/Alamy Stock Photo
p. 47 (bottom) Eric Feferberg/Getty Images
p. 51 (bottom) Magic Car Pics/Shutterstock
p. 55 (middle) Motoring Picture Library/Alamy Stock Photo
p. 61 (top) Gerard Hughes; (bottom) Motoring Picture Library/Alamy Stock Photo
p. 67 (top) Chronicle/Alamy Stock Photo
p. 73 (middle) Heritage Image Partnership Ltd/Alamy Stock Photo
p. 75 (middle left) Goddard Automotive/Alamy Stock Photo
p. 79 (bottom) Bill Philpot/Alamy Stock Photo
p. 80 Matthew Richardson/Alamy Stock Photo
p. 83 (top) LAT Images/Stringer/Getty Images
p. 85 (middle) Central Press/Stringer/Getty Images
p. 91 Retro AdArchives/Alamy Stock Photo
p. 93 (top) Simon Clay/Alamy Stock Photo
p. 96 Bob Masters Classic Car Images/Alamy Stock Photo
p. 109 (top) John Crowe/Alamy Stock Photo; (bottom) adsR/Alamy Stock Photo
p. 111 (top) Matthew Richardson/Alamy Stock Photo
p. 113 (top right) pbpgalleries/Alamy Stock Photo; (bottom right) Goddard on the Go/Alamy Stock Photo
p. 121 (top) Motoring Picture Library/Alamy Stock Photo; (bottom) Ian Bottle/Alamy Stock Photo
p. 123 (bottom) Paul Cooper/Shutterstock
p. 129 (bottom) Motoring Picture Library/Alamy Stock Photo
p. 133 (top) Retro AdArchives/Alamy Stock Photo; (bottom) Phil Talbot/Alamy Stock Photo
p. 135 (bottom) Goddard Archive/Alamy Stock Photo
p. 140 culture-images GmbH/Alamy Stock Photo
p. 143 (bottom) Magic Car Pics/Shutterstock
p. 153 (top) ZarkePix/Alamy Stock Photo; (bottom) Motoring Picture Library/Alamy Stock Photo
p. 155 (top) Magic Car Pics/Shutterstock; (middle) DPPI/Shutterstock
p. 159 (top) mauritius images GmbH/Alamy Stock Photo; (bottom) Hum Images/Alamy Stock Photo
p. 167 (bottom) Eric Feferberg/Getty Images
p. 173 (bottom) Screen Archives/Getty Images
p. 177 (top) culture-images GmbH/Alamy Stock Photo; (middle) TT News Agency/Alamy Stock Photo
p. 179 (top) Derek Seaward/Alamy Stock Photo; (bottom) Goddard Automotive/Alamy Stock Photo
p. 183 (bottom) Goddard Automotive/Alamy Stock Photo
p. 185 (top) Don Morley/Getty Images
p. 191 (bottom) DPPI Media/Alamy Stock Photo
p. 199 (top) Phil Talbot/Alamy Stock Photo; (bottom) Sutton Images/Stringer/Getty Images
p. 201 (top) National Motor Museum/Shutterstock
p. 203 (top) Goddard Archive 2/Alamy Stock Photo; (bottom) Juergen Tapp/Getty Images
p. 207 (top) Goddard Archive/Alamy Stock Photo; (bottom) Magic Car Pics/Shutterstock
p. 211 (bottom) Matthew Richardson/Alamy Stock Photo
p. 217 (top) Pascal Rondeau/Getty Images
p. 225 (top and bottom) Magic Car Pics/Shutterstock
p. 231 (bottom) Thousand Word Media Ltd/Alamy Stock Photo
p. 233 (bottom) PA Images/Alamy Stock Photo
p. 234 Jonathan Tennant/Alamy Stock Photo
p. 245 (top) Heritage Image Partnership Ltd/Alamy Stock Photo
p. 249 (top and middle) Heritage Image Partnership Ltd/Alamy Stock Photo
p. 253 (top) PR Images/Alamy Stock Photo

## Captions

p. 3: As stylish as they come, the Mercedes 300SL Gullwing in red.
p. 6: 'Any colour so long as it is black' was what Henry Ford is supposed to have said, but the first Model Ts of 1913 could be ordered in various colours.
p. 36: The streamlined Bristol 401 (see p. 48) was one of the most sophisticated British cars of the post-war years.
p. 86: The 1965 Ford/Shelby Mustang GT350, often seen with distinctive Daytona stripes down the centre line.
p. 140: The unmistakeable wedge shape of a 1974 Lamborghini Countach.
p. 186: Body kit, BBS wheels, red paint and a BMW E30 cabriolet – it must be the Eighties!
p. 222: Honda's amazing NSX was an unusual achievement: a practical supercar.